Democratic Transformations

Democratic Transformations

Eight Conflicts in the Negotiation of American Identity

KERRY T. BURCH

continuum

Continuum International Publishing Group
A Bloomsbury imprint

50 Bedford Square	80 Maiden Lane
London	New York
WC1B 3DP	NY 10038

www.continuumbooks.com

© Kerry T. Burch, 2012

ISBN: HB: 978-1-4411-1213-2
PB: 978-1-4411-7378-2

Library of Congress Cataloging-in-Publication Data
A catalog record for this book is available from the Library of Congress.

Typeset by Deanta Global Publishing Services, Chennai, India
Printed and bound in the United States of America

Truly speaking, it is not instruction, but provocation, that I can receive from another soul.

RALPH WALDO EMERSON, 1838.

Philosophy recovers itself when it ceases to be a device for dealing with the problems of philosophers and becomes a method, cultivated by philosophers, for dealing with the problems of men.

JOHN DEWEY, 1917.

Everybody has the blues. Everybody longs for meaning. Everybody needs to love and be loved. Everybody needs to clap hands and be happy. Everybody longs for faith. In music, especially in the broad category called Jazz, there is a stepping stone to all of these.

MARTIN LUTHER KING, JR, 1964.

The truth will set you free. But first it will piss you off.

GLORIA STEINEM, 1973.

CONTENTS

Prologue x

1 The pursuit of happiness 1

Transforming American scripture into a site
of democratic pedagogy 1
Citizens and idiots: An ancient Greek and Roman
snapshot of human happiness 5
Jefferson unplugged: Moving beyond idiotic
pursuits of happiness 6
Hannah Arendt and John Dewey on Jefferson's legacy 9
The pursuit of happiness and the renaissance
of civic virtue 14

2 The tyranny of the majority 21

Reflections on a democratic educational conundrum 21
Contextualizing the tyranny of the majority 24
The tyranny of the majority and the "inverted
totalitarianism" of American democracy 27
Classroom manifestations of the tyranny of the majority 31
The tyranny of the majority as a resource for cultivating
democratic moral literacy 34

3 Four score and seven years ago 37

Civic rebirth and the erotic character of
the Gettysburg Address 39

The "apple of gold" and the "picture of silver":
   What the textbooks don't say 41
Reading Lincoln as a symbol of American identity:
   Toward a new civic aesthetic 46

4 Forty acres and a mule 55

"The Colloquy in Savannah": What a black public taught
   Sherman and Stanton about democratic citizenship,
   freedom, and the pursuit of happiness 57
Forty acres and a mule, white supremacy, and
   the politics of ignorance 62
Reflections on Martin Luther King's 1968 "speech that
   never was": How the reparative principle of justice at
   stake in forty acres and a mule was denied again 66

5 The moral equivalent of war 75

A tale of two heroisms: How William James turned
   Theodore Roosevelt on his head 78
How Jane Roland Martin turns William James on
   his head: Reflections on the status of
   a Jamesian category 81
Constructing musical education as a moral equivalent
   of war: The need for a recovery of Horace Mann's lost
   Eighth Report (1844) 85

6 The business of America is business 93

Framing the contradictions at the heart of
   the "roaring twenties" 93
Coolidge, advertising, and religion: Constructing
   the business mind in the 1920s 98
John Dewey's construction of the democratic mind
   in the 1920s 102
The task before us—treating corporate personhood
   as the new *Plessy v. Ferguson* 107

7 The military-industrial complex 115

Putting the "Academic" back into the military-industrial-
academic complex 118
The difficulty of mapping the expanding boundaries
of the military-industrial-academic-media-sports-
entertainment-complex 123
Rereading the "Complex" psychologically:
Toward a theory of America's civic neurosis 126

8 The personal is political 137

Bridging the gap between feminist consciousness-raising
groups and critical pedagogy 140
Making the personal political: The education of desire
and purpose in the formation of democratic selfhood 146
Teachers as lovers or managers? Reflections on the
impossibility of teacher neutrality 152

Epilogue: Educating the souls of democratic folk 161

What jazz music can teach us about the education of
democratic souls 167
Acknowledgments 177
Further Reading 179
Index 189

PROLOGUE

Considering our national absorption in a spectacle-driven and profit-seeking media environment, coupled with a political economy which leaves citizens less and less time for civic engagement, it's worth asking: Do the American people have the capacity to enact a more democratic version of themselves? Is such a democratic transformation possible in the context of the starkest inequalities in wealth the United States has seen since 1929? As a critical response to these obstacles, how might educators develop a pedagogical art to resist America's slow-motion devolution into a regime of corporate oligarchy and permanent warfare? Questions and concerns like these about the purposes of American education in perilous times give *Democratic Transformations* its shape and substance.

The nation's greatest thinkers and artists have always understood that Americans dwell in a state of permanent crisis, owing in large measure to the absence of a prefixed or settled image of national identity. It is this very open-endedness and freedom that gives rise to all manner of conflict and anxiety in American culture. Paradoxically, however, it is this difficult feature that gives both individuals and nations the capacity as well as the confidence that they can indeed reinvent themselves. If, as Deborah Britzman has written, we can "make education from anything," we should be able to make education out of the absences and anxieties of national identity.[1]

Even as some of us individually may be prepared to acknowledge that a condition of crisis—born out of this lack of closure—is a permanent feature of American national identity, how often do our schools treat this condition as something admirable and good? How often do they treat the emotional content of crisis as a kind of civic aesthetic that contains transformational properties? Not so often, I suspect. Instead, we're encouraged in most public educational cultures to repress the crisis-ridden, messier dimensions of national identity. America's bristling yet fecund contradictions, its vexing paradoxes, its endless ambiguities, and its tragic ironies, represent the very stuff of national identity formation. Yet the moral content of this stuff, its emotional field, tends to be ignored—and with a passion. This passion to ignore tends to infantilize both students and the broader public. From the standpoint of citizenship education, the passion to ignore these existential conditions as formative influences on the national identity is tantamount to squandering opportunities to harness the educational vitality latent within these evocative signifiers. To harness this energy and redirect it toward democratic ends requires us to "do" critical pedagogy.

The problem with this requirement, however, is that many Americans seem to have developed a jaundiced view of the very term, *critical*. The practice of being critical is frequently regarded as nothing more than an unproductive tendency to complain about things we don't like and can't change anyway. As a consequence of this mentality, an appreciation of the rich beauty of the term seems to have escaped us, a token of America's increasingly carnivalesque and mean-spirited cultural environment. We need to somehow turn around this negative conception of both crisis and critical as a first step in reinvigorating democratic education. Wendy Brown brilliantly recovers the Greek etymology of *crisis* and *critique* and explains how they stem from the same linguistic source and share common meanings. Brown observes

> In ancient Athens, *krisis* was a jurisprudential term identified with the art of making distinctions, an art considered essential to judging and rectifying an alleged disorder in or of democracy . . . The sifting and sorting entailed in Greek *krisis* focused on distinguishing the true from the false, the genuine from the spurious, the beautiful from the ugly, and the right from the wrong, distinctions that involved weighing pros and cons of particular arguments—that is, evaluating and eventually judging evidence, reasons, or reasoning.[2]

In this passage, we see that *krisis* is closely aligned with the virtue of deliberation, if not critical thinking itself. Brown remarks that "its connotations are quite remote from negativity or scholasticism."[3] The etymology of critical (*kritikos*) means "to be able to judge, and to choose."[4] Based on the original definitions of both terms, then, we would be justified in claiming that individuals who wish to lead meaningful "examined lives" ought to hold these democratic virtues in the highest esteem.

Applying these insights to the negotiation of American national identity, both terms can serve a valuable purpose, insofar as their exercise stimulates our moral imaginations, and this exercise functions to keep democracies democratic. For this reason, we would do well to recover the positive ethical dimensions of these foundational Western terms and learn how absolutely crucial they are to the formation of democratic selfhood.

Democratic Transformations responds to these challenges by introducing a novel and critically eclectic approach for negotiating both the question of American identity and the moral predicaments that arise when individuals identify both with and against this contested symbolic terrain. I propose that instead of shying away from the conflicted nucleus of American identity, we confront these moral and ideological conflicts head-on, and in doing so, transform them into sites of pedagogical opportunity. As a contribution to the field of critical pedagogy, *Democratic Transformations* seeks to articulate how our perceptions of these conflicts and the existential qualities of mind such conflicts tend to generate can be revalued as part of the longer-term project of theorizing how we might learn to better integrate these marginalized features into the negotiation of American identity.

To inaugurate this project, I adopt a deliberately unorthodox method for representing eight pieces of public rhetoric found in US political culture. *Democratic Transformations* revives these iconic yet now languishing strands of public rhetoric to draw out their educational and democratic meanings. In using these phrases as points of entry to telescope the nation's defining contradictions, I hope to intensify personal encounters with how citizens navigate their way through the sometimes treacherous symbolic mind-fields of national identity. The phrases under consideration have been authored, circulated, publicly debated, and in many cases, just plain forgotten. To my knowledge, these pieces of public rhetoric, or others like them, have never been conceptualized as instruments of democratic pedagogy—until now.

One may well ask—*So what's in a phrase?* The eight phrases have been selected for analysis because each one contains an enormous potential for what I call "civic generativity." That is, as discursive windows into US political culture, they are capable of generating instructive civic controversies which, if dissected and investigated in the right way, can sharpen perceptions of American social reality and our frequently indifferent, ambivalent, or unconscious relationship to that reality. The phrases are mined as treasure troves of civic meaning, because they reflect contradictory images of what it means to be an American. Identification and analysis of contradictions—located externally in society, or internally within— constitute healthy exercises in democratic moral imagination.

The public rhetoric approach adopted here is indebted to Brazilian educational philosopher Paulo Freire (1929–97). Freire brings to our attention the idea that teachers should learn to frame the contradictions residing within the signs and symbols that circulate within peoples' everyday cultural life. Due to my own cultural location, I interpret this Freirean principle strictly in terms of US political culture. I am proposing, then, that the eight pieces of public rhetoric I have selected from American political culture can be conceptualized as rough equivalents of Freire's concept of "generative themes."

Among other things, one of Freire's enduring achievements was to take seriously the idiosyncratic colloquialisms of the adult illiterates he worked alongside. With the adoption of Freire's innovative method, everyday symbols and culturally specific figures of speech could be critically analyzed and *new meanings about them could be made to emerge if identified in dialogue and constructed as a problem in the right way.*[6] In a similar manner, my book invites readers to converse with the cultural contradictions identified within these generative themes of American culture, a conversation that can potentially alter one's vicarious symbolic relation both to national identity and to the democratic project (as interrelated significations). According to Freire, moreover, a cultures' inventory of generative themes exist as sub-units within a larger "thematic universe."[7] To deepen and extend the application of Freire's theory throughout the pages of *Democratic Transformations*, I bracket four civic tensions whose pervasiveness in American culture qualifies them to be defined as equivalents of Freire's concept of a culture's thematic universe.

As conceptual motifs, these four civic tensions are highlighted in different ways in different chapters and in different contexts. Despite their diverse expressions throughout the book, they constitute part of the larger fabric of American culture. It is this larger fabric that Freire refers to when he theorizes a culture's thematic universe. I "factor down" the thematic universe of American culture as follows: (1) individualism/individuality, (2) democracy/imperialism, (3) historical amnesia and the politics of forgetting, and (4) the ambiguous status of American exceptionalism.[8] To be sure, this framework is partial; however, despite its limited scope, it is an interpretive device that thematizes several of the nation's core contradictions that find expression in some form in every chapter of *Democratic Transformations*.

Freire defines critical thinking, what he calls *conscientization*, as "learning to perceive social, political, and economic contradictions and to take action against the oppressive elements of reality."[9] An essential component of his definition is the development of a "critical historical awareness," without which Freire argued critical thinking cannot exist. When this principle is applied to a twenty-first century American context, problems immediately arise, for American culture has accurately been described as notoriously ahistorical. The origins of this deeply ingrained collective habit is traced in part to the symbolism of the American dream, a future-directed transcendent project of reinvention which depended for its existence on individuals discarding the past as irrelevant.[10] This future-directed social imaginary tends to legitimize patterns of historical amnesia that are by now deeply etched into the public imagination. For democratic educators, the contagion of historical amnesia constitutes a problem of the first order since the recovery of democracy's memory is a necessary condition for its robust reemergence in the future.

The all-important ethical component of *conscientization* is reflected in Freire's assertion that one must "take action" as a consequence of acquiring greater knowledge of self and society. Of course, what constitutes an "action" is itself a complicated philosophical issue. For the purposes of this book, I take the view that launching a new inquiry, initiating a new conversation, or even speaking up in the classroom about some issue one cares about, could all qualify as legitimate forms of action.

Here we need to be flexible in applying Freire's theory. We need to acknowledge that "taking action against the oppressive elements of reality" might mean one thing to illiterate Brazilian campesinos in the 1960s and quite another to the privileged middle-class American citizens in the twenty-first century. In either case, the enduring educational value of thinking through a culture's contradictions is that the process often leads to further inquiries and further tasks to be fulfilled. Freire writes: "I have termed these themes 'generative' because (however they are comprehended and whatever action they may evoke) they contain the possibility of unfolding into again as many themes, which in turn call for new tasks to be fulfilled."[11] In linking the acquisition of knowledge to an imperative to act, Freire wants to unite theory and practice. The name he gives this informed type of action is *praxis*. In the following pages, I attempt to move toward this ideal unity by asking readers to imagine how each phrase might be jettisoned out of its present moribund state and recast to democratize American identity. The last section of each chapter introduces what could be called "action-oriented" public policy initiatives. These theoretical experiments in democratic renovation are inspired not only by Freire but by the tradition of American pragmatism; and they are intended to be more exploratory than explanatory, intended more to open up new conversations about old problems than to introduce a set of infallible policy initiatives.

The pieces of public rhetoric chosen for investigation span the eighteenth to the twentieth centuries. They are drawn mainly from the nation's constitutional language, from presidential speeches, and from leading public intellectuals. There are several advantages that accrue from interpreting US political history from a public rhetoric perspective. Perhaps the most notable advantage that accompanies such an approach is that these pieces of public rhetoric are closely associated with the chief architects of America's civic mythology, a set of luminaries which includes Thomas Jefferson, Alexis de Tocqueville, Horace Mann, Abraham Lincoln, Frederick Douglass, W. E. B. Du Bois, William James, Theodore Roosevelt, John Dewey, Calvin Coolidge, Dwight Eisenhower, and Martin Luther King, Jr. In the case of Chapter eight, "the personal is political," the rhetoric is not attributable to any single individual, rather this sublime piece of civic rhetoric emerged from the 1960s and 1970s women's movement. Because the schematic organization of the book permits me to foreground the writings of these pivotal figures and social movements in US political history, *Democratic Transformations* offers readers a radical democratic rereading of the American canon.

At the risk of oversimplifying the ways in which this approach works in each of the eight chapters, let me briefly illustrate how two of the nation's iconic pieces of public rhetoric can be recruited to frame educationally fecund contradictions.

- *The pursuit of happiness*: Americans are proud of their spiritual traditions yet, our culture is unabashedly materialistic. How does this contradiction manifest itself in debates over the meaning of the pursuit of happiness clause in the Declaration of Independence? What would Jefferson say about today's consumerist understanding of the pursuit of happiness? Is there a basis for thinking that we can turn the meaning of this phrase around from one grounded in material acquisition to one grounded in a democratic moral vision?

- *The moral equivalent of war*: Americans like to think of themselves as peaceful, yet US history presents a chronicle of constant warfare. How to make sense of this contradiction? Is it possible to develop a "moral equivalent" of war as William James boldly suggested in his 1910 essay by the same name? Can the passions for war and its heroic virtues be replaced by passions for peace and its heroic virtues?

Here, we glimpse how contradictions sequestered within two foundational pieces of public rhetoric can be viewed as sites of educational opportunity. It is crucial to learn to perceive contradictions because perceptions of contradiction give rise to heightened states of internal tension. These heightened states of internal tension can propel new desires to know into existence. Without the productive internal forces these states of tension propel, "desires to know" cannot, so to speak, "take flight." This theory of how desires to know can be brought about represents the core educational principle of the book. While such a learning theory is traced to Socratic pedagogy (and to the Platonic "dialectic"), key dimensions of it also finds modern expression in the writings of French educational psychologist Jean Piaget (1896–1980) and, as previously remarked, in the work of Paulo Freire.[12]

The theory of how human desires can be drawn out to imagine an envisioned good was so significant to Plato that he has Socrates declare in the *Symposium* that no one could find a better collaborator for acquiring virtue than being connected to this desire to know, to seek, and to transcend. Plato defined this transcendent desire as a form of love—what he called Eros.[13] (The assumption which permeates this book is that the practice of identifying and probing contradictions is a vital and healthy democratic activity.) It is beneficial not only because of the possibilities it opens up for stimulating one's eros (love) for a knowledge quest but because in democratic regimes such inquiries are as essential for the health of individual "psyches" as they are for the health of the "city." Put more dramatically democratic citizens require philosophy—literally, the love of wisdom and questioning—every bit as much as human beings require oxygen.

In everyday news, we look aghast at the wickedly polarizing and disheartening conflicts that occur over the contested meaning of American identity. These spectacles of conflict tend to activate difficult emotions and, precisely for this reason, these expressions are more likely to become objects of repression. Yet, it is this conflicted ideational nucleus of American identity that *Democratic Transformations* seeks to investigate and transform into a site of education. Thus, a legitimate question arises—Why go there? The assumption here is that we need to "go there" because learning how to recode the meaning of these conflicts and to respond wisely to the psychological states they engender represents an ethical endeavor that must be worked through before we can enact the nation's next chapter in democratization.

In this regard, it is crucial to note that America's premier philosopher of democracy, John Dewey, saw in social conflict a largely untapped reservoir of educative and transformational potential. Richard Bernstein adroitly interprets this Deweyan proposition:

> Conflict is not just "ineliminable" in democratic politics; it is *essential* for the achievement of social reform and justice. No longer does Dewey speak of democracy as an ideal organic unity of the individual and society. New conflicts will always break out. The key point is how one *responds* to conflict. And this requires imagination, intelligence, and a commitment to solve concrete problems.[14]

Grounded in an analysis of conflict, then, *Democratic Trans-formations* views this overall psychical terrain as one of America's great educational frontiers, a moral geography that invites our pioneering exploration.

Finally, there is one additional rationale I would mention to justify the adoption of my synergistic integration of Socratic and Freirean pedagogy, Critical Theory and American pragmatism. It can be explained by reference to two premier books in the nation's democratic canon, books that have inspired my thinking about the benefits of "difficult knowledge" as that knowledge relates to raising questions about the meaning of American identity.

In this connection, it's worth recalling why, exactly, Howard Zinn's *A People's History of the United States* and James Loewen's *Lies My Teacher Told Me* struck such a popular chord with the American public. No doubt, part of this appeal was that both authors recovered repressed dimensions of the American experience that conventional textbooks seem determined to overlook.[15] As a consequence of engaging these innovative texts, millions of Americans felt viscerally connected to the democratic tradition for the first time in their lives. The books had this "affect" on readers not because they offered "objective" representations of US history, rather it was the authors' abandonment of the false pretense of objectivity which inspired many to participate with the texts at a deeper level.[16] Readers were compelled to wrestle with the meaning of democracy in novel ways and to participate symbolically in forging a new moral identity both for themselves and for their image of American nationhood. The process was as pleasurable as it was ethically demanding. Based on this brief overview, I think it's warranted to assert these books excited the public imagination because they tacitly embodied an alternative "civic aesthetic."[17] Even though this civic aesthetic was never stated explicitly in either *A People's History* or in *Lies My Teacher Told Me*, its moral content is revealed in the authorial decisions to place renewed value on the examination of contradictions and on the difficult knowledge and emotions such examinations can be expected to generate.

In a fashion similar to these books, *Democratic Transformations* is written to highlight the nation's core contradictions and through this process jostle into being a greater awareness of the American democratic tradition, the precondition for morally renovating the national identity. In contrast to these fine authors, however—and writing as a philosopher of education—I attempt to outline the contours of a new civic aesthetic as a framework for making meaning out of these difficult-to-assimilate qualities. I argue in the Epilogue, for instance, that the cultivation of America's democratic spirit can be educationally nourished on the basis of a critical utilization of the jazz-as-democracy metaphor. This largely untapped resource can help us negotiate with greater receptivity the conflicts that bedevil American political culture. I develop the case that the epistemic attributes of this musical idiom can be conceptualized as a civic aesthetic which can encourage us to positively integrate the existential qualities of contradiction, paradox, ambiguity and irony into our civic self-conceptions.[18] Among other advantages, it can help us reconcile a sense of individuality with a viable sense of the common good. Significantly, the jazz-as-democracy metaphor can also clarify what it means to *be* democratic as opposed to merely learning *about* democracy in a procedural sense.

How we choose to negotiate the zones of tension and anxiety that saturate every dimension of national identity will, to a large extent, determine whether or not Americans can envision and enact a more democratic version of ourselves. *Democratic Transformations* marks a hopeful contribution to this perpetually unfinished enactment.

Notes

1 Deborah Britzman, *After-Education: Anna Freud, Melanie Klein, and Psychoanalytic Histories of Learning* (New York: SUNY Press, 2003), 1, 150. Britzman's concept of "difficult knowledge" is a crucial element in my book, insofar as the act of perceiving contradictions often entails encounters with difficult to assimilate forms of knowledge; at another level, Britzman's psychoanalytic notion that education can be made out of anything, in my opinion, justifies my attempt to make education both out of the phrases and out of the creative absences of American identity.

2 Wendy Brown, "Untimeliness and Punctuality: Critical Theory in Dark Times" in *Edgework: Critical Essays on Knowledge and Politics* (Princeton NJ: Princeton University Press, 2005), 5–6.

3 Ibid., 5–6. For an additional treatment of the origins of the term critical, and for a superb primer on Critical Theory, see Stephen Eric Bronner *Critical Theory: A Very Short Introduction* (New York: Oxford University Press, 2011), 1–3, 20–1.

4 *The Barnhart Concise Dictionary of Etymology*, ed. Robert Barnhart. (New York: HaperCollins, 1995), 173.

5 Paulo Freire, *Pedagogy of the Oppressed* (New York: Continuum Books, 1997), 96–104. (all subsequent reference to this source will be cited as *POP*).

6 Paulo Freire, *Education for Critical Consciousness* (New York: Continuum Books, 1973).

7 Freire, *POP*, 96–7.

8 While each of these strands of America's thematic universe are elaborated upon in varying degrees throughout the pages of *Democratic Transformations*, it may be useful to broadly frame these thematic tensions at the outset. John Dewey spent much of his career grappling with the tension between an individualist model of selfhood and a more social-oriented model he dubbed, "individuality." This civic tension appears most notably in Chapters 1, 6, and 8, but it also appears in other chapters, albeit less extensively. As an interpretive trope, the tension between the values of democracy versus those of imperialism is indebted to Cornel West's *Democracy Matters* (2004); this civic tension finds expression in Chapters 2, 5, and 7. The phenomenon of historical amnesia is wedded to what I am calling the "politics of ignorance," in that cultural forgetting is never innocent of power relations. This theme is highlighted in Chapters 1, 3, 4, and 7. Finally, the contested narrative of American exceptionalism is treated most extensively in Chapters 1, 3, 4, 5, and 7. The literature on American exceptionalism is too vast to summarize here. My thinking on the subject, however, is inspired in large part by Donald E. Pease's psychoanalytical treatment of the "fantasy" of American exceptionalism. See his "The United States of Fantasy" in *The New American Exceptionalism* (Minneapolis: University of Minnesota, 2009), 1–39. Far from seeing the fantasy of American exceptionalism as "delusional," or as a peripheral factor in the formation of state authority, Pease argues that fantasy is central to the life of nations and states even as it's seldom regarded as such. In this sense, then, the power within the narrative of American exceptionalism derives from the power of the wish fulfillments individuals' project onto the myths of the nation.

9 Freire, *POP*, 35.

10 For more on how the ideology of the American Dream relies on historical amnesia for its very existence, see Russell Banks, *Dreaming Up America* (New York: Seven Stories Press, 2008), 6, 7, 39.

11 Freire, *POP*, 102 (fn #19).

12 In a Platonic sense, the "dialectic" can be broadly understood as a method and process of dialogue between people whose purpose is to seek truths through questioning and through the identification of contradictions. See, for example, Hans- Georg Gadamer, *Dialogue and Dialectic: Eight Hermeneutical Studies of Plato* (New Haven: Yale University Press, 1980). Paulo Freire's concept of *conscientization*, defined as "learning to perceive contradictions" is roughly equivalent to Plato's dialectic. See, *Pedagogy of the Oppressed* (New York: Continuum Books, 2000); Jean-Paul Piaget's concept of equilibrium posits the notion that desires to know and other positive features occur when there is "cognitive conflict" within the learner. See Jean Piaget, *Six Psychological Studies* (New York: Vintage Books, 1967), 100–15.

13 William Cobb, trans. *Plato's Erotic Dialogues: The Symposium and the Phaedrus* (Albany: SUNY Press, 1993), 212b (p. 49). For more on Eros as a concept vital to democratic education see, Kerry T. Burch, *Eros as the Educational Principle of Democracy* (New York: Peter Lang, 2000).

14 Richard J. Bernstein, "John Dewey's Vision of Radical Democracy" in *The Pragmatic Turn* (Malden, MA: Polity Press, 2010), 84.

15 Howard Zinn, *A People's History of the United States* (New York, Harper Perennial Books, 1980/2010); James W. Loewen, *Lies My Teacher Told Me: Everything Your American History Textbooks Got Wrong* (New York: Touchstone, 1995/2007).

16 This principle is articulated quite well by Richard Rorty in his *Achieving Our Country: Leftist Thought in Twentieth-Century America* (Cambridge: Harvard University Press, 1998).

17 I would like to acknowledge my indebtedness to Jessica Heybach for suggesting how the idea of a "civic aesthetic" might be used to clarify the underlying purposes of the book.

18 See, for example, Robert G. O'Meally, ed. *The Jazz Cadence in American Culture* (New York: Columbia University Press).

CHAPTER ONE

The pursuit of happiness

Transforming American scripture into a site of democratic pedagogy

Working in tandem with their cunning advertising strategists, corporations invest billions every year to persuade Americans to believe that they lack something vital to their "happiness." This well-documented pattern makes advertising the most powerful educational force in America today.[1] It is reasonable for us to assume that this power exercises a profound influence in shaping the nation's image of the meaning of the *pursuit of happiness*[2] clause, particularly among young Americans of recent generations who have been most decisively subjected to its unremitting influence. I want to suggest that there are steep democratic costs involved in continuing to privatize our conception of this crown jewel of American political rhetoric.

From a democratic perspective, for us to reduce what Pauline Maier called "American scripture" into something that has no more than a commercial or consumer meaning is both tragic and unjustified.[3] It is tragic in that it robs the phrase of its democratic potential, and unjustified in that, during the eighteenth century at least, the phrase was seen to contain a crucial civic dimension. We need to remind ourselves that our conceptions of the meaning of the pursuit of happiness—especially its civic dimension which we've slowly forgotten over time—carry profound implications in terms of how we go about imagining our personal and national identities.

As critical educational theorists have cogently demonstrated, corporations have been predatorily taking advantage of the nation's youth for decades in America's schools. The accelerated pace of corporate influence in determining the direction of educational "reform" has had the cumulative effect not only of degrading the civic purposes of public education but also of undermining the very idea of public education itself. Today, an ever increasing number of students can now look forward to encountering TV advertising in schools, hallways adorned with glitzy advertising billboards, and curriculum packets sponsored by such renowned educational authorities as Pizza Hut, M & M's, Hershey's, Kellogg's, and McDonald's.[4]

Owing to the growing influence of corporate power within the schools, few can be shocked to learn that the meaning of the pursuit of happiness has devolved into a civically barren, utilitarian narrative of maximizing individual pleasure. The problem, as I have suggested, is that precious few Americans today realize that in the revolutionary period the pursuit of happiness was seen to contain a vital civic dimension as a condition of its own higher realization. To the extent the phrase is remembered at all today, its meaning is understood to be a wholly private, individualistic affair. With the extension of corporate power into the previously noncommercialized sphere of public education, corporate advertisers-turned-educators are increasingly in the position to educate youth desire within the schools by linking consumerism to the core meaning of human identity. In what can only be judged a remarkably successful effort to orchestrate human fantasy and desire—and thereby to corporatize selfhood—the titillating promise of infinite consumption now assumes the majestic heights of a transcendent ideal. Behold—*Homo economicus!*

Of course, the problem of *Homo economicus* has always been a factor in the negotiation of American identity. And for political theorists throughout the Western tradition, this species of character has consistently been perceived as a danger to both democratic and republican notions of selfhood, from ancient Greece and the Roman Empire up to the present moment. Since the pursuit of happiness has become yoked to consumption as an end-in-itself, today's hegemonic interpretation of the phrase's meaning poses a threat not only to American citizenship and democracy but also to the ecological health of the planet. It is my contention that in forgetting the civic and spiritual basis of this defining moral principle—or in not knowing or caring about its original conception—we unwittingly squander opportunities to revitalize the democratic project.

To redress this cultural forgetting, teachers need to develop critical pedagogies capable of engaging in what might be called the "politics of happiness." Such an approach would mine the contradictory dimensions of the phrase with a focus on rearticulating its public resonances. Hannah Arendt, in her *On Revolution*, talked about the need to recover what she called the phrase's intended "two-fold meaning" (i.e. the harmonization of its private and public dimensions). To resist the wholesale privatization of this vital strand of public rhetoric, I explore how a recovered public conception of the phrase's meaning can be deployed to restore a more robust sense of civic purpose to the nation's schools. What follows, then, is a conceptual road map for showing how the meaning of the phrase might be "turned around" from its present consumer focus on external material objects toward an alternative focus on a renewed democratic moral vision of the nation's future.

Some readers will be skeptical about the possibility of turning around or modifying the meanings we attach to the pursuit of happiness. Indeed, such attitudes are quite understandable yet they are also symptomatic of a much larger problem—the erosion of our capacity for political imagination. But even as we acknowledge the odds stacked against the possibility of transforming public opinion regarding the meaning of the phrase, we would be remiss not to acknowledge that, in the United States many social movements in the past have coalesced around politically inventive rereadings of the Declaration of Independence. Such episodes of moral renovation represent the symbolic axes upon which American identity has historically been democratized. Conversely, the most antidemocratic phases in US history have been those in which the memory of the values enshrined in the Declaration have been subject to historical amnesia. Prominent historians of the Declaration demonstrate that changing interpretations of the document's moral content, namely, questions about what exactly *equality*, *self-determination*, *right to revolution*, and *pursuit of happiness* mean at different points in the nation's history, have always been sites of contestation perpetually "under construction."[5]

To briefly illustrate: the first political party to emerge in the United States once the Constitution was ratified—the Federalists—had little interest in acknowledging much less venerating the democratic and egalitarian values of the Declaration. For decades, the volcanic political potential of the Declaration lay dormant as the Federalists succeeded in representing the text as nothing more than an expedient vehicle to announce independence. In the Federalist view, once the war against England was over, so, too, was the Declaration's usefulness. Its potential to continue shaping the national identity was effectively tamed—at least for a couple decades.

In the 1820s, however, newly assertive labor and abolitionist movements revived its public memory and civic meaning. The Declaration's forgotten egalitarian principles were imaginatively reclaimed and its meaning transformed into something democratic, future-directed and transcendent. Historian Alfred F. Young captures the transformation in American identity that emerged from this momentous rediscovery of the Declaration: "The Fourth of July, to conservatives never more than the anniversary of independence, to others had become a symbol of liberation."[6]

What occurred within these individuals, and within these larger political bodies, so that abstractions written on paper were transformed into emotionally powerful symbols of liberation? Was the value of equality reawakened as a force in the contest over the meaning of the national identity? Did many begin to realize that their own personal happiness was incomplete apart from their engaged participation in building a "more perfect union"? Whatever the ideas motivating these visionaries, their examples provide ample testimony to the fact that the most democratic phases in American history have come about as a consequence of citizens undergoing an intensified encounter with the democratic moral ideals embodied in the Declaration. Whether in reference to the abolitionists, to the trade unionists, to the suffragettes, or to the twentieth century civic rights advocates, a clear pattern emerges: The meanings we attach to the Declaration, and to the pursuit of happiness in particular, may be more fluid and susceptible to re-conceptualization than we are taught to think.

The public dimensions of the pursuit of happiness, at least within the American context, are rooted in the writings of Thomas Jefferson, George Mason and James Otis. These figures in turn were indebted to the leading thinkers of the Scottish Enlightenment. But the kernel of the idea of public happiness is also traced to Platonic, Aristotelian, Stoic and Epicurean conceptions of happiness and the social conditions that these traditions believed necessary to bring this desirable state into being. In order to recover a fuller meaning of the pursuit of happiness, then, the first step will be to establish the continuity between the civic humanism of antiquity and aspects of the American enlightenment whose ethos Jefferson so paradoxically personifies.

Citizens and idiots: An ancient Greek and Roman snapshot of human happiness

The classical Greek word for happiness is "*eudaimonia*," which means "to have a good *daimon*."[7] As Socrates describes it, a *daimon* represents an interior space coded mythically as a "third term" intermediary; this third term was named eros by Plato as a form of love which was seen to bind the divine realm to the human realm. Socrates describes his *daimon* as an "inner voice" that came to him only to advise what actions he should not take. In the Socratic tradition, we see human happiness imagined as an internal moral orientation to the self and world. Socrates claimed that this orientation could only be achieved by "taking care of the soul." In *The Apology* we observe Socrates on trial for allegedly "corrupting" Athenian youth, no doubt because he was urging them to question popular images of happiness and to take care of their souls. He defends himself by lambasting those who would reduce happiness to the pursuit of wealth:

> My very good friend, you are an Athenian and belong to a city which is the greatest and most famous in the world for its wisdom and strength. Are you not ashamed that you give your attention to acquiring as much money as possible, and similarly with reputation and honor, and give no attention or thought to truth and understanding and the perfection of your soul?[8]

There is a sense in which Socrates inaugurates the tradition of critical pedagogy by engaging in the "politics of happiness," an effort to identify the contradictions embedded within the Athenian self-conception. Later, Aristotle would continue the Socratic ethos of critically reflective citizenship by defining the most elevated form of happiness as intellectual contemplation, the *vita contemplativa*.[9] In the Stoic and Epicurean traditions, whose leading figures worked very much within the then dominant Socratic/Platonic paradigm, happiness results from the harmonious life, whereby the conflicting parts of the psyche are brought into conscious awareness through the cultivation of one's critical reason.

As is well known, one of the guiding assumptions of Aristotle's philosophy is that human beings are innately political creatures (*zoon politikon*).[10] For Aristotle, then, the condition of happiness could only come into existence within a social context, within a political order where the civic or social dimensions of being are explicitly acknowledged, valued and consciously developed. Because our sociability defines us as humans, the prospect of being self-regarding and other-regarding in a virtuous manner could only be realized through sustained civic engagement.

The idea that human beings were essentially "political animals" was so crucial to Greek democratic political culture that the term "idiot" (*idios*) was invented to describe those who could legally participate in the polis or political community, but instead chose to live a private existence. *Idiotes* is defined as "a purely private person."[11] In his oft-noted funeral oration, Pericles boasts that in democratic Athens those who took no part in civic affairs were considered to be "useless." Unlike democratic characters, they could not judge, choose, deliberate about public affairs, or become indignant at the sight of injustice. Within the democratic social imaginary, then, privately isolated individuals were disparaged as idiots because they denied themselves exposure to a diversity of external stimuli. Idiots foreclosed on the possibility that they might positively transform themselves as a consequence of their relations with others-in-community. Martha Nussbaum's discussion of Aristotle's *eudaimonism* affirms the fundamental civic character of happiness as it was understood in classical antiquity: "the sort of self-sufficiency that characterizes the best human life is a communal one and not a solitary self-sufficiency . . . a solitary life is insufficient for *eudaimonia*."[12]

Jefferson unplugged: Moving beyond idiotic pursuits of happiness

For much of the nation's history, the liberal orthodoxy or the so-called consensus interpretations held that Jefferson's political philosophy was exclusively rooted in the individualistic ethos of British philosopher John Locke.[13] Among other things, this meant that Jefferson was believed to have endorsed Locke's version of "possessive" individualism, a free-market orientation to the world anchored in the assumption that property was a natural right.

Several outstanding scholars have challenged the assumption that Jefferson was a free-market liberal in a Lockean mold.[14] These thinkers profile a "Jefferson" who rejects the notion that property was an unalienable, natural right. As strange as it may seem given Jefferson's status as a slaveholder, these authors characterize Jefferson as a communitarian and radical democratic visionary. It should be noted that my purpose here is not to deny Jefferson's obvious contradictions as a political figure or to gloss over his decades-long love affair with Sally Hemings, his slave, but rather to advance a narrower claim: that Jefferson's conception of the pursuit of happiness included a vital public dimension.

It is significant that Jefferson rejected the core assumption held by many classical liberals that purely individualized pursuits of happiness would lead "naturally" to the public interest, the general welfare or the common good. The first clue that enables us to tease Jefferson apart from Locke's possessive individualism is his exclusion of property from the roster of natural, unalienable rights enumerated in the Declaration:

> We hold these truths to be self-evident; that all men are created equal; that they are endowed by their Creator by certain unalienable rights; that among these are life, liberty and the pursuit of happiness.[15]

Consider the consequences for the future of the American identity formation had Jefferson simply adopted Locke's well known formulation of "life, liberty and *property*." Such an explicit economic rendering of the Declaration would have surely constricted the shifting boundaries of American civic identity at one of its founding moments, while at the same time providing moral legitimacy to the development of *Homo economicus*. Jefferson's demotion of Locke's principle that property was a natural right signals his belief that the principle of human rights—symbolized by the pursuit of happiness clause—must be given primacy over market-based property rights in the project of "dreaming up" America.

Moreover, Jefferson's statement that "the earth is made for the living" meant that the ideas and conceptions of past generations should never be seen as binding on present day generations. When this principle is applied to our interpretation of the pursuit of happiness clause, it indicates that today's consumerist reading of the phrase should not be seen as binding on current and future generations of Americans. At stake for Jefferson was the validity of American exceptionalism: whether the American identity formation would elevate human rights over property rights and thus vindicate the experiment, or whether the new nation through its own timidity would devolve into a dismal reflection of the values and hierarchies that defined life in "old" Europe.

The substantive moral content of Jefferson's civic image of happiness is captured by Donald H. Meyer in *The Democratic Enlightenment*:

> It is clear that by "happiness" Jefferson did not mean purely sensual gratification . . . Nor did he mean the possession of wealth, for if he had, he could very well have repeated Locke's well-known formula, "life, liberty and property." It seems evident that Jefferson was thinking of happiness in the grand sense suggested by his Epicurean ethic. Happiness is the byproduct of an active, useful, and disciplined life, the satisfaction of soul that is the reward of virtue. Happiness is to develop one's mental and moral capabilities and to live as a fully functioning person.[16]

Here a nonacquisitive or holistic model of happiness is seen to depend on the prior development of one's moral and intellectual capacities. The passage suggests what it would mean for happiness to begin to be turned around from an externalized projection onto material objects of desire and toward an internalized projection onto immaterial objects of desire (such as the development of one's civic virtue). Jefferson linked happiness to civic virtue because he knew that the people of the United States could only be relied on to engage in public affairs as a consequence of their civic virtue being consciously developed.

Jefferson argued that his decentralized "ward system" would promote the nation's democratic character, for it would create a context in which, "every man is a sharer in the direction of his ward-republic . . . and feels that he is a participator in the government of affairs, not merely at an election one day in the year, but every day."[17] To be a "participator" every day in public affairs and to be a "sharer in the direction" of one's community, it first requires identification on the part of individuals with a community or government. It also requires a desire to care about some notion of a common good. This desire to care about a common good is paramount, for it works against the reduction of politics to the assertion of one's narrow self-interest, which, properly defined, is not really "politics" at all. Jefferson consistently identifies the indispensability of education for the development of civic virtue, the precondition for the ability of democratic citizens to exercise their right to the pursuit of happiness: "I know of no safe depository of the ultimate powers of society but the people themselves; and if we think them not enlightened enough to exercise their control with a wholesome discretion, the remedy is not to take it from them, but to inform their discretion by education."[18]

Hannah Arendt and John Dewey on Jefferson's legacy

Hannah Arendt's comparative study of modern revolutions further affirms the principle that "public happiness" was identified in eighteenth century America as the central purpose of government. What may be surprising to twenty-first century readers is the degree to which the principle of public happiness was legitimized by a widely shared public consensus. According to Arendt:

> This freedom they called later, when they came to taste it, "public happiness," and it consisted in the citizen's right of access to the public realm, in his share in public power—to be a "participator in the government of affairs" in Jefferson's telling phrase. The very fact that the word "happiness" was chosen in laying claim to a share of public power indicates strongly that there existed in the country, prior to revolution, such a thing as public happiness, and that men knew they could not be altogether "happy" if their happiness was located and enjoyed only in a private life.[19]

Here we see elements of the Aristotelian/Stoic paradigm of civic humanism manifesting itself, however imperfectly, two thousand years later on American soil. As we think through the project of reframing the pursuit of happiness today, it's worth repeating that the notion of happiness in the eighteenth century was not restricted to merely enjoying one's private life, but instead was seen as something deeply entwined with one's capacity to actively participate in public affairs. Among other things, this brings to our attention that, in one of the nation's founding moments, an American public came into existence in which a conception of public happiness—anchored in idea that civic virtues required active educating—was articulated as one of the first principles that differentiated American from European identity.

In concentrating on the public dimension of happiness for the purpose of clarifying the discursive career of this moral ideal, it's important not to overlook the legitimate private dimensions of the phrase. The voluminous letters Jefferson wrote make it clear that he would endorse what Arendt calls the "twofold meaning" of happiness—the harmonization of its private and public dimensions.[20] Arendt seems confident in asserting what the happiness clause intends:

> One thing at least we may be sure: the Declaration of Independence, though it blurs the distinction between private and public happiness, at least still intends us to hear the term 'pursuit of happiness' in its twofold meaning: private welfare as well as the right to public happiness, the pursuit of well-Being as well as being a participator in public affairs."[21]

It is important to note that Arendt, following Jefferson, links well-being and civic participation to a fully developed conception of happiness. If, then, within a democratic republic, an indispensable dimension of the pursuit of happiness is being a "participator in public affairs," does it not follow that one of the purposes of such a government's system of education should be to prepare its citizens preeminently to actually *be* citizens? Arendt observed that the rapid "loss of memory" of a viable sense of public happiness in the United States—a process which, as we have seen, accelerated in the years after the adoption of the Constitution—had the effect of arresting what was truly revolutionary about the American revolution.

Jefferson's beliefs about the public dimension of happiness are for the most part only implicit in his writings. Perhaps the most radical, yet least appreciated of Jefferson's political initiatives, was his belief that every (free white male) citizen be granted 50 acres of land by the State of Virginia.[22] While this measure was defeated in the Virginia legislature, as was his far-reaching educational proposals, the point is that Jefferson envisioned a nation of small freeholders in which land ownership and wealth was relatively evenly distributed. According to Jefferson, the realization of the pursuit of happiness (with its ideal harmonization of private and public) could only occur within a democratically organized social and economic structure, as this was the only sound basis upon which richer and more engaged civic personalities could develop. His proposal to divide Virginia into highly decentralized self-governing wards was the necessary political counterpart to his desire to move toward a more general distribution of wealth. And, in turn, his call for a "general diffusion of knowledge" among the "mass of people" was the indispensable educational counterpart for achieving this overall democratic vision.

Jefferson's ideas about the requirements for creating not only democratic government but also, tougher still, a democratic people, led him to formulate his educational theory. This theory is traced in no small part to his European travels. In England and France during the 1790s, Jefferson witnessed the consequences of early capitalism: he looked aghast at the political orders that were structured by class oppression, mass ignorance and perpetual war. Writing from Paris on the pending subject of Virginia's new State Constitution, Jefferson connects the development of happiness to the development of a civically awake citizenry:

> I think by far the most important bill in our whole code is that for the diffusion of knowledge among the people. No other sure foundation can be devised, for the preservation of freedom and happiness. If anybody thinks that kings, nobles or priests are good conservators of the public happiness send them here. It is the best school in the universe to cure them of that folly.[23]

Once again, Jefferson highlights his belief that the ultimate purpose of government is not the protection of property but the ongoing task of being "good conservators of the public happiness." Put differently, the highest function of a democratic republic is pedagogical: "public happiness" is the result of the State's active involvement in developing the moral and civic character of its people. The passage above thus serves as a touchstone for challenging purely individualistic interpretations of the pursuit of happiness. Within the classical liberal understanding of the clause—in what could be called the *laissez-faire* model of the pursuit of happiness—the State is not envisioned to have a legitimate role to play in positively promoting the pursuits of happiness. Instead, the State's power in relation to happiness is understood negatively; it tells us what the State cannot do and refuses to engage the question of what a State could do positively to furnish the educational conditions in which citizens would learn how to actually *be* participatory democratic citizens.

John Dewey also recognized that Jefferson's rejection of Locke's notion that property was a natural right carried significant implications for interpreting the meaning of the pursuit of happiness. Regarding Jefferson's legacy, Dewey asserts that

> It would be absurd to hold that his personal views were "radical" beyond fear of concentrated wealth and a positive desire for general distribution of wealth without great extremes in either direction. However, it is sometimes suggested that his phrase "pursuit of happiness" stood for economic activity, so that life, liberty and property were the rights he thought organized society should maintain. But just here is where he broke most completely with Locke . . . . Jefferson held that property rights are created by a "social pact" instead of representing inherent individual moral claims which government is morally bound to maintain.[24]

Jefferson's break with Locke once again proves crucial for grasping the civic dimensions of the pursuit of happiness. Dewey highlights this break (particularly during the 1920s) because he was disturbed at how images of happiness and the American Dream were being reduced to a ritualized gospel of consumption. In contrast to this dominant narrative, Dewey noted that the exercise of one's pursuit of happiness involves many things. It involves "choosing one's career" and being able to act upon one's judgment free from constraints imposed by either "officials of government" or by "persons whose command of capital and control of the opportunities for engaging in useful work limits the ability of others to 'pursue happiness'.[25]

Although Dewey does not explicitly adopt the terminology of "civic" or "public" happiness in these passages, his analysis of the tensions operating within the contested terrain of American individualism leaves no doubt that he was criticizing a privatized and externalized conception of happiness anchored in consumption. Not unlike Socrates' critique of the soul-denying Athenian materialism more than two millennia earlier, Dewey observed that,

> We pursue happiness in these external things because, I suppose, we do not really possess our own souls. We are impatient; we are hurried; we are fretful because we try to find happiness where it cannot be got . . . without knowing it, we distrust the slow processes of growth, and we do not tend the roots of life from which a lasting happiness springs.[26]

Here, Dewey tacitly underscores the importance of civic education in fostering pursuits of happiness when he asserts that the most "easily attained source of happiness is found simply in the broadening of intellectual curiosity and sympathy in all concerns of life." In a democratic society, the broadening of intellectual curiosity and sympathy in all concerns of life are learned conditions best cultivated by the nation's public schools. If, in this connection, the pursuit of happiness was deployed as a guiding metric for rejuvenating both civic education and spiritual democracy within the schools, it would surely represent an audacious and life-affirming reclamation of this Socratic-Jeffersonian-Deweyan tradition.

Dewey, writing before Arendt, had already identified the nation's historical amnesia regarding the "spiritual element" of the American founding: "Instead of the development of individualities which it prophetically set forth, there is a perversion of the whole ideal of individualism to conform to the practices of a pecuniary culture."[27] For Dewey, the relentless penetration of the "business mind" into every recess of American cultural life was "deplorably pervasive."[28] This historical perversion of the ideal of individuality resulted in false conceptions of happiness while also undermining the very idea of a democratic American identity. Dewey explains: "the source of the American democratic tradition is moral—not technical, abstract, narrowly political nor materially utilitarian."[29] As we shall see in chapter six, at the apparent height of American prosperity in the Roaring Twenties, Dewey produced a series of scathing articles about the ways in which the moral source of the American democratic tradition was being systematically emptied of meaning through the agency of corporate power.[30]

The pursuit of happiness and the renaissance of civic virtue

How tragically ironic it is that the public schools today are organized according to pure Lockean principles: A system where property counts most and where possessive individualism is sweetly ordained in a thousand different ways. On the one hand, financing public education through local property taxes guarantees that the quality of education citizens receive will merely reproduce existing inequalities, while on the other, the deepening corporatization of public education guarantees that the schools' responsibility to educate the young for citizenship will continue to be stripped to its barest minimum. For these reasons, the current status of the pursuit of happiness as a purely private affair, an activity and state of mind that is purported to be intrinsically linked to possessive individualism as a moral ideal, should be transformed into something akin to its opposite: the pursuit of happiness as a civic affair, a moral ideal that could be used as a heuristic device to help form democratic individualities.

In his 1953 classic, *The Pursuit of Happiness*, Howard Mumford Jones stated the obvious by writing that Jefferson's agrarian republic was a "vanished ideal." Jones asked if our "industrial empire" was capable of distributing happiness in "more equal portions." "Everything will turn," he observed, "on the question whether happiness is construed in modern America as primarily an individual or primarily a social state." Jones speculated that if such a transformation were to occur in the phrase's meaning—toward a social understanding—it would have the most "radical" consequences in the fields of health care, public education and leisure.[31]

Jones assessed some 50 judicial decisions in which the pursuit of happiness held legal force and was invoked by jurists in constructing their legal reasoning.[32] All of these cases, however, were detached from public education, consisting of narrowly defined disputes over property and inheritance claims. Still, Jones's essay succeeds in raising some untimely questions: If the courts have been willing in the past to grant legal force to the "unalienable right" to the "pursuit of happiness" in select legal domains, why not grant this right legal force in the domain of public education, the premier *citizen-forming* institution in the nation? What would it mean to apply this right to the sphere of public education? How might a reconfigured pursuit of happiness clause function as a metric for restoring a sense of civic purpose to the nation's schools?

First, let's affirm that in American society since the nineteenth century the public school has always been regarded as the chief avenue through which the *citizenship* of the citizen is supposed to be educated. On this point, it is important to recall that the *Brown* decision maintained that the purpose of public education was to provide "the very foundation of good citizenship."[33] If indeed public education is to provide the very foundation of good citizenship, it seems undeniable that the educational legislation known as "No Child Left Behind" (NCLB), due to its curricular bias against civic education, suppresses the foundational civic purposes of public education. A case could be made that for young citizens today, ensnared as they are in the consequences of NCLB, their "unalienable right" to the "pursuit of happiness"—*defined here as an equal opportunity to develop one's civic selfhood*—is being systematically infringed.

Imagine, on the other hand, if the social or public dimensions of the pursuit of happiness were developed consistent with the civic humanist and radical democratic traditions. The phrase could then be rearticulated as the moral equivalent of civic virtue, a transformation which would mark a recovery of its original twofold conception. Were the phrase to be understood in this manner, as signifying a developmental, embodied form of citizenship, the schools would then have a moral and legal obligation to educate the citizenship of its citizens equally.

Such a reform would mandate the schools to reframe their underlying purposes from their current economic and "sorting" rationale to a democratic civic rationale. If the pursuit of happiness were understood in a social sense and given *legal* force—after all, it appears in the Declaration as an "unalienable right"—it might also include relocating the primary object of discrimination in public education from the traditional categories of "race" or "class" to that of the "civic potential" or "citizenship" of the citizen. This moral principle finds recent expression in Meira Levinson's *No Citizen Left Behind* (2012), in which she categorizes this same basic principle as "the civic empowerment gap."[34]

The fact is that NCLB not only devalues *civic* education but also abandons any pretense that education might possibly include the aim of *self* understanding. For this reason, the curricular imperatives sequestered within NCLB impose a striking *absence of caring* in relation to self and civic development. This "constructed absence" of caring represents a sterling example of what Elliot Eisner calls the "null curriculum." The null curriculum in this instance—what isn't taught, the questions that go unasked, the desires to know that go undeveloped—is vastly more decisive in terms of shaping our civic self-conceptions than we tend to realize.[35] While some may want to cite this absence of self and civic caring as a positive example of a politically neutral education, it would be more accurate to say that it represents a tectonic shift toward the mass production of idiocy. For in its systematic reproduction of privatized noncitizens, this "null curriculum" constitutes a form of ideological indoctrination even as it masquerades as a politically neutral education (for a fuller discussion of the question of indoctrination, see Chapter eight).

As educational purposes are further corporatized, ever larger numbers of students will continue to experience school as a joyless and demoralizing force in their lives. The cultivation of fear, guilt, and inadequacy within the space of the public school can only impede the capacity of individuals to pursue happiness with a wholesome discretion. The absence of robust practices of democratic citizenship within the schools also means that the nation's pedagogically fertile civic controversies will not be properly encountered, further squandering opportunities for students to develop a passion for civic mindfulness. As Gerald Graff and, more recently, Diana Hess convincingly show from different disciplinary angles, giving full treatment to controversial issues within the classroom represents the best curricular avenue for developing critically reflective democratic citizens.[36]

It is difficult to imagine how democratic civic education can be revitalized in the nation's schools without a prior recovery of the public dimensions of the pursuit of happiness clause. Both the ancients and Jefferson had it right in attaching civic virtue to their understanding of happiness. By imaginatively recovering the phrase's repressed civic dimensions, we can position ourselves to re-code the meaning of this crown jewel of American political rhetoric beyond the narrow parameters of possessive individualism. If we can accomplish this moral and intellectual task, the pursuit of happiness will come to mean something much richer than the titillating promise of infinite consumption. It could fulfill, in a new age, under novel circumstances, its majestic form as a democratic and transcendent moral ideal, an ideal whose restorative power would give point and direction to a much-needed renaissance of civic virtue within the nation's schools.

Notes

1 For a sobering update on the exponentially expanding role of advertising in the lives of children since 1980, including within the schools, see the documentary film, *Consuming Kids: The Commercialization of Childhood* (Northampton, MA: Media Education Foundation, 2008).

2 To avoid unnecessary distractions for readers, I will italicize the phrase under consideration in each of the eight chapters the first time it occurs, while all subsequent references will appear in plain text.

3 Pauline Maier, *American Scripture: Making the Declaration of Independence*. (New York: Vintage Press, 1997). While it is true that Maier used the term "American scripture" to refer to the Declaration as a whole, the pursuit of happiness clause can be safely regarded as the moral core of that secularized scripture.

4 See, Trevor Norris, *Consuming Schools: Commercialism and the End of Politics*. (Toronto: University of Toronto Press, 2011); Deron Boyles, ed. *Schools or Markets? Commercialism, Privatization, and School-Business Partnerships*. (Mahwah, NJ: Lawrence Erlbaum, 2005); Alex Molnar, *School Commercialism: From Democratic Ideal to Market Commodity*. (New York: Routledge Books, 2005). Henry Giroux and Grace Pollack, *The Mouse That Roared: Disney and the End of Innocence* (Lanham, MD: Rowman & Littlefield, 2010).

5 See for example, Staughton Lynd, *The Intellectual Origins of American Radicalism*. (New York: Pantheon Books, 1968); Pauline Maier, *American Scripture: Making the Declaration of Independence*. (New York: Vintage Press, 1997); Philip Detweiler, "The Changing Reputation of the Declaration of Independence: The First Fifty Years," *William & Mary Quarterly*, 19, 4. Oct. 1962.

6 Alfred Young, *The Shoemaker and the Tea Party: Memory and the American Revolution*. (Boston: Beacon Press, 1999), 147.

7 F. E. Peters, *Greek Philosophical Terms: A Historical Lexicon*. (New York: New York University Press, 1967), 66.

8 Plato, *The Last Days of Socrates*. (New York: Penguin Classics, 1993), 53.

9   Aristotle, *The Nicomachean Ethics*. Ed. D. Ross. (Oxford: Oxford University Press), 1097a–99b.

10 Ernest Barker, ed. & trans. *The Politics of Aristotle* (New York: Oxford University Press, 1974), 4–5.

11 The concept of "idios" is discussed in Arlene Saxonhouse, "The Philosopher and the Female in the Political Thought of Plato." In *Feminist Interpretations of Plato*, ed. Nancy Tuana (University Park: Penn State University Press, 1994), 78–9.

12 Martha Nussbaum, "The Vulnerability of the Good Human Life: Relational Goods." In *The Fragility of Goodness: Luck and Ethics in Greek Tragedy and Ethics*. (London: Cambridge University Press, 1986), 344–5.

13 See for example, Carl. L. Becker, *The Declaration of Independence: A Study in the History of Political Ideas* (New York: Random House, 1958); Louis Hartz, *The Liberal Tradition in America* (New York: Harvest, 1955).

14 See Richard K. Matthews, *The Radical Politics of Thomas Jefferson: A Revisionist View*. (Lawrence: University of Kansas Press, 1984); Garry Wills, *Inventing America: Jefferson's Declaration of Independence* (New York: Vintage Press, 1978).

15 The Jefferson draft of the Declaration of Independence along with Congress' editorial changes, including the clauses that were struck out for criticizing the slave trade, can be found in Pauline Maier, *American Scripture: Making the Declaration of Independence* (New York: Vintage Books, 1997), 236–41.

16 Donald H. Meyer, *The Democratic Enlightenment* (New York: G. P. Putnam's Sons, 1976), 123.

17 Letter to Joseph C. Cabell (1816). Merrill D. Peterson, Ed. *Thomas Jefferson, Writings* (New York: The Library of America, 1984), 1377–81. (hereafter, *TJ Writings*).

18 Saul K. Padover, Ed. *Thomas Jefferson on Democracy* (New York: Mentor Books, 1939), 89–90.

19 Hannah Arendt, "The Pursuit of Happiness." *On Revolution* (New York: Penguin Books, 1963), 127.

20 Ibid., 132.

21 Ibid., 132.

22 "Draft Constitution for Virginia. Section IV: Rights, Private and Public." *TJ, Writings*, 343.

23 *TJ Writings*, letter to George Wythe, August 13, 1786, 857–9.

24 John Dewey, *Freedom and Culture* (New York: Prometheus Books, 1989), 123.

25 Ibid., 123.

26 John Dewey, "In Response," *John Dewey: The Later Works, 1925–53. Volume 5: 1929–30*. Edited by Jo Ann Boydston, (Carbondale: Southern Illinois University Press, 1984), 422.

27 John Dewey, *Individualism Old and New* (New York: Prometheus Books, 1999), 9.

28 Ibid., 29.

29 Dewey, *Freedom and Culture*, 124.

30 John Dewey, "The House Divided against Itself"; "America—By Formula"; "The United States, Incorporated." *Individualism Old and New* (see fn #27).

31 Howard Mumford Jones, *The Pursuit of Happiness* (Ithaca: Cornell University Press, 1953), 162–5.

32 Ibid., 167–8.

33 The relevant passage reads: "[Education] is the very foundation of good citizenship . . . it is the principle instrument in awakening the child to cultural values, in preparing him for later professional training, and in helping him adjust normally to his environment." *Brown v. Board of Education*, 347 U.S. 483 (1954). For a trenchant critique of *Brown* as a "magnificent mirage," see Derrick Bell, *Silent Covenants: Brown v. Board of Education and the Unfulfilled Hopes for Racial Reform*. (New York: Oxford University Press, 2004).

34 Meira Levinson, *No Citizen Left Behind* (Cambridge: Harvard University Press, 2012), 31–41.

35 Elliot Eisner, "The Null Curriculum." In *The Educational Imagination: On the Design and Evaluation of School Programs* (New York: Macmillan Publishing, 1978), 94–7.

36 Diana E. Hess, *Controversy in the Classroom: The Democratic Power of Discussion* (New York: Routledge, 2009).

CHAPTER TWO

The tyranny of the majority

Reflections on a democratic educational conundrum

Most Americans, if asked the question—"Do you believe in the principle of majority rule?—would respond in the affirmative. If pressed, some might add that the principle of majority rule is the moral cornerstone of democratic culture and without it no democracy would be possible. But is it good enough to simply believe in this principle in the abstract? For what if, after lodging power with a majority, the people who constitute that majority exercise their power in an unjust manner? What if the majority acts in a tyrannical fashion? The educational conundrum that the concept of *the tyranny of the majority* generates can be stated as a question: How can members of a majority learn to see what they have been conditioned by virtue of their majority status, not to see?

We are indebted to the brilliant French aristocrat, Alexis de Tocqueville, for introducing the tyranny of the majority into the American political lexicon. As a consequence of his extensive travels throughout the United States in 1831, Tocqueville developed the concept and continued to wrestle with it as a theoretical model for interpreting the new world experiment in democracy. In *Democracy in America*, he adroitly frames the tyranny of the majority as the ultimate democratic conundrum:

> The maxim that in matters of government the majority of the nation has the right to do everything I regard as unholy and detestable; yet, I place the origin of all powers in the will of the majority. Am I contradicting myself?[1]

Tocqueville may not be contradicting himself. He just succinctly captures one of the paradoxes within democracy itself: there is no guarantee that the power expressed by popular majorities will actually reflect core democratic values. Tocqueville further pinpoints the nature of the conundrum:

> So, what is a majority taken as a collective whole, if not an individual with opinions and quite often interests, in opposition to another individual whom we call a minority? Now, if you admit that an all-powerful man can abuse his power against his opponents, why not admit the same thing for a majority? Have men, united together, changed their character? Have they become more patient of obstacles by becoming stronger? For my part, I cannot think so and I shall never grant to several the power to do anything they like which I refuse to grant to a single one of my fellows.[2]

As a thought-experiment, we could recalibrate the question posed to our hypothetical American at the outset of the chapter in order to throw light on the substance of this paradox. The question might be rephrased this way: "Would you believe in the rule of the majority if you thought that those who constituted the majority were an assemblage of idiots (in the formal sense of the term), racists and war-lovers?" This modified formulation of the question should give us a serious pause. Among other things, it suggests that a purely mechanical or procedural conception of majority rule is an insufficient basis for claiming it to be "democratic."

No doubt the most egregious twentieth century example of a popular majority exercising its power *against* democratic values and principles was when the 1932 parliamentary elections in Germany resulted in a triumph for the fascist Nazi party.[3] Although it could be said that the Nazi victories at the polls were mechanically or procedurally democratic, it is perfectly obvious that the Nazi's and their civilian supporters embodied and put into action values and principles that contradicted core democratic values and principles.

Can we safely conjecture that the power exercised by popular majorities is not inherently democratic or inherently antidemocratic? The invention of the structure itself—that of representative government—is certainly of democratic origin. Still, it is difficult to overlook the numerous historical examples in which individuals and groups inhabiting these "democratic" structures have become severely detached from the ideals that gave rise to them. Is resolution to this conundrum, then, simply a matter of whether or not one happens to agree with what the majority does in any given exercise of its power? On what grounds, if any, can we judge whether an exercise of majority power is tyrannical or democratic? What are we to make of Tocqueville's assertion that, "[i]f ever freedom is lost in America, blame will have to be laid at the door of the omnipotence of the majority."[4]

The operative assumption in what follows is that the principle of majority rule only achieves moral legitimacy to a degree to which the people who constitute a majority somehow become awake to the democratic values. In thinking through this core structural contradiction we are reminded that the fulfillment of the democratic project consists of more than the formal creation of electoral majorities. For democracies to move toward greater realization of their moral ideals in a broader cultural sense, self-identified members of popular majorities must learn to heed those moral and democratic qualities that would enable them to become cognizant of the potential of popular majorities, and of themselves, to believe and to act contrary to the democratic values.

This chapter takes up the question of how students and citizens alike might become more conversant with the potential of popular majorities to act against the democratic values. This type of civic awareness will necessarily be more difficult to achieve for those whose identities, opinions and common sense is privileged by virtue of some form of majority status. In contrast, individuals who occupy a minority position based on race, class, sexual orientation, ideology, religion and the like, scarcely require any coaching in grasping the merit of Tocqueville's concept—they will have experienced the truth of it up close, and often painfully. Precisely because of its ability to illuminate the invisible character of hegemonic power, Tocqueville's theory of the tyranny of the majority ought to be integrated into our pedagogical quivers more frequently and rigorously than it has been in the past. Multicultural educators of all stripes should be able to recognize that their own projects have grown directly out of the recognition that popular majorities always have the potential to become tyrannical; indeed, without the prior ascendancy of this form of political and cultural power, there would be no need for the development of a multicultural ethos to begin with.

As a heuristic device, the concept has the power to rupture the frequently unconscious normalization of majority opinion and privilege that many of us unwittingly internalize. Tocqueville offers an unparalleled outsiders perspective of those majoritarian American attitudes and habits of mind which, if not properly understood and resisted, could further contribute to the moral and spiritual degradation of democracy. Put differently, a better understanding of this piece of public rhetoric will illuminate not only the neofascist or totalitarian potential of American democracy but also what's required educationally to confront this impulse head-on.

The chapter is divided into four sections. Each one highlights a different theoretical facet of the concept: An historical overview of manifestations of the tyranny of the majority; an analysis of the concept in relation to the fascist or totalitarian potential of American democracy; and an exploration of the tyranny of the majority as it manifests itself within the American classroom. Finally, I summarize the tyranny of the majority as a pedagogical motif that, if properly deployed, can enrich both the development of a democratic moral literacy and a critical multicultural ethos.

Contextualizing the tyranny of the majority

Not unlike the principle of public happiness examined in Chapter one, the underlying principle and insight that informs the concept of the tyranny of the majority represents a problem that extends deep into the history of Western political theory.[5] Though Tocqueville did not invent the concept he did extend its theoretic tradition by using it as an incisive model to interpret the American nineteenth century political and cultural landscape. We would do well then to first take a brief look at how the tyranny of the majority has manifested itself historically both before and after Tocqueville's intervention.

To begin with, it is crucial to recognize that Plato's animus against democracy is traced to his conviction that popular majorities, as the moral foundation of democratic regimes, could all too easily transform themselves into horrifying expressions of political, social, and psychological tyranny. For Plato, the chief problem with democratic regimes was that they had no "foundations"—they were a bizarre of moral relativisms.[6] To illustrate this point, let us recall that Plato was 35 years old when he witnessed how a "democratic" jury issued the death sentence to Socrates due to his annoying habit of questioning/badgering people about what it means to be good, just, and happy. Paradoxically, although the 500 jurors in this infamous trial were *de jure* democratic citizens, a strong case can be made that those who voted for the execution of Socrates acted as *de facto* antidemocratic citizens.[7] Genuinely democratic jurors would have surely acquitted Socrates of the charges filed against him and honored his ennobling service to the City; they would have never ordered him, by law, to drink the deadly hemlock poison. One reason why the execution of Socrates is such an iconic event in Western intellectual history is because it still produces vexing but necessary questions about the relationship of philosophy to democracy and to what extent democracy can be said to exist without the benefit of philosophy's critical spirit.

Turning to US history, it is no exaggeration to say that the specter of the tyranny of the majority hung like a fearsome cloud over deliberations at the 1787 Philadelphia convention. The device of the Electoral College, among other notable things, was intended to stymie both the formation and the power of popular majorities. It stands today as a sparkling emblem of the framers distrust of the common people and therefore of democracy itself. This distrust of human potential and educability is one of the central pillars of the Electoral College. In Madison's Federalist 10, rightfully considered one of the most significant political texts in US history, the prospect of the tyranny of the majority lurks behind his analysis of "the problem of a majority faction."[8] Madison's proposed remedy for alleviating the "unjust" and "wicked projects" of popular majorities was, in his words, to "extend the sphere." According to Madison, through a process of continual geographical expansion, the political contradictions occasioned by the exercise of democracy within the existing oligarchic order, would be "less apt to pervade the whole union than a particular member of it" than if no such expansion occurred.[9]

Thus, conquering the vast continental frontier through a policy of empire was regarded as a crucial element in preventing popular majorities from coalescing into a majority faction. In Madison's view, majority factions had an "inherent" tendency to disturb what the powerful called their "liberty," liberty being equated with the preservation of America's race and class based oligarchy. In a sense, then, the linkage between the tyranny of the majority (read: fear of democracy) and the imperative of "extending the sphere" illustrates how domestic contradictions within the US political economy shaped, and still shape, the direction of US foreign policy.

The concept can also be used to shed light on the contradictory and paradoxical dimensions of American democracy during the twentieth century civil rights movement. Recall that popular majorities throughout the American South in the 1950s and 1960s tenaciously opposed racial integration. Imagine, for example, if these white majorities had been given the opportunity to repudiate the Supreme Court's 1954 *Brown* decision through a popular referendum. We can safely assume that this landmark decision would have been defeated across the South. Of course, such a maneuver was not an available option, but the larger point is that racist popular majorities came into formation and were sustained not on the basis of democratic values but in violent opposition to them. It would be accurate to say, then, that the celebrated "checks and balances" built into the constitutional structure and symbolized in this instance by *Brown* worked to delegitimize the exercise of power by a popular majority that was *a priori* detached from the core democratic value of equality (to name but one democratic principle the popular majority failed to heed).

Based on this brief review, the tyranny of the majority can be defined as a *multilayered exercise of majoritarian power*. It is a kind of power that manifests itself conspicuously in the legal and political domains of society, as we have seen. However, the effects of this form of power on identity formation occur much less tangibly in the cultural domain. Arguably, the *experiential* or *psychological* consequences of the tyranny of the majority are expressed most profoundly yet most elusively within our everyday lives. It is "elusive" because it's an exercise of power that insinuates itself into our patterns of speech, our patterns of thought, and even into what could be called our political unconscious. By reading the tyranny of the majority in part as a series of psychological internalizations, as inscribed patterns of thinking and feeling borne out of majority power, we may inch closer to diminishing the negative consequences of that power.

The tyranny of the majority and the "inverted totalitarianism" of American democracy

Tocqueville observed that while the United States was "the most democratic country in the world,"[10] dimensions of its national character could, under certain conditions, devolve into despotism or tyranny. "If despotism were to be established in present-day democracies," Tocqueville wrote, "it would probably assume a different character; it would be more widespread and kinder; it would debase men without tormenting them."[11] He groped for the right terminology to capture this new phenomenon: "I, too, am having difficulty finding a word which will convey the whole idea I have formed; the old words despotism and tyranny are not suitable."[12]

Tocqueville did not consider the devolution of American democracy as an inevitable event. But through his perceptive French eyes, he thought he had spied some of its early cultural symptoms: "I know of no country in the world where there prevails, in general, less true freedom of discussion than in America."[13] Tocqueville consistently expresses great unease about the fate of critical thought within democracies that exist under the spell of commercial power and interest. What Tocqueville feared most about democracy in the United States was that its burgeoning commercial culture, combined with the values of radical individualism, would unleash privatizing forces that would eventually overwhelm the civic values which sustained the idea of citizenship and shared visions of a common good.[14]

Tocqueville described an historical context in which a new and potentially dangerous form of power showed evidence of informing the values and mental habits of the dominant culture. He focused attention on how the American people all too often displayed a troubling degree of conformity and self-adoration. In the following passage, he identifies a set of learned personality traits not easily reconciled with the core democratic values:

> In America, the majority draws a formidable ring around thought. . . . One would think at first glance that in America minds were all formed on the same model, so much do they follow exactly the same paths . . . The majority thus lives amid a perpetual adoration of itself; only foreigners or experience can make certain truths reach the ears of Americans.[15]

Without too much difficulty we can see how the traits that Tocqueville describes Americans as having are, in and of themselves, the result of an absence of critical self-reflection. Tocqueville interpreted the absence of such democratic sensibilities paradoxically as the consequence of majority rule. When a society is organized according to the principles of equality and majority rule, he argued, there is a tendency for powerful "conforming" forces to take shape within the society, both politically and culturally. Tocqueville warned that the tyranny of a majority would exercise its most destructive effects when and if a species of radical individualism somehow transformed commercial values into religious objects of devotion. Roger Boesche articulates Tocqueville's understanding of this potential problem:

> Tocqueville was suggesting that democracy has two key characteristics in tension with each other: citizenship and commerce. Over time there is a tendency for the demands and pleasures of the commercial ethic to undermine the ethic of citizenship, that is, for private interests to bring an eclipse of public life.[16]

The reason that Tocqueville took serious note of the proliferation of private or civic associations that honeycombed the United States was that he saw their further development as the only means through which to counter the eclipse of public life. In explicitly linking the fate of American democracy to the vibrancy of its civil society, Tocqueville affirms the idea that the quality of democracy relies just as much on what *happens outside the State* than with what happens inside it. He regarded institutions of civil society not only as the most promising development of modern democracy but also as the best safeguard against the formation of majority tyranny. "In democratic countries" he wrote, "the knowledge of how to form associations is the mother of all knowledge since the success of all others depends on it."[17]

Active participation within civil society, in this view, is the primary means through which democratic citizens can escape a sense of their own individual powerlessness. They do this by forming into political bodies that transcend their isolated individual existences. Tocqueville realized that a nation of isolated individuals closed-off from one another would be a nation of ciphers and not citizens; the danger would be that political and cultural conditions might then arise in which no countervailing power would exist to temper the totalizing effects of an atomistic, profit-seeking commercial culture.

In such a cultural climate, of course, narratives of happiness would be given a commercial rather than a civic meaning. How ironic that Tocqueville claimed he rarely saw a "happy" person in America! He observes: "A lot of modest fortunes spring up. Their owners have enough physical comforts to have a liking for them but not enough to be content."[18] For Tocqueville, as for many other foreign observers, the dominant American character they identified was constantly in search of "fugitive delights." "In America, I have seen the freest and the best educated men in the happiest circumstances the world can afford; yet, it seemed to me that a cloud usually darkened their features, [they] constantly muse on the good things they are missing."[19] Once again we see why the future health of American democracy depends in large measure on challenging the commercial or corporate construction of happiness. This realization suggests that teachers should deploy the concept of the tyranny of the majority to engage in the politics of happiness, specifically to interrogate how the corporate model of happiness operates to politically demobilize the nation's citizenry.

In attempting to map what this new form of tyranny in America would look like, Tocqueville offers this remarkably prescient perspective:

> I wish to see with what new features despotism might appear in the world. I see an innumerable crowd of men, all alike and equal, turned in upon themselves in a restless search for those

petty, vulgar pleasures with which they fill their souls. Each of them, withdrawn and apart, is like a stranger to the destiny of all the rest. His children and his personal friends constitute to him the whole of mankind; as for the remainder of his fellow citizens, he stands alongside them but does not see them; he touches them without feeling them; he exists only in himself and for himself; if he still retains his family circle, at any rate he may be said to have lost his country. Above these men stand an immense and protective power which alone is responsible for looking after their enjoyments and watching over their destiny . . .. I have always believed that this type of organized, gentle, and peaceful enslavement just described could link up more easily than imagined with some of the external forms of freedom and that it would not be impossible for it to take hold in the very shadow of the sovereignty of the people[20]

Boesche effectively connects Tocqueville's warning about the decay of citizenship to the emergence of the tyranny of the majority: "When Tocqueville linked 'interests,' 'narrow individualism,' 'private life,' 'love of gain,' and 'business careers,' he quite clearly was illustrating that the acquisitive ethic of the bourgeoisie was not only incompatible with participatory democracy but also the key factor in the new despotism that he feared. Only when this functional relation is kept in mind between commercial culture and acquisitive individualism can one understand Tocqueville's idea of the tyranny of the majority."[21]

Sheldon Wolin has coined the term "inverted totalitarianism" to describe the contemporary incarnation of the tyranny of the majority in US political culture. Wolin points out how the fascisms that emerged in Italy and Germany in the 1920s and 1930s went to great lengths to mobilize their citizenry on behalf of its ideals through organizing marches, endless meetings and other mass spectacles. "In contrast," writes Wolin, "inverted totalitarianism thrives on a politically demobilized society, that is, a society in which the citizens, far from being whipped into a continuous frenzy by the regime's operatives, are politically lethargic, reminiscent of Tocqueville's privatized citizenry."[22] One measure of the degree to which the public's vigilance has been eroded with respect to democratic norms and basic civil liberties is suggested in a recent article by Daniel Ellsberg. In commenting on the government's declassification of *the Pentagon Papers* 40 years after Ellsberg unofficially released these documents to the press, he observed that "all of the crimes that forced President Nixon to resign in 1974, are now legal." "Under the new laws, Nixon would have stayed in office, and the Vietnam War would have continued at least several more years."[23]

As the permanent warfare state becomes increasingly institutionalized, the "military-industrial complex" seems correspondingly immune from the scrutiny that is routinely directed toward other government programs, such as those that support health, education and social welfare. Wolin links this ominous development to the new face of the tyranny of the majority:

> Identification with militarism and patriotism, along with the images of American might projected by the media, serves to make the individual citizen *feel stronger,* thereby compensating for the *feelings of weakness* visited by the economy upon the overworked, exhausted, and insecure labor force. For its antipolitics inverted totalitarianism requires believers, patriots and nonunion "guest workers." (my emphasis).[24]

Based on the preceding analysis it would appear that images of happiness as well as the imperatives of the permanent warfare state represent two dimensions of American political culture that invite critical inquiry from a Tocquevillian tyranny of the majority perspective.

Classroom manifestations of the tyranny of the majority

To clarify some of the claims and observations made so far about dimensions of the tyranny of the majority, I discuss examples from my own teaching experience as well as from Megan Boler's experiences found in her cogently written article, "Teaching for Hope: The Ethics of Shattering World Views." Boler describes some of the difficulties she encountered in her classroom when she attempted, through her critical pedagogy, to "make students go where they didn't want to go." Although Boler does not adopt the tyranny of the

majority to help her interpret the problems brought about by the consequences of her critical pedagogy, it is evident that these problems
can be usefully explained in reference to Tocqueville's concept.[25]

Recently I taught a course in philosophy of education which
was presented to undergraduates as an excursion into the most
controversial issues facing American education and society. Students
were told at the outset of the course that the primary learning would
not grow out of the *content* of the course per se but rather out of the
process—how we would encounter and negotiate the many sharp
differences which were bound to emerge as we studied the war in
Iraq and same-sex marriage, to name two controversial issues we
were going to tackle. Despite my hopes for raising the collective
level of dialogue in the classroom, I think I failed to lead the class
into these ideal regions of communication. It was as if a prior silent
covenant had been enacted among the students in order to avoid
facing the latent discord and division which simmered beneath the
surface of our friendly civility. Of course, teachers dedicated to the
multicultural project and committed to renegotiating the national
identity formation are almost always bedeviled by their students'
expressions of silence, ignorance, hostility or indifference to the
critical inquiries they initiate into the reproduction of national
identity, even as other students seem to love the process.

A sizeable portion of the problem of why students dread or are
averse to civic controversy may be attributable to the power and
influence of the tyranny of the majority, whereby, as Tocqueville put
it, "a formidable ring is drawn around thought." This ring drawn
around thought is a subtle yet powerful force which constricts what
is deemed permissible to think and to say out loud. In discussing
both the war in Iraq and same-sex marriage, many students who
had been vocal in earlier meetings now exhibited an odd friendly
indifference.

Students eventually wrote position papers on the legal and moral
principles at stake in the debates over same-sex marriage. These
papers were based on excerpts from two opposing US Supreme Court
rulings, *Bowers v. Hartwick* (1986) legalizing the criminalization of
sodomy by the State and *Lawrence v. Texas* (2003) which reversed
Bowers.[26] Surprisingly, many of these "private" papers favored
same-sex marriage: this immediately raised the question in my
mind why so few students had articulated these opinions in class. It
was striking to see such a discrepancy between what students were

willing to discuss in their papers and what they were unwilling to discuss in class. Only later did I realize that I had experienced the invisible hand of the tyranny of the majority drawing a formidable ring around thought and speech.

The same pattern also held true for discussions about the war in Iraq. Again, a discrepancy emerged between private and public expression: those few students who were willing to express opposition or doubts about the war did so privately in their papers but rarely if ever in the public realm of the classroom. While many factors are involved in explaining this phenomenon, including, of course, my own biases, limitations, and personality as a teacher, I believe Tocqueville's theory of the tyranny of the majority goes a long distance in placing these types of inhibitions to thought and speech in a beneficial political context. Inhibitions to class dialogue may also be traced in part to the learned notions of "civility" that work against the possibility of discussing culturally divisive issues. Cris Mayo contends that these norms of civility often disguise the operation of privilege when they are used to ignore or smooth over the consideration of controversial issues. The apolitical civility that Mayo identifies can be usefully conceptualized in terms of this Tocquevillian theme.[27]

In her article, Boler enumerates three main categories of students that educators tend to encounter: first, those who are excited by attempting critical theory; second, those who angrily and vocally resist attempts to do critical theory; and third, those who "appear disaffected, already sufficiently numb so that (our) attempts to ask them to rethink the world encounter only vacant and dull stares."[28] Her analysis focuses on the second category of vocal, angry resisters to critical theory. These students, while not silent like the third group, still embody central aspects of Tocqueville's theory and reinforce the benefits of introducing a "foreign" set of eyes to the project of negotiating one's relation to the national identity.

Based on her reflections on students' resistance, Boler writes that "I am learning to accept that people will not go where they don't want to go."[29] While Boler's assertion may be true in one sense; in another, I think it's also true that critical pedagogy sets for itself precisely the ambitious task of encouraging students to go where they didn't previously want to go. As democratic civic educators, we are engaged in "educating student desires" to value and desire things that they didn't necessarily value or desire before (such as critical inquiry, the value of the common good, or to recognize their majority-derived privilege). It seems to me that those students of ours who inhabit (often unconsciously) a white male majority status, for example, and tend to resent having this status pointed out to them are ideal candidates for reading Tocqueville's writings on the tyranny of the majority. Those who identify themselves as members of any majority could benefit from studying a theory which illuminates the very ideological problem they personify.

The third category of student to which Boler refers, the "silent majority," is not explicitly treated in her article; yet, this group is most illustrative for inquiry into contemporary expressions of the tyranny of the majority. It is significant that two of Boler's key principles share important conceptual affinities with Tocqueville's theory. First, the tyranny of the majority, as an interpretive frame, could accurately be located under the canopy of Boler's "pedagogy of discomfort" since it can be deployed to frame new and discomforting questions about the politics of majority privilege.[30]

In addition, Tocqueville's observations about the conformist tendencies of US culture seem to approximate what Boler refers to as "inscribed habits of emotional inattention."[31] This concept captures the operative essence of the tyranny of the majority: dominant ways of seeing—and not seeing—become unconsciously internalized making them difficult to identify and transcend. These learned and often unconscious patterns of inattention help to reproduce the kind of heteronomous individuals that Tocqueville feared most: "idiotic citizens" whose scope of civic discourse is anchored firmly and "sweetly" in a set of self-congratulatory platitudes. These platitudes—as constitutive elements of the majority culture's thematic universe—embody contradictions that ought to become sites of critical analysis precisely for the discomfort such inquiries are capable of eliciting.

The tyranny of the majority as a resource for cultivating democratic moral literacy

We need to think critically about our own congratulatory and mythological self-conceptions since the spiritual rejuvenation of American democracy depends in part on our recognition of the oppressive potential of majoritarian power. Pedagogically understood as a means for identifying and questioning the silences, opinions and common sense of the majority culture, the concept of the tyranny of the majority offers educators a theoretical compass for prying open new space from which to interrogate the moral authority and privileges which accrue from any majority-derived status. These sensibilities are exactly the type that engagement with Tocqueville's concept can help to cultivate. For this reason, democratic-minded teachers should be encouraged to deploy the tyranny of the majority as a resource for cultivating what could be called a democratic moral literacy.

Notes

1 Alexis de Tocqueville, *Democracy in America*, trans., by Gerald E. Bevan, and with an introduction by Isaac Kramnick (New York: Penguin Books, 2003), 292. (All subsequent references to this book will be cited as *DIA*.).

2 *DIA*, 293.

3 Robert O. Paxton, *The Anatomy of Fascism* (New York: Vintage Books, 2005), 67.

4 *DIA*, 304.

5 For an excellent historical survey of this theme, see Roger Boesche, *Theories of Tyranny From Plato to Arendt*. (University Park, PA.: The Pennsylvania State University Press, 1996). All subsequent references to this book will be cited as *TOT*.

6 Joe Sachs, trans. Plato, Republic (Newburyport, MA: Focus Books, 2007). See Book VIII, 543a–69c. Also Sara Monoson's, Plato's Democratic Entanglements (Princeton, NJ: Princeton University Press, 2000) discusses Plato's ambiguous treatment of democracy.

7 The source I use for the number of jurors comes from James A. Coloaiaco, *Socrates against Athens: Philosophy on Trial*. (New York: Routledge, 2001), 14.

8 James Madison, Federalist 10. In *The Federalist Papers*, Alexander Hamilton, James Madison, John Jay. (New York: Mentor Books, 196), 77–84.

9 Ibid., 83–4.

10 *DIA*, 596.

11 *DIA*, 804.

12 *DIA*, 805.

13 *DIA*, 297.

14 For a comprehensive treatment of this theme, see Roger Boesche, "Privatization and the Eclipse of Public Life." In *TOT*, 211–16.

15 *DIA*, 244–5.

16 Boesche, 213.

17 *DIA*, 600. For an in-depth analysis of the concept of "Civil Society", see Don Eberly, ed. *The Essential Civil Society Reader: The Classic Essays*. (Lanham: Rowman & Littlefield, 2000).

18 *DIA*, 617.

19 *DIA*, 622–3.

20 *DIA*, 805–6.

21 *TOT*, 219.

22 Sheldon Wolin, *Democracy, Incorporated: Managed Democracy and the Specter of Inverted Totalitarianism*. (Princeton, NJ: Princeton University Press, 2008), 64.

23 David Edwards, "Ellsberg: All the Crimes Committed Against Me Are Now Legal." The Raw Story, June 9, 2011; available from: <http://www.rawstory.com/rs/2011/06/09/ellsberg-all-the-crimes-nixon-committed-against-me-are-now-legal.

24 Wolin, 199.

25 Megan Boler, "Teaching for Hope: The Ethics of Shattering World Views." In Jim Garrison and Daniel Liston, eds *Teaching, Loving and Learning: Reclaiming Passion in Educational Practice* (New York: RoutlegeFalmer, 2004), 117–31.

26 For a transdisciplinary text which focuses on the same-sex marriage controversy, see *Same-Sex Marriage: Pro & Con, A Reader*. Edited by Andrew Sullivan (New York: Vintage Books, 2004), 86–120.

27 Cris Mayo, "Civility and Its Discontents: Sexuality, Race and the Lure of Beautiful Manners." *Philosophy of Education* 2001; 78–87.

28 Boler, 117.

29 Ibid., 123.

30 Ibid., 120–3.

31 Ibid., 122.

CHAPTER THREE

Four score and seven years ago

Although a prominent fixture on the landscape of America's civic mythology, it's worth asking if the rhetoric of *four score and seven years ago* contains any potential today to function as an instrument of civic meaning. Unfortunately, the rhetoric of the Gettysburg Address, including its opening phrase, appears to have become a dead letter for a large number of Americans. Nowadays, to the extent it is considered at all, four score and seven years ago comes to us as a linguistic end in itself, a phrase whose meaning is limited to a silky and clever way of saying "eighty-seven years ago." Seldom are we encouraged to explore the meaning of this phrase beyond its status as a graceful, biblical reference to the number 87 and to what "our fathers brought forth." The question arises: What was Abraham Lincoln intending to convey with the strategic use of this phrase?

The contention here is that a critical reappraisal of how exactly this strand of public rhetoric fits into the overall logic of the Gettysburg Address can yield insight not only into the imagined character of the national identity but also into the first principles of the American democratic tradition. The Gettysburg Address could be regarded as Lincoln's syllabus for democratic renewal: He uses a funeral oration to teach the nation about how the better angels of its nature had been unwisely repressed and how that repression might be lifted.

The common assumption is that Lincoln, in harkening back to what "our fathers brought forth," was celebrating *both* the patriots of 1776 who authored the Declaration of Independence and the Constitutional framers of 1789. In collapsing the nation's two founding moments into a unitary whole, however, this view tends to assume that Lincoln was expressing a self-evident moral equivalence between the nation's two founding documents. To the extent this assumption prevails, the deeper significance of what Abraham Lincoln so boldly yet slyly announced in the first six words of the Gettysburg Address will continue to elude us.

Of course, 87 years before the speech was given in 1863, is 1776. Thus the textual absence of the 1789 Constitutional framers in Lincoln's formulation means something. The omission is itself part of the lesson Lincoln bequeaths to the nation. Far from using the phrase as a neutral linguistic mechanism to refer to the 1776–89 period as a unitary whole, Lincoln tacitly encourages us to examine the fundamental contradiction at the center of the negotiation of American identity: the contradiction between the Declaration of Independence and the Constitution, the two symbolic birth certificates of the nation. According to Lincoln, the moral vision contained within the Declaration should have primacy over the procedural instrument which is the Constitution.[2]

If the symbolic meaning of the phrase is to be imaginatively retrieved, we need to revisit the story of Abraham Lincoln as pedagogue-in-chief. John Patrick Diggins succinctly captures the unique pedagogical ambition of the 16th president: "Abraham Lincoln teaches us how to read the Declaration of Independence."[3] This is no small teaching! In fact, given the American penchant for historical amnesia, Lincoln's desire to teach the nation how to "read" the Declaration may qualify as the highest order teaching any sitting president has sought to undertake.

Four score and seven years ago can thus serve as a point of entry that encourages inquiry into why Lincoln considered the Constitution—taken by itself without anchorage in the Declaration—to be morally and politically deficient. Such an education into reading the Declaration begins by appreciating not only the potential harmony between these two charters (a possibility Lincoln fully recognized) but also the *nature of the contradiction* between them. Exploring the nature of this contradiction is a first step in recovering the first principles of American democracy, which, in turn, is the necessary precondition for identifying and theorizing the proper aims of a democratic education. Not only was Lincoln assuming the role of the nation's teacher *par excellence* in persuading Americans not to forget the spirit of 1776, his civic pedagogy also reflects a decidedly erotic character. To pursue this line of analysis, we need to take a closer look at the metaphors of death, rebirth and creation at the heart of the Gettysburg Address.

Civic rebirth and the erotic character of the Gettysburg Address

In his first inaugural address, desperately trying to avert the collapse of the union, Lincoln urged Americans to remember those "mystic chords of memory" that supposedly connected them not only to the "better angels of their nature" but also to the transcendent meaning he believed had energized the spirit of 1776.[4] However, the war did come, and two years later, in the Gettysburg Address, Lincoln once again found himself urging Americans to exercise their power of memory as an instrument of national survival. By 1863, the "mystic chords of memory" imagery, while an aesthetic delight, must have appeared tragically naïve if not deceptive to many. How, then, was Lincoln to breathe new life into these transcendent if largely forgotten ideas? His opening words, as we have seen, direct us to 1776, a move consistent with Lincoln's project of elaborating a novel interpretation of the Declaration of Independence.

In the Gettysburg speech, Lincoln performs a rhetorical act of civic remembrance, a politically inventive act in which an alternative vision of the past (recovering the values and principles of the Declaration) is said to exist in harmonic accord with an alternative vision of the future (performing "the unfinished tasks" necessary for a "new birth of freedom" and for creating a "government of, by and for the people").[5] As an erotic teacher, the aim of Lincoln's civic pedagogy is to cultivate a future-directed idea of national completion, an image of wholeness that can only be "brought forth" when symbolically "conceived" in relation to the philosophical spirit of 1776.

Eros, the ancient Greek term that describes a form of love, is a symbol uniquely endowed to help us grasp the deeper layers of meaning of the Gettysburg Address. While popular conceptions typically reduce eros to the realm of sexuality, let us recall that Plato wrote the *Symposium* to articulate the powerful educational dimensions of the concept. In his classic treatise on love, Plato has Aristophanes define eros as "the desire for wholeness," a theme in symmetry with Lincoln's identification of the "unfinished work" facing the nation.[6] The life-enhancing energies of eros have long been recognized as vital to the process of self knowledge and to the development of community. Rollo May tells us that "eros is a state of being," an ardent desire which provides the condition of possibility for an individual to be "magnetized" toward the vision of an imagined good, for oneself or for one's larger community.[7] One of the defining strands of eros therefore consists of a passion for changing things for the better, individually and civically.

With this broad understanding of eros in mind, it is easier to recognize how Lincoln's consistent use of birth imagery—"brought forth," "conceived," "created," and "new birth of freedom"— affirms the erotic character underlying the Gettysburg Address. Not only are these erotic signifiers woven into the fabric of the speech but they also emerge from a background of contradiction and are presented as resolutions to that contradiction.

Indeed, it is precisely a heightened awareness of this contradiction that prompts Lincoln the teacher to ask Americans to reconnect to their democratic tradition as a way out of their collective predicament. The desire to move toward and connect to something better, whether to a person, to an object of knowledge, or to a sense of national wholeness, is not only an erotic energy but is also educable. Similarly, Lincoln wanted Americans to reinvent themselves in light of what was "truly good," holding that such goodness would be impossible to bring forth without a prior grounding in the values and principles enshrined in the Declaration. That Lincoln's civic pedagogy has an erotic character is also evidenced by his ability to fashion Gettysburg as an aesthetic event in which the teacher, representing beautiful ideas, succeeds in stimulating a desire among citizens to reinvent the nation on the basis of a common good of equality of opportunity, that is, on the basis of a philosophical idea.

The validity of interpreting Lincoln as an erotic pedagogue-in-chief is further reinforced by examining a rarely discussed fragment in his writings.

The "apple of gold" and the "picture of silver": What the textbooks don't say

It is significant that Lincoln bestowed greater value onto the Declaration than he did to the Constitution. He reveals this bias most vividly in an 1861 allegory which describes the Declaration as an "apple of gold" and the Constitution as a "picture of silver." He observes: "The *picture* was made *for* the apple—*not* the apple for the picture."[8] Lincoln's purpose in making this analytical distinction is properly regarded as "pedagogical" because he wants to change the national perception as to how these foundational texts relate to one another. At one level, this distinction is crucial because for Lincoln the Declaration symbolically represents the emotional and moral content of the nation's democratic identity more so than the Constitution. In Lincoln's view, the Constitution's sole purpose was to carry out the prior values of the apple of gold. Our schools consistently overlook the value of Lincoln's theoretically rich attempts to conceptualize the paradoxes and contradictions at the nucleus of the American founding. This absence of curricular attention therefore limits how we go about deciding which values and which questions should be actively encountered and worked through in the process of constructing America's civic self-conception.

Allen Guelzo remarks how Lincoln's forays into constitutional theory remain a source of anxiety for specialists in the field: "And even among Lincoln's admirers, there is a running current of discomfort at Lincoln's apparent willingness to set the Constitution below the Declaration . . . . More recently voices on the political left like Garry Wills, Charles L. Black and Mark Tushnet have actually applauded Lincoln for dumping the Constitution in favor of the Declaration."[9] It was not that Lincoln thought the Constitution should be set "below the Declaration" because it had covertly written the legal protection of slavery into several clauses or because the Constitution existed in conflict with the principle of human equality in the Declaration. It would be more precise to say that, for Lincoln, without the prior guidance of the Declaration's values and principles, the Constitution would continue to function as no more than an *amoral* legal framework. Such a framework—in which naked power relations (self-interest) determined the national structure of values—would have the long-term effect of restricting the boundaries and purposes of the national identity. By 1863 Lincoln was wrestling with the idea that a virtuous citizenry could never develop through the procedural "checks and balances" of the Constitution or through its enumeration of individual rights and immunities. The legal structure, to be democratic, required a prior moral and philosophical purpose to justify itself and to give the legal edifice proper direction.

Garry Wills gives resonance to the transcendental aura of the Gettysburg Address and, in doing so, suggests the triumph of Lincoln's civic pedagogy:

> Lincoln is here not only to sweeten the air of Gettysburg, but to clear the infected atmosphere of American history itself, tainted with official sins and inherited guilt . . . he performed one of the most daring acts of open-air slight-of-hand ever witnessed by the unsuspecting. Everyone in that vast throng was having his or her intellectual pocket picked. The crowd departed with a new thing in its ideological luggage, that new constitution Lincoln had substituted for the one they brought there with them. They walked off, from those curving graves on the hillside, under a changed sky, into a different America. Lincoln had revolutionized the Revolution, giving people a new past to live with that would change their future indefinitely.[10]

It is difficult to escape the conclusion that Lincoln believed the Civil War had occurred, in large measure, because the nation had first *forgotten* and then only gradually *remembered* the Declaration. Only when Americans could fully, rather than inchoately recover the values contained within the Declaration would American political culture achieve its moral bearings.

As previously indicated in the "Fragment on the Constitution and Union," Lincoln describes the values, principles and the "philosophical cause" underlying the Declaration as an "apple of gold." Lincoln's musings on the relationship between the two charters in this fragment, as in other writings, appear to affirm the idea that he did not conceive of these texts as morally equivalent.

The assertion of that *principle*, at that time, was the word fitly spoken which has proved an apple of gold to us. The Union, and the Constitution, are the *picture of silver*, subsequently framed around it. The picture was made, not to *conceal* or *destroy* the apple; but to *adorn*, and *preserve* it. The picture was made *for* the apple—*not* the apple for the picture.[11]

When Lincoln declares that the picture was made *for* the apple, *not* the apple for the picture, he deems the substantive moral content of the Declaration paramount; it precedes and trumps in value the legal, procedural instrument that is the Constitution. Pausing at the metaphorical level, the *apple* symbolizes knowledge or the knowledge-quest, the search for new meanings and possibilities, while *gold* has been deemed more valuable than silver. These associations suggest that the *apple of gold* is a perfectly fitting symbol for *eros*! As an erotic metaphor, then, the *apple of gold* can be seen as a symbolic representation of the first principles of American democracy. Among other principles, this would include equality of opportunity, liberty, justice, and hope for a common good.

Lincoln is emphatic that the existence of the apple of gold has a "philosophical cause." This indicates his conviction that the spirit of 1776 was rooted in a philosophical idea that ran deeper than either the desire for political independence or for material acquisition. This philosophical idea consisted of something "entwining itself more closely about the human heart" than even our "great prosperity." It "is the principle of 'liberty to all'—the principle that clears the *path* for all—gives *hope* to all—and, by consequence, *enterprise* and *industry* to all."[12]

Here, Lincoln defines the ideal architecture of the American mind, the symbolic incarnation of a new type of individual whose reason for being is more oriented to a philosophical principle than to anything else. If we were to treat Lincoln's use of "philosophical" from an etymological standpoint, as the "love of wisdom," then we could hazard that American identity would need to partake of this type of love as a condition for performing the "unfinished work" necessary to actualize its democratic potential.

In a speech in Baltimore in 1864, Lincoln gives a stunning update to the apple of gold/picture of silver allegory. He does so by drawing upon the biblical images of "wolves and sheep" as a way to work through the contradictory interpretations of "liberty" reflected in the Declaration and Constitution:

> The world has never had a good definition of the word liberty, and the American people, just now, are such in want of one. We all declare for liberty, but in using the same word we do not all mean the same things . . . The shepherd drives the wolf from the sheep's throat. For which the sheep thanks the shepherd as his liberator, while the wolf denounces him for the same act, as the destroyer of liberty, especially as the sheep was a black one. Plainly the sheep and the wolf are not agreed upon a definition of the word liberty; and precisely the same difference prevails today among us human creatures, even in the North, and all professing to love liberty.[13]

In this simile, it is the figurative Declaration or the apple of gold (as the watchful shepherd) that protects the black sheep (the oppressed) from the aggressive wolf (unregulated commerce) which, in turn, acts to opens up the free space necessary for the enactment of "life, liberty and the pursuit of happiness." It was this founding principle that Lincoln considered universally valid and which made the American experiment "exceptional" and worth defending by armed force.

Lincoln ends the fragment on a prophetic note. "So let us act, that neither *picture*, or *apple* shall ever be blurred, or bruised or broken. That we may so act, we must study, and understand the points of danger."[14] Given Lincoln's first words of the Gettysburg Address, we may speculate that for him, one of the main "points of danger" confronting the nation was the problem of historical amnesia, a learned condition in which the memory of the apple of gold was erased from the nation's register of lived values. For this reason, Lincoln instructs the nation to first "read" the Declaration, but also to read it "philosophically" as the best means for relearning what would be required to give birth to a more democratic America.

Another point of danger standing in the way of Lincoln's desire to reinvent American selfhood was the Supreme Court, whose 1857 *Dred Scott* decision denied that the framers of the Constitution had ever anticipated that those "held in servitude" would become citizens. The Court further ruled that Congress had no authority to prohibit legally obtained property (slaves) from being located anywhere in the United States, including the western territories. Lincoln responded to this logic in his debate with Stephen Douglas, not by parsing the language of the Constitution but by anchoring his counter-argument in his interpretation of what he thought Jefferson (and his committee) had intended to say in the Declaration:

> I think the authors of that notable instrument intended to include all men, but they did not intend to declare all men equal in all respects. They did not mean to say all were equal in color, size, intellect, moral development, or social capacity. They defined with tolerable directness, in what respects they did consider all men equal—equal in "certain inalienable rights, among which are life, liberty and the pursuit of happiness." This they said, and this they meant. They did not mean to assert the obvious untruth, that all men were actually enjoying that equality, nor yet, that they were about to confer it immediately upon them. In fact, they had no power to confer such a boon. They meant simply to declare the right, so that enforcement of it might follow as fast as circumstances should permit. They meant to set a standard maxim for free society, which should be familiar to all, and revered by all; constantly looked to, constantly labored for, and even though never perfectly attained, constantly approximated, and thereby constantly spreading and deepening its influence, and augmenting the happiness and value of life to all people of all colors everywhere.[15]

Once more we encounter Lincoln's narrative of an equality-based American identity, an identity that is *perpetually unfinished*, ever spreading and deepening, "augmenting the happiness and value of life to all people of all colors everywhere." Noble-sounding rhetoric like this inspired Diggins to observe that, "in Lincoln American political thought ascended, and, ascending, reached spiritual ecstasy."[16] Indeed, the ascent to spiritual ecstasy is accomplished through Lincoln's adroit use of a democratic public rhetoric. We might add that Lincoln's civic pedagogy, with its perpetually unfinished and future-directed character, resonates with a hopeful, philosophical eros.

Reading Lincoln as a symbol of American identity: Toward a new civic aesthetic

Nowhere is the legitimacy of Lincoln's moral stature challenged as forcefully as it is in the writings of the historian Lerone Bennett. In 1999, Bennett expanded his earlier work on Lincoln into a 626 page book, *Forced into Glory: Abraham Lincoln's White Dream*.[17] Bennett contends that Lincoln was "forced into glory" entirely against his will by abolitionists and radical republicans who had agitated in favor of emancipation since before 1861, a course of action that Lincoln worked hard to avoid.

Bennett defines the method of his book: "this is *not* a biography: this is a political study of the uses and abuses of biography and myth, and it suggests, among other things, that your identity, whatever your color, is based, at least in part, on what you think about Lincoln, the Civil War, and slavery."[18] Bennett makes a valid point: our identities as Americans are based in part on what and how we think about Lincoln, the Civil War, and slavery. This observation affirms the idea expressed throughout this book, that our conception of the past—or lack thereof —shapes our identities in powerful ways that are not always immediately apparent. To illustrate this principle, echoing Lincoln, I have suggested that our identification with the Declaration of Independence, or lack of it, decisively shapes who we think we are as a "democratic people." Bennett similarly emphasizes the Declaration as a symbolic touchstone of American identity but rejects the assumption that Lincoln actually believed in it:

> I have compared Lincoln here not with twentieth-century leaders but with the White men and women of his own time, and I have suggested that one of the reasons we are in trouble racially in this country is that we have systematically downplayed and suppressed the White men and women who, unlike Lincoln, really believed in the Declaration of Independence. I have suggested finally that Lincoln is a key, perhaps the key, to the American personality and that what we invest in him, and *hide* in him, is who we are. In the end, then, *Forced Into Glory* is not so much about Lincoln as it is about race, heroes, leadership, political morality, scholarship, and the American Dream.[19]

Much of Bennett's book is an effort to highlight "what has been hidden" in Lincoln and how this repression misshapes American identity today. His project of uncovering these repressed pieces of historical knowledge and using them to puncture an overinflated version of the national ego has the potential to intensify our encounter with the conflicted values at stake in the negotiation of the national identity. For, if Lincoln is "the key" to the American personality, and if what we "invest" and "hide" in him constitutes "who we are," it becomes crucial to identify these repressions and to wrestle with the contradictions of the Lincoln myth.

Bennett writes that Lincoln was adept at "evading moral crises" by seeking "rhetorical solutions" in order to avoid available substantive solutions: "It was his art to say nothing eloquently in support of abstract political principles that were true everywhere and nowhere and that he had no intention of doing anything about anywhere."[20] Lincoln's tendency to "evade moral crises" through the adroit use of public rhetoric, according to Bennett, reached its zenith in the Gettysburg Address. Bennett is troubled by the fact that Lincoln's three minute, 272 word speech said nothing about slavery, the Emancipation Proclamation, the New York City race riots which had occurred three months before, and not a word *"that the White forefathers blew it, that the graves of Gettysburg were contained in the Constitution as the plant is contained in the seed."*[21] Regarding this last claim, readers will recall that Lincoln's intent in uttering four score and seven years ago was to indicate—albeit, indirectly—that the Constitutional framers had, in effect, blown it. Bennett seems to detach Lincoln's phrase from having any connection to the Declaration.[22] Nor does *Forced into Glory* treat Lincoln's "Constitutional Fragment." How, then, to make sense out of these conflicting narratives of Lincoln?

One way to transcend the either/or conceptual frameworks that usually govern interpretations of Lincoln is to examine what Frederick Douglass and W.E.B. Du Bois wrote about Lincoln and his legacy. It is striking that their accounts bear little relation *either* to Bennett's deconstructive approach *or* to those which reinforce an uncritical glorification of Lincoln. It is further striking that these two eminent social critics think through the Lincoln problem first by privileging the qualities of contradiction, irony, and paradox and then by weighing how these qualities help clarify Lincoln's self-transformation. In critically addressing the Lincoln problem, these figures provide useful models for negotiating the psychic turbulences reverberating within the national identity.

The most comprehensive public statement Douglass makes about Lincoln occurred in 1876, at the unveiling of the Freedmen's Monument in Washington, D.C. The still controversial monument was being dedicated to the memory of Abraham Lincoln, whose stony likeness is shown standing tall with a black child kneeling by his side, looking upward. Douglass' commemoration begins on a critical note:

> It must be admitted—truth compels me to admit, even here in the presence of the monument we have erected to his memory, that Abraham Lincoln was not, in the fullest sense of the word, either our man or our model. In his interests, in his associations, in his habits of thought and in his prejudices, he was a white man. He was preeminently the white man's President, entirely devoted to the welfare of white men. He was ready and willing at any time during the first years of his administration to deny, postpone, and sacrifice the rights of humanity in the colored people in order to promote the welfare of the white people of his country.[23]

Douglass chronicles how he and his followers had been "grieved, stunned, and greatly bewildered" by Lincoln's tepid war policy and his determined efforts to alleviate the national crisis through a program of deporting blacks to Africa. However, after reminding his audience of the moral calamities which Lincoln enabled in the first years of his administration, Douglass offers a startling psychological analysis of Lincoln. He speculates—paradoxically—that it was Lincoln's inherited racial animus *against* blacks that helped secure the union on the basis of emancipation.

> I have said that President Lincoln was a white man and shared towards the colored race the prejudices common to his countryman. Looking back to his times and to the condition of his country, we are compelled to admit that this *unfriendly feeling on his part may be safely set down as one element of his wonderful success in organizing the loyal American people for the tremendous conflict before them, and bringing them safely through that conflict* (my emphasis).[24]

Douglass' claim that Lincoln's "unfriendly feeling" toward blacks enabled him to better perceive what "the loyal American people" could accept in terms of making the war a war for abolishing slavery is an amazing and seldom considered perspective. Douglass says tellingly of Lincoln: "He knew the American people better than they knew themselves."[25] How intriguing! Let us assume for the moment that Douglass is correct. What might be the likeliest clue that Lincoln possessed valuable insight into the national psyche? This inquiry suggests that the most likely clue sequestered inside the phrase four score and seven years ago is the moral imperative of recovering the "apple of gold" as the only legitimate basis for reconstructing the national identity. Such an imperative was paradoxical: on the one hand, Lincoln identified with the racial "prejudices common to his countrymen," while on the other, Douglass tells us that Lincoln "loathed and hated slavery."[26] In Douglass's estimation, the 16th President was a divided being presiding over a divided nation.

Over time Douglass developed an appreciation not only for the enormous predicaments Lincoln faced but also for how skillfully he "directed" those moral predicaments:

> He was assailed by abolitionists; he was assailed by slaveholders; he was assailed by the men who were for peace at any price; he was assailed by those who were for a more vigorous prosecution of the war; and he was assailed for not making the war an abolition war; and he was most bitterly assailed for making the war an abolition war.[27]

Writing 50 years after Douglass, W.E.B. Du Bois is similarly attentive to the contradictions and paradoxes reflected in Lincoln's character. "Abraham Lincoln," he observed, "was a Southern poor white, of illegitimate birth, poorly educated and unusually ugly, awkward, ill-dressed. He liked smutty stories and was a politician down to his toes."[28] Despite this rather unappealing portrait, Du Bois gives Lincoln credit for having the courage to change his inherited patterns of thinking:

> He had little outwardly that compelled respect. But in that curious human way he was big inside. He had reserves and depths and when habit and convention were torn away there was something

left to Lincoln . . . so that at the crisis he was big enough to be inconsistent—cruel, merciful; peace-loving, a fighter; despising Negroes and letting them fight and vote; protecting slavery and freeing the slaves. He was a man—a big, inconsistent, brave man.[29]

Twice in this passage Du Bois alludes to Lincoln's virtuous inconsistency. Lincoln's inconsistency presupposes a person who is beset by inner conflict over competing values and truths, some that are culturally conditioned and deeply rooted, others that are recently formed or forming. It would appear that the severe tension wrought by these opposing forces is precisely what generated in Lincoln the desire to transcend himself and to rise "up out of his contradictions." In another attempt to read meaning into Lincoln's "war within," Du Bois again evaluates his moral character as a study in contradiction and self-transformation through "upward struggle."

The world is full of people born hating and despising their fellows. To these I love to say: See this man. He was one of you and yet he became Abraham Lincoln. Others may refuse to believe his taste in jokes and political maneuvers and list him as an original abolitionist and defender of Negroes. But personally I revere him the more because up out of his contradictions and inconsistencies he fought his way to the pinnacles of earth and his fight was within as well as without.[30]

Lincoln's personal struggles in working through the contradictions of his own character, of course, mirrored countless individual struggles that were roiling the nation. It is significant that Douglass and Du Bois both interpret the meaning of the Lincoln myth by theorizing the fluid, evolving intersection between his personal psychology and the national psychology.

In his survey of African-American historiography, David Blight writes that the work of Douglass, Du Bois, and Nathan Irwin Huggins, among others, reflect a kind of methodological orientation which makes productive use of the qualities of contradiction, irony, and paradox. These existential qualities permitted Douglass and Du Bois to think more perceptively about Lincoln and about the future of America's democratic experiment.[31] These undervalued faculties of knowing—as instruments of meaning-making—introduce fresh difficulties and uncertainties into the process of interpreting our personal and civic identities, not to mention what these faculties might portend for our interpretation of Abraham Lincoln. Since these three qualities constitute *experiences*, *feelings*, and *perceptions*, they meet the criteria for being classified as "aesthetic properties." Applied to the negotiation of the national identity, these aesthetic properties can be seen to form a kind of "civic aesthetic," a new sensibility that has the potential to reframe how we come to know and vicariously identify with the conflicting principles of American identity.

To conclude, I want to draw attention to something Richard Rorty wrote in reference to Lincoln in his insightful book, *Achieving Our Country* (1998). He lamented the fact that, "it rarely occurs to present-day American leftists to quote Lincoln."[32] In echoing and extending Rorty's point, I want to suggest that "left-minded" folk should quote Lincoln in their writing more often than they do. And insofar as teachers are concerned, they should be encouraged to deploy his myth in the classroom as a heuristic device to illuminate not only his ample contradictions but also his mature redemptive wisdom, reflected in his willingness to improvise, to rethink, and finally to act on behalf of a hope for a new kind of human fraternity. After all, Lincoln's effort to return the nation's attention to the underlying meaning of "1776" through his Gettysburg Address was tantamount to calling for a radical improvisation in how Americans defined themselves. As we shall soon see in the next chapter, such a complex achievement can never be finished once and for all, but must be continually enacted and re-enacted, *ad infinitum*. In this interminable process, Lincoln can still teach us important things as we think through the educational project of democratizing American culture and identity.

Notes

1 The phrase originates in Prov. 25:11 (Solomon): "Like golden apples in silver settings are words spoken at the proper time."

2 Abraham Lincoln, "Fragment on the Constitution and the Union." *The Collected Works of Abraham Lincoln*. Vol. IV, Roy Basler, Ed. (New Brunswick, N.J.: Rutgers University Press, 1953), 168. This source will be cited as *CW* in all subsequent references.

3   John Patrick Diggins, *On Hallowed Ground: Abraham Lincoln and the Foundations of American History* (New Haven: Yale University Press, 2000), 41.

4   Richard Hofstader, ed. *Great Issues in American History: From the Revolution to the Civil War,* 1765–1865 (New York: Vintage Press, 1982), 389–97.

5   Ibid., 414–15. Among other sources, my analysis of the Gettysburg Address is indebted to Garry Wills, *Lincoln at Gettysburg: The Words That Remade America* (New York.: Touchstone Books, 1992).

6   William Cobb, trans. *Plato's Erotic Dialogues: The Symposium and the Phaedrus* (Albany, NY: SUNY Press, 1993), 31 (or 193a).

7   Rollo May, "Eros in Conflict with Sex," *Love and Will* (New York: W.W. Norton, 1969), 72–81.

8   *CW*, 168.

9   Allen C. Guelzo, "Apple of Gold in a Picture of Silver: The Constitution and Liberty." In *The Lincoln Enigma: The Changing Faces of an American Icon.* Ed. Gabor Boritt (New York: Oxford University Press, 2001), 89.

10 Garry Wills, *Lincoln at Gettysburg: The Words That Remade America* (New York: Touchstone Books, 1992), 38.

11 *CW*, 168–9.

12 *CW*, 168.

13 Abraham Lincoln, "Address at Sanitary Fair," Baltimore, Maryland. *The Portable Abraham Lincoln*, ed. Andrew Delbanco (New York: Viking Books, 1992), 305–7.

14 *CW*, 168.

15 *CW*, Vol. II, 405–6

16 John Patrick Diggins, *The Lost Soul of American Politics: Virtue, Self-Interest, and the Foundations of Liberalism* (New York: Basic Books, 1984), 333.

17 Lerone Bennett, Jr. *Forced Into Glory: Abraham Lincoln's White American Dream* (Chicago: Johnson Publishing, 1999). In February 1968, *Ebony* magazine published his first treatment of Lincoln under the title, "Was Abe Lincoln a White Supremacist?" Bennett's answer to this question remains, "yes."

18 Ibid., 3.

19 Ibid., 3.

20 Ibid., 556.

21 Ibid., 557–8.

22 Ibid., 564.

23 Frederick Douglass, The Freedmen's Monument Oration, April 14, 1876.Washington, D.C. In *The Life and Times of Frederick Douglass* (Mineola, NY: Dover Publications, 2003), 353–4.

24 Ibid., 357.

25 Ibid., 357.

26 Ibid., 357.

27 Ibid., 356.

28 W.E.B. Du Bois, "Abraham Lincoln" (May 1922). *W.E.B. Du Bois: Writings* (New York: Literary Classics, 1986), 1196.

29 Ibid., 1196.

30 W.E.B. Du Bois, "Again, Lincoln" (September 1922). *W.E.B. Du Bois: Writings* (New York:Literary Classics, 1986), 1198–9.

31 David W. Blight, "In Retrospect: Nathan Irvin Huggins, the Art of History, and the Irony of the American Dream." In *Beyond the Battlefield: Race, Memory and the American Civil War* (Amherst, MA: University of Massachusetts Press, 2002), 272–3.

32 Richard Rorty, *Achieving Our Country: Leftist Thought in Twentieth-Century America* (Cambridge: Harvard University Press, 1998), 10. Rorty's phrase includes Walt Whitman as a figure American leftists seldom quote. For the sake of clarity, I choose to omit this from the text.

CHAPTER FOUR

Forty acres and a mule

The phrase, *forty acres and a mule* means something quite significant to many African-Americans, but for a majority of white Americans, it unfortunately means little to nothing. For those of us in the white majority culture, curiosity about the meaning of the phrase, or interest in its teeming moral and political symbolism, simply doesn't seem to exist. This largely unselfconscious absence of interest is symptomatic of a deeper problem. The civic indifference that such an attitude reflects bears the imprint of white privilege, or, as some would have it, white supremacy. For white Americans in particular, we need to learn to recognize how this worldview insinuates itself in our thinking and in the choices we make about what's worth being curious about both within our own minds and in the world outside.

This type of learning occurs best when we first acknowledge the performative and thus the ethical dimensions of ignorance. Along with Shoshana Felman and others, we can define ignorance not so much as a quantitative lack of knowledge but as a qualitative "passion to ignore."[1] For those of us in the majority culture, we often develop tenacious though frequently unconscious emotional investments in not knowing or in ignoring certain things, particularly about those patterns of inattention that accompany our majoritarian status (as we've seen in chapter two). I argue in this chapter that not knowing or caring about the full story behind forty acres and a mule impedes the progressive evolution of the nation's democratic identity. For this reason, then, I investigate this forgotten strand of public rhetoric to make its moral and political symbolism not only apparent but also richly significant to the project of reconstructing American democracy.

Among the few citizens for whom the phrase still retains a semblance of meaning, it stands as a largely forgotten indictment of the US government for violating its promise to provide 40 acres of land to the newly freed at the conclusion of the Civil War. In fact, there had already been Congressional plans for land redistribution championed by the Radical Republican leaders, Thaddeus Stevens and Charles Sumner, during and after the war, but these efforts were defeated. Both proposals used "forty acres" as a standard for the acreage to be granted to the newly freed as compensation for their decades of unpaid labor. Stevens and Sumner fought valiantly for the moral principle that an authentically democratic citizenship for the emancipated could be brought into being only when a new class of black landholders was created. The prospect of a mass emergence of "landless citizens" was considered by these democratic leaders to be a contradiction—a betrayal of the very possibility of a redemptive American democratic vision.

The reason the slogan exists at all in the popular imagination, or at least in the popular black imagination, is due not so much to the ultimately defeated pieces of legislation proposed by Stevens and Sumner. The origin of the phrase is traced to January 1865, when General William Tecumseh Sherman, having just finished the devastating "march to the sea," issued Special Field Order 15.[2] It set aside "forty acres and a mule" for the newly freed along the coastal areas of South Carolina and Georgia, a swath extending some 100 miles in length and 30 miles inland. This was the "officially stated promise" that was "taken back" by President Andrew Johnson when he began rescinding these land grants in late 1865. Thus began the process of returning the federal lands to the confederate aristocracy. In light of this past, scholars and activists today point to these events as a moral and legal basis for black reparations.[3] For the newly freed, despite their eventual status as formal citizens, the consequences of enforced landlessness—economic and political dependency—crippled their ability to actually *be* citizens.

"The Colloquy in Savannah": What a black public taught Sherman and Stanton about democratic citizenship, freedom, and the pursuit of happiness

Our discussion of forty acres and a mule would be fundamentally different today if General Sherman had not wired President Lincoln and General Ulysses S. Grant in late 1864 requesting a change in their military strategy. After having secured Atlanta (and Lincoln's reelection in 1864) Sherman outlined a bold and daring plan of attack. Instead of engaging Confederate forces located northwest of Atlanta as they had agreed upon, Sherman proposed to disengage most of his forces from those beleaguered Confederate positions and to march 65,000 soldiers 400 miles eastward to the Atlantic coast. At first, Lincoln and Grant balked. But Sherman persisted and finally was authorized to embark on his cunning military tactic. The underlying purpose of Sherman's tactical improvisation could be described as one of the original "shock and awe" military campaigns in U.S. history: "My aim," Sherman wrote later, "was to whip the rebels, to humble their pride, to follow them to their inmost recesses, and make them fear and dread us."[4] The change in military strategy had immediate consequences: Without this resort to total war, there would have been no refugee problem, no "Colloquy in Savannah," no Field Order 15, and consequently, no distribution of 40 acre plots to 40,000 newly emancipated black farmers (albeit, for only a year).

As Sherman's army scorched and burned its way across Georgia, thousands of slaves descended upon the Union lines. By the time Sherman reached Savannah, tens of thousands had descended upon the Union columns. By the time Sherman's army reached Savannah, a huge refugee problem had emerged (estimated at 150,000). The refugee crisis prompted the Secretary of War Edwin Stanton to travel to Savannah for a meeting with Sherman. Importantly, Stanton also requested a meeting with the representatives of the black leadership in order to ask the newly freed "what they wanted for themselves."[5] There were 20 representatives from local black churches at what has been called the Colloquy in Savannah, held on January 12, 1865. The delegation appointed Garrison Frazier as their chief spokesman, a 67-year-old preacher who had been free for eight years. When asked what he understood by slavery and what the President's 1863 Emancipation Proclamation meant, Frazier said:

> Slavery is receiving by irresistible power the work of another man, and not by his consent. The freedom, as I understand it, promised by the proclamation, is taking us from under the yoke of bondage and placing us where we could reap the fruit of our own labor, and take care of ourselves, and assist the government in maintaining our own freedom.[6]

Stanton then asked how they planned to "take care of themselves" and maintain their freedom, to which Frazier responded:

> The best way we can take care of ourselves is to have land, and turn it in and till it by our own labor. . . . We want to be placed on land until we are able to buy it and make it our own.[7]

Frazier and his people were not asking for "free land" but for land grants that would eventually be purchased. The Colloquy in Savannah educated both Sherman and Stanton. It was a seminar of sorts which gave them confidence in the capacity of the recently enslaved to be virtuous, property-owning citizens. That various trades and other organizations were represented by these 20 leaders, suggests that even in oppressive circumstances black people were able to coalesce into viable, autonomous publics. Overnight, Stanton and Sherman formulated Field Order 15, a plan which became effective only days after their extraordinary meeting. Totaling 800,000 acres, these lands were to be divided into 40-acre plots and distributed among the heads of families of the newly freed. Since Sherman's army had a surplus of mules which were no longer needed for military use, livestock were to be distributed as well, thus rounding out the phrase, "forty acres and a mule."

In recalling the Colloquy in Savannah, we need to attach meaning to what Garrison Frazier did not say. He did not say what his people needed was formal citizenship and the right to vote. While it is safe to assume that Frazier and his compatriots would not oppose these procedural rights—neither the 14th nor

15th Amendments had materialized yet— he emphatically said that land, and land only, was the key to securing black livelihood. Stanton was keenly aware of the swarm of tricky political questions taking shape over the undefined civic status of the emancipated. He initiated Field Order 15 because he knew that land would be an essential if controversial component in fulfilling the substantive citizenship of the newly freed. The fact that Stanton would instruct his aide to transcribe the proceedings of the colloquy indicates that he wanted to bestow as much historical significance to this public forum as possible. To his credit, Stanton encouraged the oppressed to speak in their own voice; these voices can speak to us today if we are willing to listen.

Only three months after Field Order 15, in March 1865, Congress established the Bureau of Refugees, Freedmen, and Abandoned Lands (commonly referred to as the Freedmen's Bureau). Headed by General Oliver Howard, its task was to organize the myriad activities required to facilitate the transition of the emancipated from servitude to freedom, from adjudicating land claims and work contracts to setting up schools and hospitals. Impressively enough, by June 1865, 40,000 freedmen were settled on some 400,000 acres which became known as "Sherman's Land." Imagine what these recently emancipated and now land-owning people were feeling— the exhilaration and the hopefulness—working their own land for their own money!

Lincoln's murder marks another turning point in the history of forty acres and a mule. President Andrew Johnson made no bones about the fact that he was a committed white supremacist. He opposed citizenship and voting rights for blacks and was vehemently opposed to granting *any* lands to the freedpeople. Through a series of executive pardons and amnesties issued in the summer of 1865, Johnson nullified the deeds to land organized under the auspices of Field Order 15. According to Howard's *Autobiography,* Johnson was not content with emasculating Field Order 15, he also ordered hundreds of thousands additional acres removed from control of the Freedmen's Bureau.[8] These reversals culminated in October 1865 at Edisto Island, South Carolina. Howard was instructed by Johnson to inform thousands of landed black farmers that the lands they had been told was theirs, was no longer theirs.

Historian Eric Foner describes the October 1865 meeting at Edisto Island as "one of the most poignant encounters of the entire

Reconstruction era."[9] It's also accurate to identify the meeting at Edisto Island as both the symbol and reality of the failure of Reconstruction. More than 2000 people attended the meeting. To capture this moment in its full pathos, I quote Howard directly:

> The auditorium and galleries were filled. The rumor preceded my coming had reached the people that I was obliged by the President's orders to restore lands to the old planters, so that strong evidence of dissatisfaction and sorrow were manifested from every part of the assembly. In the noise and confusion no progress was had till a sweet-voiced negro woman began the hymn "Nobody knows the trouble I feel—Nobody knows but Jesus," which, joined in by all, had a quieting effect on the audience. Then I endeavored as clearly and gently as I could to explain to them the wishes of the President . . . My address, however kind in manner I rendered it, met with no apparent favor. They did not hiss, but their eyes flashed unpleasantly, and with one voice they cried, "*No, no!*" Speeches full of feeling and rough eloquence came back in response. One very black man, thick set and strong, cried out from the gallery: "Why, General Howard, why do you take away our lands? You take them from us who are true, always true to the Government! You give them to our all-time enemies! That is not right![10]

This rarely discussed fragment tells us that these communities were alert to their own interests. They surely understood the language of the democratic heart well enough to see land ownership as the mother of all other freedoms. Denied land, denied the means of economic independence, denied their share of the apple of gold, these aspiring citizens were now being told that they were to be economically dependent on their former slave-masters. Thus, Edisto Island signifies the officially sanctioned undoing of their unalienable right to the pursuit of happiness. In a state of exhilaration one year and despair the next, is there any wonder why African-Americans responded musically to their dashed democratic dreams with the blues idiom?

Just as the Colloquy in Savannah highlights the destructive consequences of black landlessness to any decent notion of American citizenship, so, too, does Howard's Edisto Island testimony highlight the fact that these "Americans" knew intuitively that their unalienable right to the pursuit of happiness was being violated. While this unalienable "natural right" had not yet been formally extended to these persons by the (legal) State, symbolized by the Constitution, we could say it had already been extended to them by the (moral) nation, symbolized by the Declaration of Independence. As we've seen in Chapter four, Lincoln employs the "apple of gold" metaphor to help explain the moral identity of the nation to the nation: "the principle of liberty to all, hope to all, enterprise and industry to all."

As these land reforms on the southeast coast of the United States were turned back with brutal efficiency, the elections of 1866 enabled Radical Republican leaders in Congress to wrest the control of reconstruction policy from President Johnson. In the House of Representatives, Thaddeus Stevens called for a bold plan of land redistribution that extended far beyond the southeastern coastal areas identified within the Sherman Reservation. This legislation called for the distribution of "forty acres each to one million freedmen," land that was to be expropriated from 70,000 elite landholders within the confederate power structure. Stevens insisted on mandating the "forty acres of land" clause, reminding lawmakers that land ownership was far more vital to black citizenship than the procedural right to vote.

> Whatever may be the fate of the rest of the bill, I must earnestly pray that this may not be defeated. On its success, in my judgment, depends not only the happiness and respectability of the colored race, but their very existence. Homesteads to them are far more valuable than the immediate right of suffrage, though both are their due.[11]

As it happened, the defeat of this legislation squandered what could have been an exceptionally grand chapter in the unfolding of America's democratic experiment. W. E. B. Du Bois described this loss in both domestic and global terms: "To have given each one of the million Negro free families a forty-acre freehold would have made a basis of real democracy in the United States that might easily have transformed the modern world."[12] On striking display here is the contrast between what a democratic State could have offered the newly freed in terms of substantive freedom and what a timid "liberal" State did offer: empty-shelled procedural rights that didn't meaningfully exist until a century later. To echo a theme discussed in earlier chapters, we could also say that their unalienable right to the pursuit of happiness turned out to be very much "alienable." Indeed, the tragedy of enforced black landlessness as well as the denial of their pursuit of happiness was soon compounded by the tragedy of the 14th Amendment. The original purpose of this legislation was intended to benefit those denied citizenship due to slavery by granting equal citizenship to all "persons" born on American soil. Yet, starting in the 1880s, corporate lawyers succeeded in using the 14th Amendment to define corporations as "persons" that now would be accorded the same protections and due process that human persons were due. How to begin to grasp the human costs associated with the denial of such constitutional guarantees? Is there a contemporary "moral equivalent" of forty acres and a mule that could be redeemed today?

Forty acres and a mule, white supremacy, and the politics of ignorance

In "The Propaganda of History," Du Bois chronicles how educational institutions and the textbook industry combined to impose a stream of white supremacist representations upon generations of Americans in the decades after Reconstruction. Writing in 1935, Du Bois quotes extensively from these textbooks, showing how they all boiled down to the articulation of one outstanding principle: *black people are incapable of citizenship*. A cruel paradox thus emerged: first, blacks were denied land as the basis of genuine citizenship, and then, Americans were subjected to white supremacist propaganda in textbook histories, films, and print media informing them in objective tones that, when given the opportunity, "the colored" were incapable of exercising citizenship. Reflecting on the power and scope of this ideological indoctrination, Du Bois blasts the custodians of official knowledge:

> In propaganda against the Negro since emancipation in this land, we face one of the most stupendous efforts the world ever saw to discredit human beings, an effort involving universities, history, science, social life and religion.[13]

One enduring consequence of these "stupendous efforts" was to stitch white supremacist assumptions so deeply into the fabric of American identity that white privilege would appear natural and thus invisible. There are many ways to define and conceptualize this racist ontology (race supremacy as a mode of being).[14] I think "white supremacy" can usefully be likened to an octopus with a thousand tentacles reaching out in every direction. Rather than trying to capture this creature in its global aspect, here I want to isolate one tentacle in particular.

From an educational point of view, one danger of internalizing white supremacist assumptions and patterns of thought is that our desires to know get preempted (or repressed). Those in the dominant white culture seldom develop curiosity about the supposedly "inferior" culture's history, literature, art, and the like. "They" are not "us" and therefore not worth knowing about. The general white ignorance of forty acres and a mule aptly symbolizes this inscribed pattern of inattention. As outlined in the introduction to this chapter, I use the term *ignorance* here not to denote a lack *of* knowing but to denote an attitude *toward* knowing: ignorance is none other than a passion to ignore. It is a universal part of human being. The lived myth of white supremacy depends on individuals developing specific passions to ignore. Such ignorance is properly regarded as "political" because that which is ignored is always that which would jeopardize the privileged position of its adherents. For example, greater knowledge about the historical context of forty acres and a mule would force those of us in the majority culture to acknowledge how factors of race and class interacted to deny full citizenship and freedom to African-Americans during and after Reconstruction. One way to begin to release ourselves from the tentacles of white supremacy, then, is to learn to perceive the internalized patterns of inattention that constitute whiteness as a license to ignore.

Despite advances in recent years regarding "the color line," it would be naive to conclude that the tentacles of white supremacist ideology no longer reach into the country's most esteemed journals, professional magazines, documentary films, and classrooms. Take, for example, a recent article in the *Chronicle of Higher Education* by John David Smith, "The Enduring Myth of Forty Acres and a Mule." The author contends that the "myth" of the phrase is that no promise of land was ever made to the freedmen in the first place:

> What does history teach us? Yes, the historical record disproves assertions that the federal government reneged on promises to grant the freedpeople forty acres and a mule.[15]

It's worth noting that Smith, a history professor, never quotes from Field Order 15, for to do so would risk demolishing his entire argument. As previously established, Field Order 15 was a federal, executive decree that functioned as law until President Johnson rescinded it through issuing letters of amnesty to confederate landholders. Before we pass judgment on the quality of Smith's scholarship too hastily, however, it would behoove us to examine the relevant sections of Field Order 15. Articles 1, 3, and 5 read:

> The islands from Charleston south, the abandoned rice-fields along the rivers for thirty miles back from the sea, and the country bordering the St. John's River, Florida, are *reserved and set apart for the settlement of the negroes.*
>
> Whenever three respectable negroes, heads of families, shall desire to settle on land . . . the Inspector of Settlements and Plantations will himself, *give them a license to settle such island or district* and afford them such assistance as he can to enable them to establish a peaceable agricultural settlement . . . *so that each family shall have a plot of not more than forty acres of tillable ground.*
>
> In order to carry out this system of settlement, a general officer will be detailed as Inspector of Settlements and plantations whose duty it shall be to visit the settlements . . . and who will furnish personally to each head of a family, subject to the approval of the President of the United States, *a possessory title in writing,* giving as near as possible the description of the boundaries; and who shall adjust all claims or conflicts that may arise under the same, subject to the like approval, *treating such titles altogether as possessory.*[16] (My italics)

Amazingly for Smith, "the historical record" indicates that no promise of land was ever extended. Scholarship like this harkens back to the nineteenth century textbooks that Du Bois lambasted.

Not surprisingly, the author also reproduces the fiction that the Congressional efforts to secure land for the newly freed had nothing to do with "reparations":

> Significantly, proponents of land distribution *never defined their plans as reparations to former slaves for their centuries of servitude and unrequited labor.* Rather, Congressional Republicans used the prospect of distributing land to punish ex-Confederates, as well as to garner political support of black people and to establish the freedpeople as a landholding class, thereby guaranteeing their economic freedom.[17]

Senator Sumner's 1867 bill and debates surrounding it are part of the historical record. These debates expose the fallacy of the claim that the provision of land was "never" linked to a principle of reparations. Sumner explicitly connected the acquisition of land to economic independence and to the development of full citizenship, measures that were said to be justified given the scale and duration of the past injury. In the Senate debate that followed the introduction of Sumner's bill, one skeptical senator, Mr. Fessenden of Maine observed with astonishment that providing land to former slaves "is more than we do for white men." Sumner's reply is crucial:

> White men have never been in slavery; there is no emancipation and no enfranchisement of white men to be consummated. I put it to my friend, I ask his best judgment, can he see a way to complete and crown this great and glorious work without securing land for the freedmen?[18]

This exchange makes plain that legislation for the provision of land to the newly freed was absolutely intended to serve a reparative function: land was regarded as the *consummation* of their franchise. It's hard to escape the conclusion that Smith's neo-confederate interpretation of the phrase is comfortably ensconced in the fiction of his "colorblind objectivity." The author is intent not to arouse the readers' curiosity; he wants us to dismiss the radical political implications of the phrase. More than anything else, it seems that the article is designed to halt the spirit of inquiry, a hallmark of the politics of ignorance.

Reflections on Martin Luther King's 1968 "speech that never was": How the reparative principle of justice at stake in forty acres and a mule was denied again[19]

As is well known, Martin Luther King's analysis of American society was further radicalized during the late 1960s.[20] King came to understand that the formal fulfillment of civil rights (the focus of the 1963 March on Washington) could not alone meet the requirements of a consummated citizenship for African-Americans. Stormy events of the late 1960s led King inexorably to the conclusion that economic structures of inequality had to be challenged and reconfigured for African-American citizenship to be substantively fulfilled.

King's increasingly radical critique of the US political economy, then, is tantamount to a recovery of the moral principle implicit within our phrase. It would be accurate to say that King's political transformation was brought about, in large part, by his search for a contemporary moral equivalent of forty acres and a mule. In 1968, King declared:

> In 1863 the negro was given abstract freedom expressed in luminous rhetoric. But in an agrarian economy he was given no land to make liberation concrete. After the war the government granted white settlers, without cost, millions of acres of land in the West, thus providing America's new white peasants from Europe with an economic floor. But at the same time its oldest peasantry, the Negro, was denied everything but a legal status he could not use, could not consolidate, could not even defend.[21]

King's democratic vision for "making liberation concrete" posed a visceral threat to the powers that be. Serious domestic reconstruction couldn't occur so as long as the nation's resources were being diverted to the Vietnam War. Part of the overall political predicament, then, was that any meaningful remedy would require that Americans learn to see what they had been conditioned not to see: the ways in which militarism, racism, and poverty were structurally interdependent.

In framing the triplets of social misery as a conceptual whole, King placed the whole edifice of white supremacy in his theoretical crosshairs. In response to King's scathing and cogent analysis, it appears that powerful forces within the system placed King in their *literal* crosshairs.[22]

As King's political analysis sharpened, the idea of launching The Poor People's Campaign was inaugurated. The campaign was originally planned to arrive in Washington, D.C., in April 1968, with a major public address to be given by King in mid June. The Poor People's Campaign was to be an indefinite encampment of half amillion of America's poorest citizens on the National Mall. It was envisioned as a sustained series of protests and acts of mass civil disobedience designed to disrupt the operations of government. The campaign was to demand that legislation be adopted to address the unmet needs of the poor (black and white). King told his aides that the summer of 1968 was shaping up to be a "national showdown for non-violence . . . a last chance to arouse the American conscience toward constructive democratic change."[23] Unlike the 1963 March on Washington, however, the civil rights movement and the anti-war movement had now joined forces, greatly amplifying their power to challenge the structural inequalities of American society.

William F. Pepper asserts that the main reason the "moral leader of America" was "executed" by an "act of State" was King's determination to publicly and eloquently link the war in Vietnam to the continuation of racial and class injustice at home:

> If the wealthy, powerful interests across the nation would find Dr. King's escalating activity against the war intolerable, his planned mobilization of a half a million poor people with the intention of laying siege to Congress could only engender outrage—and fear. This possibility simply could not be allowed to materialize, and neither could Martin King's crusade against the war be permitted to continue.[24]

Had King not been assassinated, he would have delivered to the nation another historically significant speech. In all probability, its power to reshape the nation's self conception would have surpassed even that of his iconic 1963 speech. The phrase forty acres and a mule, if not explicitly mentioned by King, would have *implicitly formed the moral core* of this tragically extinguished public address. The principle of reparative justice, coupled with a withering critique of the war system, would have been eloquently articulated to the nation in terms that people could not easily ignore. King's relentless focus on economic inequality, his opposition to the "madness" of Vietnam, and his turn toward "democratic socialism," all suggest that the public rhetoric he would have put into circulation that June afternoon would have rekindled America's democratic spirit in powerful ways. As we can surmise from his 1967–68 writings, the culminating speech of the Poor People's Campaign would have given King an opportunity to articulate an alternative narrative of cultural heroism.

> Why has our nation placed itself in the position of being God's military agent on earth, and intervened recklessly in Vietnam and the Dominican Republic? All these questions remind us that there is a need for a radical restructuring of the architecture of American society. For its very survival's sake, America must re-examine old presuppositions and release itself from many things that for centuries have been held sacred. For the evils of racism, poverty and militarism to die, a new set of values must be born. Our economy must become more person-centered than property and profit-centered. Our government must depend more on its moral power than on its military power.[25]

As King ratcheted-up his language of critique, it's not difficult to grasp why the interests of the national security state—as opposed to the democratic interests of the nation—would be threatened by King's ability to mobilize Americans on behalf of the purposes and values that transcended those imposed by the warfare state. As Pepper observes, "this possibility simply could not be allowed to materialize." Martin King was assassinated on April 4, 1968. The Poor People's Campaign that had been planned for the spring and early summer of 1968 did indeed take place without its leader, but the movement was badly shaken and demoralized. Due to the assassination, it bears repeating that Americans were denied not only an opportunity to listen to one of the moral leaders of the nation address the intensifying political crisis but they were also denied an opportunity to see in that speech a blueprint for recalibrating our national priorities. National press coverage of what could be called the "second march on Washington" was barely visible, save as a token of abject failure. The official story line, familiar to most, is that a "racist lone nut," James Earl Ray, shot King and fled to Montreal, Canada. He was then arrested at London's Heathrow Airport 6 weeks later, tried and convicted to life imprisonment. End of story—or is it?

To conclude, I want to make something of a conceptual leap and read the King assassination through the pedagogical lens of forty acres and a mule. This leap can be justified by recalling that King's public career was rooted in acknowledging that the promises made to African-Americans for full citizenship had been broken and were in need of repair. The phrase forty acres and a mule symbolized this broken promise. As late as 1968, as we've seen, King argued that this enforced landlessness was one compelling reason why some form of restitution should be forthcoming. This conceptual leap is further justified when we consider the verdict of a wrongful death civil suit, *King v. Jowers et al.* 1999.[26] As I hope to show, *King v. Jowers* shares a curious yet unmistakable affinity with forty acres and a mule. First, the jury's verdict:

> **The Court:** In answer to the question did Loyd Jowers participate in a conspiracy to do harm to Dr. Martin Luther King, your answer is yes. Do you also find that others, including governmental agencies, were parties to this conspiracy as alleged by the defendant? Your answer to that one is also yes. And the total amount of damages you find for the plaintiffs entitled to is one hundred dollars. Is that your verdict?
>
> **The Jury:** Yes (In unison).[27]

To read the trial record of *King v. Jowers*, even if only for a few hours, some untimely questions are raised: Why is it that so few Americans know that 12 jurors (six black, six white) found that certain "governmental agencies" (read: Army intelligence units) had been dispatched to Memphis in April 1968 and were found to be "party to the conspiracy"? What institutional powers would stand to benefit from this alleged act of State? Would it be unwarranted to speculate, based on the juries' verdict, that the motive behind the assassination may have also included an attempt to kill the *idea of reparative justice* implicit within King's political vision?

It should be acknowledged that the politics of ignorance has already done its work in lulling the nation into a state of forgetfulness about the principles of equality and justice at stake in both our phrase and in King's assassination. This inquiry suggests that to forget these moral principles is to forget knowing the only real basis upon which American democracy can be reconstructed. Martin King's vision for America's democratic transformation was all about redeeming the promise of forty acres and a mule in contemporary terms. But this redemption, he saw, couldn't be enacted in the context of a permanent war society (any more than it can be enacted today under similar circumstances). Remarkably enough, then, our inquiry into a nineteenth-century piece of public rhetoric leads directly to a twentieth-century piece of public rhetoric for democratic reconstruction. This image of reconstruction is beautifully expressed in King's Riverside Church speech, "Beyond Vietnam: A Time to Break the Silence." Among its many memorable passages, this one stands out: "A nation that continues year after year to spend more money on military defense than on programs of social uplift is approaching spiritual death."[28] As we will see in chapter seven, in the decades since King spoke these words, the nation has continued to spend far more on military defense than on programs of social uplift, a pattern that few could deny has had a corrosive effect on the soul-life of the nation.

In adopting forty acres and a mule as a vehicle of inquiry and public memory recovery, we can see more clearly the unfinished character of American democracy. And we can see why its progressive reconstruction remains indivisibly linked to recovering the value of King's framework for explaining how militarism, racism, and poverty were structurally interdependent in 1968 America. Today, nearly a half-century later, it appears that the civic disease which King so insightfully diagnosed as the nation's preeminent soul doctor has now penetrated into the deepest recesses of American culture and identity. Thus, rejuvenating the soul-life of the nation depends in large part on our capacity to remember and act upon King's mature and radical critique of 1968 America. King's radical democratic vision offers both a lucid description of what ails the country and a method for stimulating its progressive enactment. The task for educators is therefore to fight against the tendency to subject King's richly significant democratic legacy to the machinations of historical amnesia.

Notes

1 For a penetrating discussion of this general theme, see Shoshana Felman, "Psychoanalysis and Education: Teaching Terminable and Interminable" in *Jaques Lacan and the Adventure of Insight: Psychoanalysis in Contemporary Culture* (Cambridge: Harvard University Press), 69–97. For a series of equally penetrating essays which link ignorance specifically to issues of race in America, see Shannon Sullivan and Nancy Tuana, eds *Race and Epistemologies of Ignorance* (Albany: SUNY Press, 2007).

2 See Claude F. Oubre, *Forty Acres and a Mule: The Freedmen's Bureau and Black Land Ownership* (Baton Rouge: Louisiana State University Press, 1978).

3 See, for example, Randall Robinson, *The Debt: What America Owes to Blacks* (New York: Dutton Books, 2000); Manning Marable, "Forty Acres and a Mule: The Case for Black Reparations." In *The Great Wells of Democracy: The Meaning of Race in American Life* (New York: Basic Books, 2002), 223–53.

4 William T. Sherman, *Memoirs* (New York: Penguin Classics, 2000), 608–9.

5 Benjamin P.Thomas and Harold Hyman, *Stanton: The Life and Times of Lincoln's Secretary of War* (New York: Alfred Knopf, 1962), 343–4.

6 See "Colloquy with Colored Ministers," *The Journal of Negro History*, 16, 1, Jan. 1931, 88–94. For a more recent account of the colloquy, see Eric Foner, *Forever Free: The Story of Emancipation and Reconstruction* (New York: Vintage 2005).

7 Ibid., 91.

8 "The Abandoned Lands," *Autobiography of Oliver Otis Howard*, Vol. 2 (New York: The Baker & Taylor Company, 1907), 229–44.

9 Foner, *Forever Free*, 76.

10 Howard, *Autobiography*, 238–9.

11 Thaddeus Stevens, "Damages to Loyal Men." *The Selected Papers of Thaddeus Stevens*, Vol. 2: April 1865/August 1868, ed. B. W. Palmer (Pittsburgh: University of Pittsburgh Press, 1998), 276–95.

12 W. E. B. Du Bois, *Black Reconstruction in America* (New York: Atheneum, 1935), 602.

13 Ibid., 727.

14 For a cogent set of essays on the myriad ways in which white supremacy manifests itself, see William Ayers & Bernadine Dohrn,

Race Course: Against White Supremacy (Chicago: Third World Press, 2009).

15 John David Smith, "The Enduring Myth of Forty Acres and a Mule," *Chronicle of Higher Education*, 49, 24 (2007), B11.

16 Special Field Order 15 (January 1865) http://teachingamericanhistory. org/library/index.asp?documentprint=545.

17 Smith, *Chronicle*, B12.

18 Charles Sumner, "Further Guaranties in Reconstruction: Loyalty, Education, and a Homestead for Freedmen; Measures of Reconstruction: Not a Burden or Penalty." *Charles Sumner Collected Works XI* (Boston: Roberts Bros, 1883), 127.

19 This rather unorthodox section title is premised on the claim that King's famous 1963 "I Have a Dream" speech has exercised a material effect on American self-conception: It is my belief that the speech he would have given in spring 1968, had he not been assassinated, would have had a potentially greater effect on American self-conception than even the 1963 speech. For an earlier version of this essay, one which articulates "educational reparations" as a contemporary moral equivalent of forty acres and a mule, see Kerry T. Burch, "Forty Acres and a Mule as a Pedagogical Motif," *Philosophical Studies in Education* (2008) Vol. 39, 118–30.

20 See Michael Eric Dyson, "America Must Move Toward a Democratic Socialism: A Progressive Social Blueprint." *I May Not Get There With You: The True Martin Luther King, Jr.* (New York: Touchstone, 2001), 78–100.

21 Martin Luther King, Jr. *Where Do We Go From Here: Chaos or Community?* (Boston: Beacon Press, 1968), 79.

22 Exactly one year prior to his murder, on April 4, 1967, at New York's Riverside Church, King gave a speech ("Beyond Vietnam: A Time to Break the Silence") that denounced not only the war in Vietnam but also the political economy that generated it. http://mlk kpp01. stanford.edu/index.php/ecyclopedia/documentary/doc_beyond_ vietnam/accessed April 4, 2010.

23 See Stephen B. Oates, "The Hour of Reckoning." *Let the Trumpet Sound: The Life of Martin Luther King, Jr.* (New York: New American Library, 1982), 459–62.

24 William F. Pepper, *An Act of State: The Execution of Martin Luther King* (London/New York: Verso, 2003), 7.

25 King, *Chaos or Community?*, 133.

26 *Coretta Scott King, et al. v. Loyd Jowers, et al.*, filed November 15, 1999. Case No. CT-97242. Circuit Court of Shelby County,

Tennessee, 30th Judicial District, Memphis. The verdict was returned December 8, 1999. Obviously there are different and generally less stringent evidentiary standards for civil cases as against criminal cases; still, for anyone interested in this controversial set of events, *King v. Jowers* is required reading.

27 See *The 13th Juror: The Official Transcript of the Martin Luther King Assassination Conspiracy Trial.* (Lexington, KY: MLK the Truth, 2009), 742.

28 http://mlk kpp01.stanford.edu/index.php/ecyclopedia/documentary/ doc_beyond_vietnam/accessed April 4, 2010.

CHAPTER FIVE

The moral equivalent of war

Just over 100 years ago, William James (1842–1910) began his last published essay "The Moral Equivalent of War" on a note of ironic understatement. He reminded Americans that "the war against war is going to be no holiday excursion or camping party."[1] Not for a moment did James harbor any illusions about the tremendous difficulties involved in waging a moral and educational struggle to dethrone the primacy of war within the negotiation of American identity. James regarded such a Herculean task as a long-term, indeed, interminable project of cultural reformation, one that would have to be creatively invented and enacted across multiple generations. As a kind of moral and intellectual jump-start, the purpose of the James' essay was to kindle the idea among Americans that new excitements and outlets of heroic energy needed to be identified and drawn-out if the nation was to move toward a just "socialistic-equilibrium."

By the time that James' last-published essay reached its first national audience in *McClure's Magazine*, he had already wrestled with the problem of defining the meaning of the phrase in *The Varieties of Religious Experience*.[2] In his first experiment in constructing this sublime if elusive piece of public rhetoric, James suggested perhaps the purest example of the phrase's meaning was embodied by "monkish" types of individuals who had the strength, daring, and courage to take vows of poverty. James wanted to show that such expressions of moral strength and courage did not have to depend on the culture of war for their inspiration. However, as a practical matter, as a matter of radicalizing American democracy, one severe difficulty with this first iteration of the concept was that it represented a model of living that scarcely any Americans, then or now, would ever find appealing. James' later efforts to theorize a moral equivalent of war, to expand its conceptual boundaries and to deepen its critical democratic content, included an invitation for others to pioneer alternative interpretations of the concept.

As a committed pacifist, it is a testament to James' fierce independence that he would criticize those in his own peace party for failing to appreciate the moral legitimacy of the so-called martial virtues, those virtues and social dispositions which formed the core of military identity. Among the four martial virtues that James singles out as the "enduring cement of a permanent peace," "the rock upon which states are built" are *intrepidity, contempt of softness, surrender of private interest* and *obedience to command*."[3] Readers today may well be horrified at James' valorization of these potentially fascist traits.[4]

It is crucial to note, however, that James qualifies his proposal with a rather profound caveat: the *violent ends* to which these virtues had historically been directed, would have to be "reeducated" and their energies redirected toward *nonviolent ends*. This claim of course is hotly contested, but it is also potentially one of the richest educative tensions James bequeaths to us. Here, the viability of the concept hinges on whether or not one believes the passions for war can be transformed into passions for peace and to what extent, if any, the metaphorical strategies James puts into play are the best instruments for bringing about such forms of psychic and social transformation.

For James, it made no sense for members of the peace party to pretend, as did many of his fellow Mugwumps, that the aggressive and competitive dimensions of the human psyche could or even should be eliminated.[5] "The military feelings are too deeply grounded," he observed, "to abdicate their place among our ideals until better substitutes are found than the glory and shame that come to nations as well as to individuals from the ups and downs of politics and the vicissitudes of trade."[6]

Since James assumed that the hurly-burly of American politics and trade would never be able to match the emotionally transcendent power of the "military feelings," he believed that alternative forms of purpose needed to be invented. What was needed was the building up of alternative myths of cultural heroism, a task which required innovative forms of civic pedagogy. Thus, James urged Americans to "foster rival excitements" and to "invent new outlets for heroic energies." Otherwise, without these civic innovations, there would be no way to displace or decenter the increasingly hegemonic power the military feelings were exerting over the character of the national identity.[7] James issued his summons to the nation:

> What we now need to discover in the social realm is the moral equivalent of war: something heroic that will speak to men as universally as war does, and yet will be as compatible with their spiritual selves as war has proved itself to be incompatible.[8]

James understands that his vision of a peaceful "socialistic-equilibrium" could never be achieved unless citizens acted with what he called "civic courage" to renovate cultural institutions and inaugurate new modes of selfhood. James further contends that the ultimate problem Americans faced, or rather refused to face squarely, has been the collective failure to release ourselves from "*the fear of emancipation from the fear-regime.*"[9] James puts this cogent phrase in italics to underscore his belief that the real threat to peace and to American democracy did not come from enemies abroad but rather from an "inner unwillingness" to acknowledge our lack of aesthetic and moral imagination and to act upon this realization by developing these very faculties. The work of constructing a moral substitute for war was intended to compensate for these aesthetic and moral deficiencies. James wants to remind Americans that psychological and emotional sources of imagination and civic courage lay dormant and pedagogically undeveloped within the martial virtues. James' obviously knew his "postulate for utopia" wouldn't be fully realized in his lifetime, yet he held that, in the long run, the slow workings of reason could be recruited to help sublimate and rechannel the warrior energies within.[10]

In our search for critical pedagogies to challenge the militarization of American identity, James' essay serves as a theoretical compass inviting us to rethink what the first principles of peace education or the first principles of democratic education ought to be. How might the nation's intimate romance with the culture of war be unsettled, ruptured, or otherwise decentered? If we stroll with James and consider his central claims, insights, and assumptions, we cannot help but ask more penetrating questions about how contemporary moral equivalents of war might be theorized, and how these moral renovations might contribute to the evolution of a political culture less enchanted by the charmed aura of criminality that enables America's permanent warfare state.

A tale of two heroisms: How William James turned Theodore Roosevelt on his head

In the late 1890s, the United States embraced a full-throated policy of imperial conquest, symbolized by a brutal counterinsurgency war in the Philippines (1899–1902). James was gravely disturbed not only by these events but also by a series of speeches that Theodore Roosevelt gave extolling the virtues of a "manly" imperialism. It is well known that Roosevelt was an apologist for American imperialism; he liked to talk unabashedly about the therapeutic effects of war on the moral development of individuals, nations, and civilizations. Roosevelt identified this worldview as the "doctrine of the strenuous life."[11] Paradoxically, James had the utmost disdain for this doctrine even as he seemed to embrace certain elements of it. He considered Roosevelt's doctrine to represent hollow, abstract thinking at its worst. Arising from these circumstances, then, James can be seen as positioning his essay "The Moral Equivalent of War" as a counterweight to Roosevelt's Doctrine of the Strenuous Life. The bitter public clash between James and Roosevelt over the meaning of the national identity—in a sense, their clash over what it means to be an American hero—spotlights the defining contradictions pulsating within the negotiation of national identity at the turn of the last century.

"I wish to preach, not the doctrine of ignoble ease," Roosevelt intoned, "but the doctrine of the strenuous life, the life of toil and effort, of labor and strife; to preach that highest form of success which comes, not to the man who desires mere easy peace, but the man who does not shrink from danger, from hardship, and who out of these wins the splendid ultimate triumph."[12] Roosevelt's doctrine thus embodies the assumption that war has an intrinsic role to play in the moral development of "real men."

Roosevelt, in fact, indirectly accuses James of treason. In a direct slap to James (who was his former teacher at Harvard), Roosevelt declared that he had "scant patience" with those "who make a pretense of humanitarianism to hide and cover their timidity, and who cant about 'liberty' and the 'consent of the governed,' in order to excuse themselves for their unwillingness to play the part of men." In another thinly disguised salvo aimed at the Anti-Imperialist League, of which James was a well-known member and acting Vice President, Roosevelt opined: "As for those in our own country who encourage our foe, we can afford contemptuously to disregard them; but it must be remembered that their utterances are not saved from being treasonable merely by the fact that they are despicable."[13]

In 1899, at precisely the time the Spanish-American War was turning ominously into the Philippine-American War, James responded. In an editorial published in *The Boston Transcript*, "Governor Roosevelt's Oration," he accused Roosevelt of still being in the adolescent stage of moral development.

> [He] treats human affairs from the sole point of view of the organic excitement and difficulty they bring, gushes over war as the ideal condition of human society, for the manly strenuousness which it involves, and treats peace as a condition of blubberlike and swollen ignobility, fit only for huckstering weaklings, dwelling in gray twilight and heedless of the higher life.[14]

James spies in Roosevelt's attitude toward the glorious benefits of war, a fatal attraction to a set of dangerous abstractions. "Not a word of the cause—one foe is as good as another; not a word of the conditions of success . . . Governor Roosevelt's abstract war worship carries no test of what is better or worse in the way of wars."[15] Roosevelt's propensity for abstraction reaches its highest pitch when he categorizes humankind according to a civilization/ barbarism binary opposition. Of course, if one accepts Roosevelt's bedrock assumption that "civilization" and "barbarism" are objectively existent categories, it provides a readymade moral justification for waging permanent war. For, as Roosevelt reasons, "In the long run civilized man finds he can keep the peace only by subduing his barbarian neighbor; for the barbarian will only yield to force."[16] In other words, without the presence of war, the progress of civilization (read: white men) would degenerate.

On this point, Kristin L. Hogansen has shown that America's turn toward imperialism during the 1890s was caused as much by domestic gender anxieties as it was by the traditional roster of foreign policy considerations, such as seizing natural resources or in "protecting civilization." According to Hogansen, many influential imperialists understood that generations of "manly men" had been produced as a result of the centuries-long process of conquering the nation's vast continental frontier. But with no surplus geographical space to serve as a crucible upon which to forge manly men, anxiety arose in elite quarters about the precarious future of American manhood.[17] Many believed that the impending gender crisis could be averted by "taming and civilizing" new frontiers through territorial expansion. Even the administrative experience garnered as a consequence of colonial expansion was valued for its ability to open up new *bureaucratic* frontiers of masculine control. Such an expansion of American power would thus provide American men opportunities to become men through their surely benevolent rule over distant colored people. Based largely on this imperial strand of American exceptionalism, within a decade the United States violently wrested control of the Philippines, Hawaii, Guam, Cuba, and Puerto Rico.

In stark contrast to this narrative of imperial heroism, James never considered the Filipino's insurgent leader, Emilio Aguinaldo, a soulless barbarian, as did Roosevelt. Significantly, James's view of American exceptionalism prohibited him from denying any other people their right to self-determination. Owing to James' abiding respect for human dignity and plurality, he refers to Aguinaldo as the carrier of a sacred purpose—national independence—and favorably compares his armed resistance to US imperialism to George Washington's armed resistance to British imperialism.[18] From this angle of consideration—from a position of radical empathy—James succeeds in identifying the fundamental moral weakness of Roosevelt's ideology of permanent war. James was convinced that Roosevelt's doctrine was dangerous to the future of American democracy. It was dangerous because the strenuous life as conceived by Roosevelt would automatically transform all wars and all desires for territorial expansion into inherently ennobling enterprises. Promoting a myth of heroism on the basis of such bright and shining abstractions would create persons incapable of recognizing the souls of other people. James wrote that there was "no sign" American policymakers ever once considered that "the Filipinos could have any feeling or insides of their own."[19]

He compared the brutal US treatment toward the Filipinos to the way big corporations in America had been and were still brutally crushing their smaller competitors. With regard to crushing the Filipino resistance, James observed, "it was merely a big material corporation against a small one, the 'soul' of the big one consisting in a stock of moral phrases, the little one owning no soul at all."[20]

James was repelled by any doctrine or mode of perception that would ignore the situated concrete reality and moral equality of all human beings.[21] This radical empathy for the other undermines every dimension of the imperial project. Here, we see how James attempts to turn Roosevelt's doctrine on its head: James wants to "tap into" the energies contained within the martial virtues, much like Roosevelt, and he also seeks to transform their objects of devotion—to redirect their ends in view. In doing so, James attempts to change, or at least modify, the ontological status of these signifiers. James rejects the idea that the energies latent within the martial virtues are intrinsically warlike—they may start out that way in any given individual life, but he insists these energies can be redirected toward peaceful ends.

James turns Roosevelt on his head in another important sense. Notice that Roosevelt meets the crisis of the closing of the frontier with a demand to seize more land and conquer new frontiers indefinitely through violent force. James suggests an alternative vocation: Not to seize foreign lands through conquest but to withdrawal those desires, energies, and projections from the traditional physical frontier and turn them toward an interior, moral frontier, one susceptible to pedagogical intervention and possible democratic transformation. The severe tension between James and Roosevelt on the morality of this war thus reflects a deeper tension between two myths of cultural heroism within American culture and two irreconcilable versions of American exceptionalism.

How Jane Roland Martin turns William James on his head: Reflections on the status of a Jamesian category

In 1987 Jane Roland Martin published what could fairly be described as a feminist deconstruction of James' controversial essay. Martin rejects the core assumption of James' argument, namely that the martial virtues are capable of being redeemed through enlightened and sustained educational intervention. Martin further maintains that it would be impossible to "detach" the martial virtues from war in any significant way. And even if we could detach them, she says, such masculine virtues by themselves would never be sufficient to create the conditions for peace. In no uncertain terms, Martin declares, "those who belong to the peace-party today must *extinguish* the higher aspects of militarist sentiment, not succumb to them."[22] Martin seems to make no distinction between the martial virtues theorized by James and the martial virtues theorized by Roosevelt. From Martin's perspective, the four martial virtues James highlights are too ontologically "finished" as masculine essences to be worth educating.

Martin takes James to task for his exclusion of "womanliness" as a set of qualities that, if properly valued by men and women alike, would go a long way toward constructing a less violent world. As a critical response to this lacuna in James' thought, Martin develops the case that the educational philosophies of Charlotte Perkins Gilman and Maria Montessori are well suited to fill the gender gap within James' text. For example, in her utopian novel *Herland* (1915), Gilman develops a theory of "mother love" that binds together a fictive harmonious community, while Montessori develops a theory of peace education for children with an ethic of caring at its center. Martin's legitimate claim is that our visions of a peaceful world should be grounded in the principle of gender balance. As she puts it, "Men, women, children: it is difficult to imagine any proposal for peace that fixes on one of these elements to the exclusion of the others being adequate to the task."[23] On Martin's reading, the sole contribution of James' essay is negative; that is to say, in its omission of gender balance as a moral principle in peace advocacy and education, "it brings to our attention a fundamental barrier to the achievement of that kind of peace which is not merely a state of expected war."[24]

To further expose James' masculine prejudices, Martin takes exception to James' suggestion that one possible moral equivalent of war could be found in the recruitment of "the whole youthful population" to serve as "an army of youth enlisted against Nature." It is widely accepted that these passages from James served as the moral and intellectual touchstone that inspired the New Deal's

Civilian Conservation Corps (CCC). This fact fails to impress Martin; discussion of the CCC as a viable moral equivalent of war is absent from her text:

> James is able to call this practice an *equivalent* of war because the function he attributes to war is that of preserving the martial virtues and the benefits accruing to society from them. Assuring us that soldiers in an 'army enlisted against Nature would get "the childishness knocked out of them" and would return to society having "paid their blood-tax," he goes on to describe a war against nature as a force able to discipline a whole community as only war itself has been able to do heretofore.[25]

Martin frames James' martial "virtues" as actual vices, vices whose substance and form cannot be educated or otherwise "turned around." James' metaphoric repertoire should give educators serious pause today. In his confidence that these qualities or human energies could be fundamentally transformed, James appears to reflect a postmodern view in which putative universal categories—definitions of "masculine" and "feminine," for example—are understood to contain no prefixed intrinsic character. This interpretive conflict forces upon us two questions: (1) In what ways could Martin be correct when she says it would be futile and even dangerous to share in James' confidence in the power of education to transform these so-called masculine traits? (2) Or, is James correct when he proposes that the fluid, evolutionary dimensions of human character and culture means that these traits can be positively transformed?

Jacques Barzun, for one, has defended James against those who have been critical of his sexist/militarist lexicon. Barzun regards the CCC as a sterling example of what James intended. He notes that in the Depression-era 1930s, "armies of youth" were enlisted to build dikes for rivers and irrigation and fire lines to protect the nation's woodlands. They were also "serving the nation" by planting hundreds of thousands of trees. Barzun then asks, with some justification: "Are these acts of hostility toward 'nature' or of tenderness towards fruits and trees?"[26] Implicit within Barzun's defense of James is the notion that the CCC was properly understood more as a campaign *for* nature than a war *against* it.[27]

Martin evinces little confidence in what James would recommend today in terms of developing suitable moral equivalents of war: "Were James alive today he might well foreswear his war against nature and offer in its stead organized sports or perhaps space exploration. The peace party among us, however, must forswear his entire project of finding a *moral* equivalent of war for the simple reason that there can be no such thing."[28] In urging today's peace-party to forswear the project of "finding" a moral equivalent of war, and in her rejection of the educability of the martial virtues, Martin attempts to turn William James' essay on its head.

The absence of a principle of gender balance in James' formulations is a theoretical conundrum of the first order. But in Martin's laudable desire to bring James' gendered biases into sharp relief, she takes her critique one step further and denies in principle the possibility that *any* "moral equivalents of war" could ever be usefully theorized and brought into being (as an individual act or as a practice of innovative democratic institution-making).

However, this conundrum is somewhat lessened, if we recall that James never made the claim that his model of the concept was the only one imaginable. And if we were to construe the theoretical boundaries of James' concept more broadly, and see its purpose serving mainly to spark a process of revitalizing America's discourse on heroism, then our conundrum is further relieved, particularly its gendered dimensions.

In grappling with the notorious problems posed by James' essay, Jean Bethke Elshtain asks if his "dream is a dream worth dreaming."[29] Unlike Martin, however, Elshtain responds in the affirmative. She does so by focusing on James' more generalized call for Americans to undertake projects of peaceful heroic action as a counterpoise to the culture of permanent war: "The dream I am dreaming . . . is not one of solemn deed doers but of zestful act takers, experimenting with new possibilities playfully but from a deep seriousness of purpose."[30]

Elshtain's dream, then, comes quite close to describing the overarching purpose of James essay, broadly conceived. According to James: "The only thing needed henceforward is to inflame the civic temper as past history has inflamed the military temper."[31] Of course, this formula begs many questions, chief among them being: How best to "inflame" democratic civic tempers within the public school curriculum? What would it mean to construct a moral equivalent of war as an educational principle that would not be symbolically fastened to the martial virtues?

In the remaining pages, I develop a foundation for curricular reform intended to kindle the democratic moral imagination of the nation's youth. As such, this initiative could be classified as a contemporary moral equivalent of war. It is a broadly constructed model of the concept, one that takes its inspiration from James' essay but is not beholden to it in all of its particulars. Nor is it a model that seeks to resolve the interpretive quagmire over the proper status of the martial virtues within antiwar pedagogies. It is, rather, a model rooted in the recognition that musical education has the capacity to generate powerful human emotions, "moral" and "civic" and "educable" emotions that, if developed pedagogically in the right way, could easily rival the "transcendent" power of the "military feelings." While I argue for a recovery of a robust musical education in the following section, in a broader sense, this argument should also be seen to include a curricular recovery of the humanities in general, as they are inextricably entwined.

Constructing musical education as a moral equivalent of war: The need for a recovery of Horace Mann's lost Eighth Report (1844)

Although few Americans realize it, the nation's chief architect of public education, Horace Mann (1796–1859) strongly believed in the moral potential of music to awaken and harmonize the conflicting passions of the soul. Depending on the type of music listened to or sung by the young, Mann wrote that some of the passions elicited would be ecstatic, some joyful, while others could be suffused with grief, tragedy, and melancholy. In the lost or, more accurately, repressed Eighth Report, Mann describes the intellectual and physical benefits that music brings to youthful hearts, minds, and bodies. He elaborates what it is exactly that makes music such an emotionally powerful vehicle of human flourishing:

> The social and moral influences of music far transcend, in value, all its physical or intellectual utilities. It holds a natural relationship or affinity with peace, hope, affection, generosity,

charity, devotion. There is also a natural repugnance between music and fear, envy, malevolence, misanthropy.[32]

In this passage, Mann introduces a set of moral virtues whose pedagogical development today through music could profoundly assist us in the task of educating democratic temperaments. Unfortunately, generations of American teachers haven't been given sufficient opportunity to read Mann's eloquent testimony on behalf of musical education. The reason for this curricular omission is that Lawrence Cremin, editor and custodian of Mann's canonical writings, apparently considered Mann's Eighth Report not significant enough to include in his edited volume, *The Republic and the Schools: Horace Mann on the Education of Free Men*. In a dismissive summary of the Eighth Report, Cremin remarks: "One is somewhat overwhelmed by these grandiose arguments for a little singing in the schools."[33] Or: "One wonders again at the quaintness of remarks about how music curbs the passions."[34] While Mann successfully broached the subject of the vital connection between musical education and democratic culture and identity, Cremin clearly undervalues this connection.

Martha Nussbaum however does appreciate the reproductive links that connect musical education to democratic culture. In Nussbaum's recent book, *Not for Profit: Why Democracy Needs the Humanities*, she offers compelling arguments for integrating vocal music into the nucleus of the public school curriculum. She credits her own thinking on the subject to our nineteenth century school reformer: "Horace Mann argued that vocal music, in particular, tends to unite people of diverse backgrounds, and to reduce conflict."[35] Nussbaum points out that the most highly developed public music programs in the nation, such as the Children's Chicago Choir, function as virtual laboratories for creating democratic dispositions in those youth fortunate enough to have access to these aesthetic opportunities. Her account of what might be called the "democratic-spiritual benefits" of musical education deserves extended quotation:

> The choir gives children the opportunity for an intense experience side by side children from different racial and socioeconomic backgrounds . . . since the choirs sing music from many different cultures, they learn about other cultures, and they learn that

these cultures are available to them; they transcend barriers that expectation and local culture have thrown in their way, showing that they can be world citizens. By learning to sing the music of another time or place, they also find ways of showing that they respect someone else, that they are willing to spend time learning about them and taking them seriously . . . In all these ways, they learn about their role in the local community and the world that can lead to many forms of curiosity, as choir alumni go on to study political science, history, language, visual art.[36]

Music, then, emerges as an activity whose ideal expressions contain significant moral, social, and political meanings. It is in this holistic sense that a reinvigorated musical education in the schools could function as a *kind* of moral equivalent of war. Insofar as vocal music has the potential to awaken one's aesthetic and moral sensibilities—that is, to awaken one's feeling function—it would seem to represent a vital curricular precondition for the promotion of human flourishing within the schools. The humanities in general represent the best curricular avenues available for awakening students to their feeling function and to their underdeveloped aesthetic and moral sensibilities. Although a bold recovery of the humanities and musical education could not by itself magically halt the further institutionalization of America's permanent war society, such a reform would at least make the schools less complicit than they are today in reproducing compliant citizen-warriors.

During the 1840s, Mann argued that music was undervalued within the Common Schools owing to the repressive legacy of the Pilgrim Fathers:

We are an un-musical,--not to say, an anti-musical people. No hereditary taste for the art has descended to us. Our Pilgrim Fathers were too stern a race to afford them either leisure or inclination to cultivate music as a refinement or embellishment of life, the mass of the population have been strangers, if not worse than strangers, to the art.[37]

How can we expect America's youth to enact a more democratic version of themselves when the educational structures they inhabit continue to make them "worse than strangers" not only to music but also to the arts and humanities in general? Perhaps this systematic curricular omission should be regarded as an act of public neglect, one whose consequences impose forms of civic impairment on the nation's youth. That President Barack Obama would embrace the legitimacy of an educational discourse which, by definition within NCLB, demotes the value of the humanities, suggests that his administration's educational policy is in dire need of a pragmatist-inspired moral renovation. Given that Obama's own educational career has been shaped by incredibly rich encounters with the humanities, it is dismally ironic that his administration's educational policies and priorities pay so little heed to the role of the arts and humanities in the educational process. According to James T. Kloppenburg's informative account of President Obama's educational experiences, throughout his past, the nation's forty-fourth president has consistently "found himself practicing forms of *pragmatist improvisation* as he tried to bring together multiple traditions and strategies of social action."[38] Based on this democratically-indebted pattern of conduct, there is perhaps a gleam of hope that Obama may yet act to transcend the spiritually-impoverished conception of education that his present administration embodies.

In the meantime, as an antidote to existing historical trends and educational dogmas, we need to recover the power and beauty of Mann's Eighth Report and use it as a conceptual road map for depuritanizing—and thus for re-aestheticizing—the public school curriculum. Even though the Eighth Report concerns musical education, on my reading, it is easily interpreted as a defense of the humanities across the board. In particular, because of music's ability to touch the deepest wellsprings of human being, and because of its potential to foster rival excitements and create new outlets for heroic energy, a revitalized musical education would appear to qualify as a useful Jamesian moral equivalent of war.

Notes

1 William James, "The Moral Equivalent of War." *William James: The Essential Writings*, edited by Bruce W. Wilshire. (Albany: SUNY Press, 1984), 349. (All subsequent references to this article will be designated as MEW.)

2 William James, "The Value of Saintliness." *The Varieties of Religious Experience*. (New York: The Modern Library, 2002), 401. As many have pointed out, James' "Moral Equivalent of War" appeared in pamphlets and in speeches before 1910, such as at Stanford University in 1906, but when the article appeared in *McClure's Magazine* (May–October 1910, Vol. 35, 463–8) it reached 450,000 subscribers nationwide.

3 James, MEW, 358.

4 It is interesting to note that while James wants to fulfill these character traits by radically modifying their violent aims, Theodor Adorno identifies several of these same qualities as the basis for fascist culture. See his, "Education After Auschwitz." *Critical Models: Interventions and Catchwords*. (New York: Columbia University Press, 1998), 191–204.

5 For an excellent treatment of James' critique of the "Peace Party" as well as his anti-imperialist convictions, see Robert L. Beisner, "William James: Paradise Lost." In *Twelve against Empire: The Anti-Imperialists, 1898–1900*. (New York: McGraw-Hill, 1968), 35–52. For an analysis of James' complicated relationship to the Civil War and how it led to his later efforts to construct moral equivalents of war, see George M. Frederickson, *The Inner Civil War: Northern Intellectuals and the Crisis of the Union*. (New York: Harper & Row, 1965), 217–8.

6 James, MEW, 349.

7 William James, "Remarks at the Peace Banquet." *The Works of William James: Essays in Religion and Morality*. (Cambridge: Harvard University Press, 1982), 120–1.

8 James, Varieties of Religious Experience, 401.

9 James, MEW, 355.

10 James, "Remarks at the Peace Banquet," 123.

11 Theodore Roosevelt, "The Strenuous Life." In *The Strenuous Life: Essays and Addresses*. (New York: The Century Co., 1902) Speech given to the Hamilton Club, Chicago, Illinois, April 10, 1899 (all subsequent references to this book will be cited as DSL).

12 DSL, 1.

13 DSL, 18–19.

14 William James, "Governor Roosevelt's Oration". *The Works of William James: Essays, Comments, and Reviews*. (Cambridge: Harvard University Press, 1987), 163.

15 Ibid., 163.

16 DSL, "Expansion and Peace," 31.

17 Kristin L. Hoganson, *Fighting for American Manhood: How Gender Politics Provoked the Spanish-American and Philippine-American Wars.*(New Haven: Yale University Press, 1998), 138–9.

18 William James, "The Philippine Tangle" (1899). *The Works of William James: Essays, Comments, and Reviews.* (Cambridge: Harvard University Press, 1987), 155.

19 William James, "The Philippine Question" (1899). *The Works of William James: Essays, Comments, and Reviews.* (Cambridge: Harvard University Press, 1987), 160.

20 Ibid., 160.

21 For elaboration on this defining Jamesian principle, see his "On a Certain Blindness in Human Beings." *William James: The Essential Writings,* edited by Bruce W. Wilshire. (Albany: SUNY Press, 1984), 326–42.

22 Jane Roland Martin, "Martial Virtues or Capital Vices? William James' Moral Equivalent of War Revisited." *Journal of Thought,* 22, Fall 1987, 42.

23 Ibid., 32.

24 Ibid., 33.

25 Ibid., 34.

26 Jacques Barzun, *A Stroll with William James.* (New York: Harper & Row, 1983), 173n. Not surprisingly, in Martin's footnote 6, she takes issue with Barzun's defense of James militaristic metaphors.

27 The ethnographic accounts and testimonies of thousands of CCC enrollees, provide ample evidence that the CCC was profoundly valued and seen as educationally transformative by virtually every albeit male participant, from 1933 to 1945. Upon examination, it is not difficult to regard the CCC as one of the most enlightened pieces of public policy in American political history. The last CCC camp established was named in honor of its moral and intellectual architect: Camp William James. See Gerald E. Myers, *William James: His Life and Thought.* (New Haven: Yale University Press, 1986), 601, fn 150.

28 Martin, 42.

29 Jean Bethke Elshtain, *Women and War.* (New York: Basic Books, 1987), 231.

30 Ibid., 258.

31 James, MEW, 360.

32 Horace Mann, "Eighth Report" (1844). *Life and Works of Horace Mann*, Vol. III (Boston: Lee and Shepard Publishers, 1891), 456–7.

33 Lawrence Cremin, Ed. *The Republic and the School: Horace Mann on the Education of Free Men*. (New York: Teachers College Press, 1957), 11.

34 Ibid., 56.

35 Martha Nussbaum, *Not for Profit: Why Democracy Needs the Humanities*. (Princeton University Press, 2010), 116.

36 Ibid., 113.

37 Mann, Eighth Report (1844), 460.

38 James T. Kloppenburg, *Reading Obama: Dreams, Hope, and the American Political Tradition*. (Princeton, NJ: Princeton University Press, 2011), 79.

CHAPTER SIX

The business of America is business

Framing the contradictions at the heart of the "roaring twenties"

What, after all, put the "roar" in the roaring twenties? Arising from a cacophony of cultural voices, the metaphoric roar of the 1920s could be understood as the sound heard from coast to coast as Americans encountered a set of transformations at what seemed like warp speed. It was the 18th Amendment to the US Constitution prohibiting the sale of alcoholic beverages which, in giving organized crime a new lease on life, also elevated millions of Americans to the status of criminals as they congregated to drink in "speak-easies." It was the sound of clashing mentalities reverberating between the advocates of religion and those of science, symbolized by the 1926 Scopes "monkey trial" in Dayton, Tennessee. It was phonograph record players, for the first time being sold nationwide carrying with them the melodious and beautifully subversive sounds of jazz music. It was the forlorn yet hopeful calls of America's artists, from the Harlem Renaissance to the Lost Generation, admonishing their compatriots to recover their democratic souls amid the resurgent racism of the Ku Klux Klan and the hurly-burly of profit-seeking. It was the dull, clinical buzzing sound of Sacco and Vanzetti being electrocuted in 1927 for crimes many Americans were convinced they never committed. The roar emanated from these and many other sources. The core conflict investigated in this chapter, however, can be framed as a conflict between the values and principles of business and those of democracy. I employ President Calvin Coolidge's aphorism, *the business of America is business* as a vehicle to try and make education out of this defining national contradiction.

On January 17, 1925, as the 30th President of the United States, Calvin Coolidge spoke to the American Society of Newspaper Editors in Washington, D.C. The title of Coolidge's speech, "The Press under a Free Government," gave the president an opportunity to praise the 1st Amendment principle of the freedom of the press in front of a receptive audience of true believers. This eminently forgettable speech would probably not be remembered today but for one rhetorical turn of phrase that Coolidge uttered about the character of American national identity.

Most of the sources that cite the phrase, whether school textbooks or scholarly articles, adopt the abbreviated version of Coolidge's now vaguely familiar aphorism. The full passage is worth noting:

> After all, the chief business of the American people is business. They are profoundly concerned with production, buying, selling, investing and prospering in the world. I am strongly of the opinion that the great majority of people will always find these the moving impulses of our life.[1]

Of course, few could take issue with Coolidge's unremarkable observation that the quest for material well-being has been and will continue to be a "moving impulse" in American life. As a piece of public rhetoric, however, this statement may *become* remarkable and educative when it is transformed into a site of critical pedagogical analysis. It may, in other words, achieve a new meaning when the phrase is used to pose questions about the contradictory-laden relationship between business and the national identity. In a broad Freirean sense, Coolidge identifies a "generative theme" within American culture, one that reflects a cultural contradiction worth framing for the educational possibilities it opens up. For when we begin to examine the contentious relationship between these symbolic fields of value, fruitful questions are raised about national identity as an arena of conflict. If, for example, we were to assume that the business of America is business, does this mean that business executives should be the dominant voice in defining the nation's purposes and priorities? Coolidge was committed to this very proposition.

As a life-long career politician, Coolidge never had any personal experience with business of any sort. Still, he was a fervent evangelist for the interests of big business, a point over which historians from opposite ends of the ideological spectrum agree.[2] When we consider the extreme *laissez faire* public policies Coolidge pursued in office, it is difficult not to read his public rhetoric as an effort to conflate what might be called the business or corporate interest with the national interest. Implicit within the assumption that a seamless relation exists between the identity of the nation and that of business are two corollary principles. First is the belief that business interests and values should be the chief factor in the negotiation of American identity. Indeed, the *laissez faire* economic model championed by the Republican administrations of Harding and Coolidge and Hoover (extending from 1920 to 1932) was promised to enable business to assume its proper role as the nation's leading moral authority. This was to be accomplished not only by a governmental policy of "leaving business alone" in a negative sense but also by reducing taxes on corporations and their profits in a positive sense.

The second corollary principle is that the appropriate image for American selfhood within a *laissez faire* economic and political order is that of "rugged individualism," an image often described as "possessive" or "acquisitive" individualism. According to this model, the individual is above all an atom of self-interest and is theorized to exist prior to and apart from "society"; indeed, this model was imagined to embody an hostility to the State and hostility to any State action that would purport to redress collective grievances. It is thus an individualism that reflects the conservative reluctance to engage in State-sponsored collective social action of any kind under any circumstances.

During the halcyon 1920s, conservatism's ideological architects, such as Coolidge's Secretary of the Treasury, Andrew W. Mellon (reputed to be the richest man in America), argued that only when market forces were unhampered by State "interference" could the conditions for creating and sustaining individual freedom and liberty be effectively established. In this way, the core moral principles of American conservatism find eloquent expression in the person and the politics of Calvin Coolidge. Through his presidency, conservatism's political and moral principles had triumphed, and its *laissez faire* economic and social ideologies seemed vindicated by what came to be known as the Coolidge Prosperity. For several decades, then, Coolidge's elective years (1924–28) were uniformly regarded as the high tide of twentieth century American conservatism, a status it retained until Ronald Reagan emerged in 1980 as the titular crown prince of a conservative restoration. Indeed, one of Reagan's first official acts as President was to remove the portraits of Jefferson and Truman from the oval office and replace them with one of Coolidge.[3]

However, just as "Silent Cal" Coolidge was enjoying wide popular support throughout the country on the basis of the prosperity he came to symbolize, John Dewey was publishing a series of essays outlining why the real business of America should not be seen so much as business but as democracy. Dewey warned Americans that the cultural dominance of the "business mind" was usurping the very conditions in which democratic values and habits of mind could be developed. Residing at the core of Dewey's alternative civic pedagogy was the assumption that there was a pronounced contradiction between the interests of the nation and the interests of business.

Today, in the wake of the 2008 elite-inspired Wall Street economic implosion, the same basic conflict appears to be intensifying. We need to pay attention to this cultural thematic, for the manner in which we decide to negotiate its conflicting elements may well determine whether or not American democracy *has* a future.

Dewey introduced the concept of "individuality" to stand as the ideal model of selfhood for a democratic society. In every important respect, this civic formation represents an historical extension of the democratic and republican models of selfhood highlighted in previous chapters. Dewey theorized that, as a precondition for individuality to come into being, an interrelated civic and educational ingredient would be required within the nucleus of that identity. Its self-conscious "making" as a cultural formation would depend on social relationships performing a vital educative growth function. And it was precisely this function which distinguished *individuality* from the restricted or "fenced in" models of *individualism* that Dewey criticized. During the 1920s, therefore, the model of individualism touted by conservative antistatist ideologues existed in severe yet potentially fertile tension with the model of individuality touted by one of the nation's premier democratic thinkers.

In what follows, these two defining generative themes—the status of business in relation to the national identity and the tension between individualism and individuality—are theoretically fleshed out in three sections. The first section describes the parameters of the business mind exemplified by the Coolidge presidency in the 1920s. Of particular importance will be to emphasize the fact that, for the first time in US history, advertising emerged as a powerful new educational force in shaping the negotiation of American identity. Through their well-planned campaigns to "engineer consent" corporate advertisers ordained the business mind as *the* American mind.[4] According to Dewey, the success of this project, at least during the Coolidge Prosperity, permitted corporate power to play not only an expanded role within the negotiation of the national identity but also more importantly one that worked against the construction of democratic individualities. The second section sketches the parameters of the democratic mind as John Dewey envisioned it as a counterpoise to the dominant business mind. The aim is to identify the conceptual linkages between democracy as a mode of being and that of "individuality" as an indispensable component of that being.

Finally, in presuming the validity of Dewey's evaluation of the contradictions between the business mind and the democratic-mind, and extrapolating from those insights in view of today's circumstances, I call on democratic minded teachers across the nation to begin transforming the doctrine of "corporate personhood" into a site of critical analysis within their classrooms. While it is true that corporate personhood as a "legal fiction" (itself a common legal term) was not invented during the Coolidge years, arguably the grand ideological synthesis effected between business and advertising and religion during Coolidge's presidency helped establish the moral legitimacy and "naturalness" of this profoundly antidemocratic doctrine. One useful way to contextualize corporate personhood, then, would be to view it as the *legal and moral extension of the principle that the business of America is business*. As the ideological linchpin of the business mind—as the *sine qua non* of its cultural and political dominance—it would be naïve for us to think that corporate power in America can ever be substantively decentered so long as the doctrine permits corporations to elevate themselves above the norms of democratic accountability. The purpose here is not to offer a comprehensive exposition of corporate personhood but rather to scrutinize some of the doctrine's most glaring contradictions and to suggest future lines of critical pedagogical intervention.[5]

Coolidge, advertising, and religion: Constructing the business mind in the 1920s

What did Coolidge and other leading Republicans mean when they promised the nation a "return to normalcy"? They meant above all that the national government would no longer be as concerned as they had been with disturbing questions about war, war profiteering, bitter labor disputes, racial justice, or with any other "progressive" reform effort which characterized the decade before World War I. Once the Great War ended, leading progressives such as John Dewey, Jane Addams, W. E. B. Du Bois, and others saw that radical change was much needed in 1920s America: child labor was still the law of the land, unions were still illegal, the prohibition era had led to astounding levels of political corruption and criminality, the anti-trust laws put into place during the Roosevelt and Wilson administrations' were deliberately ignored, and the Ku Klux Klan was enjoying a resurgence of membership and respectability. The subtext of the slogan "return to normalcy," then, could be construed to mean "let's sweep issues of democracy and social justice under the carpet and get on with the business of business."

For the purposes of this essay, Coolidge's administration is historically noteworthy because it symbolizes the historical moment in which big business was effectively repackaged and *spiritualized* by a reinvigorated advertising industry. Taking a cue from advertising intellectuals like Edward Bernays and Bruce Barton, businesses organized themselves into civil associations and lobby groups at an unprecedented rate in order to enhance their national stature as the nation's new moral authorities.[6] Frederick Lewis Allen, one of the most astute observers of the 1920s, captured the essential thrust of the Coolidge administration: "Calvin Coolidge honestly believed that by asserting himself as little as possible and by lifting the tax burden on the rich he was benefitting the whole country—as perhaps he was . . .. the great god business was supreme in the land, and Calvin Coolidge was fortunate enough to become almost a demi-god by doing discreet obeisance before the alter."[7]

In the same speech that Coolidge asserted that the business of America was business, he added that material prosperity would turn to a "barren scepter in our grasp if things of the spirit did not come first." Coolidge's oft-noted "moral idealism" is on full display as he continues: "Of course, the accumulation of wealth cannot be justified as the chief end of existence . . . so long as wealth is made the means and not the end, we need not greatly fear it. *And there never was a time when wealth was so generally regarded as a means, or so little regarded as an end, as today*"[8] (my emphasis). Coolidge's expression of moral idealism merits further consideration simply because it's belied by a mountain of counterevidence.

From both historical and literary perspectives, Coolidge's assertion contradicts most of what has been written about the period, from William Allen White's *A Puritan in Babylon* and Frederick Lewis Allen's *Only Yesterday* to F. Scott Fitzgerald's *The Great Gatsby* and Sinclair Lewis's *Babbitt*, to mention a few well-known sources. These historical and literary accounts of the 1920s suggest that Americans were being massively persuaded (by design) to make consumption and wealth an end in itself. As suggested by the trailblazing work of Stuart Ewen, by the 1920s the advertising industry had moved far beyond its previous role of merely describing products factually. Now, aided by radios and "moving pictures" and print media that could reach audiences nationwide, it was the advertisers' intention to appeal to individuals' fantasies and desires at unconscious levels. This sophisticated, Freudian-inspired development gave the industry an unrivalled influence in representing consumerism as the "end of existence" and in codifying the business mind as the de facto moral compass of American life.

Perhaps Coolidge permitted himself to nurse this idealistic notion because his own personal attitude toward the seductions of materialism was one of stoic indifference. As the title of White's definitive biography indicates, Coolidge was no doubt a frugal Yankee, a "Puritan in Babylon." Yet Coolidge refers to the attitude of the American people in the passage, not to his own personal attitude. Coolidge's insistence on this point represents a level of denial that, upon further examination, could illuminate the nature of his enormous popularity.

Arguably, moral pronouncements like this from the President softened any guilt that Americans may have felt for treating wealth very much as the end of existence. Within Coolidge's moral pedagogy, it is telling that the nation was *never* served up any jeremiads in the traditional sense of the word. One can search Coolidge's writings far and wide and never find a trace of him ever admonishing wayward citizens to right a wrong they were daily complicit in. Instead, they were served up what Walter Lippmann slyly called "Puritanism de luxe."[9] Lippmann meant that Coolidge's public personae as an austere and thrifty Yankee helped modernizing Americans reconcile what had been two warring factions within the national psyche: The Puritan ascetic model of self based on a sublimation of the appetitive desires versus a secular model of self that gave freer rein to material pursuits. In making the unvarnished pursuit of wealth reconcilable with a Christian spirituality traditionally at odds with America-as-Babylon, Coolidge gave Americans permission to indulge their consumer appetites with religious fervor even as they identified with Coolidge's comforting platitudes that they really only cared about wealth as a means, and not as an end, of existence.

To understand how the values of business and the values of religion were effectively fused together by advertising intellectuals, perhaps the most revealing artifact that emerged from the Coolidge Prosperity would be Bruce Barton's *The Man Nobody Knows*, a book that topped the nonfiction bestseller list for two years (1925–26).[10] Barton, a leader in the industry and political ally of Coolidge, offered Americans a stunning rereading of the life of Jesus as a "business entrepreneur." In the author's creative if tortured hermeneutic, the carpenter from Galilee is recast as the "founder of modern business," as someone who "picked up twelve men from the bottom of the ranks of business and forged them into an organization that conquered the world." Millions of readers must have noticed that the institutional structure that Jesus had apparently invented looked identical to the structure of the modern corporation. In strategically placing a religious halo over the corporation and business activity generally, *The Man Nobody Knows* amplified the moral *zeitgeist* of the Coolidge Prosperity.

Coolidge was more than an enthusiastic supporter of the advertising industry, for he also claimed that "advertising ministers to the spiritual side of trade."[11] Coolidge understood that the "ministry" of advertisers was none other than to reeducate human desire to want to buy things. Would this notion qualify as another example of Coolidge's moral idealism? In a 1926 address to an annual convention of advertisers, Coolidge underscored the positive educational role advertising plays in forming the desires and habits of the American people.

> When we stop to consider the part which advertising plays in the modern life of production we see that basically it is that of education. It makes new thoughts, new desires, and new actions. Advertising creates and changes the foundation of all popular action, public sentiment or public opinion. It is the most potent influence in adopting and changing the habits and modes of life, affecting what we eat, what we wear and the work and play of the whole nation.[12]

We could speculate that the new thoughts, new desires, and new actions orchestrated by the new techniques and instruments of mass persuasion now at the disposal of the advertisers, furnished the ontological justification for the reproduction of a capitalist model of consumer individualism. As a newly forming individualism, it was an identity "structured" to be in a perpetual state of need for material things and for tokens of symbolic prestige located outside the self. When we consider the enormous success advertisers achieved in elevating consumption to the status of a redemptive religious activity, they should be given credit for their pedagogical brilliance in catapulting a corporatized image of happiness and what it means to be human far past alternative narratives of identity.

Once the Stock Market Crash of 1929 brought the curtain down on the roaring twenties, and the Great Depression ensued, the foundational assumptions underpinning the legitimacy of *laissez faire* economic policies and its supporting ideology of consumer individualism were suddenly "gone with the wind." The radical break between the Coolidge Prosperity and the New Deal clearly represents a discontinuity in the reproduction of national identity. What is the meaning of this discontinuity, and why is it important? Among other things, the apparent absence of a prefixed, objectively existent national identity affirms the idea that national identity above all is a *moving* and *contested* symbolic formation that is artificially or pedagogically constructed.

The individual/State relation was negotiated in a modified form during the New Deal; child labor was abolished, unions were legalized and importantly, the business class could no longer credibly represent themselves as religious icons. The democratic principle of power-sharing and negotiating in good faith with labor was imposed on the business class because of the election of popular majorities from 1932 to 1944, majorities which permitted President Franklin D. Roosevelt (at times) to act contrary to the interests of what he called the "economic royalists." Once again, as in previous chapters, we see how these discontinuities suggest that national identity formation is more improvisational and susceptible to transformation than we tend to think.

John Dewey's construction of the democratic mind in the 1920s

In his book *Individualism Old and New*, Dewey sought to theorize an image of individuality that would be consistent with democratic values and principles but would also be flexible enough to keep pace with the bewildering transformations occurring in the opening decades of the twentieth century. Dewey wrote that while "rugged individualism is praised as the glory of American life," a tectonic shift in identity formation was occurring and that the nation's traditional image of individualism had "little relation to the moving facts of that life."[13] Dewey searched for a new language and symbolic inventory to better capture what he meant by "individuality." The new conception would have to transcend the traditional eighteenth and nineteenth century version of individualism as well as its twentieth century corporate version. Dewey observed that "the United States has steadily moved from an earlier pioneer individualism to a condition of dominant corporateness."[14] He regarded the new and uncritical veneration of the business mind as one of the single biggest obstacles preventing the development of democratic individualities:

> Attention has recently been called to a new phenomenon in human culture: the business mind, having its own conversation and language, its own interests, its own intimate groupings in

which men of this mind, in their collective capacity, determine the tone of society at large as well as the government of industrial society, and have more political influence than the government itself . . . the fact significant for present discussion, is that we now have, although without formal or legal status, a mental and moral corporateness for which history offers no parallel.[15]

When Dewey conceptualizes "a mental and moral corporateness" for which "history offers no parallel," in effect he is telling us that a new paradigm for defining human identity had emerged, a construct which reproduced its own species of individualism. Dewey is suggesting that we need to take seriously the consequences for democratic citizens of being subjected to the corporate mentality as the *dominant* mentality. As a rejoinder to the rise of corporate power, Dewey emphasized the moral and educational principle that a democratic negotiation of American identity, for it to be a "democratic negotiation," must be grounded in a respect for the interplay and balance of forces within the arena of culturally contested values. In drawing attention to the corrosive effects of commercial power on the formation of democratic values, Dewey aligns himself with thinkers treated in earlier chapters, such as Jefferson and Tocqueville. It will be recalled these thinkers feared that the seductive enticements of commercial values would someday overwhelm the civic values upon which democratic republics depend for their existence.

Again and again, Dewey returned to the contradiction between capitalist individualism on the one hand and democratic individuality on the other. He tartly pointed out that "an economic individualism of motives and aims underlies our present corporate mechanism, and undoes the individual. Hence it operates to limit individuality, to put burdens on it, to confuse and submerge it."[16] To lift a concept from Tocqueville, Dewey saw a kind of consumer-oriented "tyranny of the majority" operating within the Coolidge Prosperity. He pointed out that "we live exposed to the greatest flood of mass suggestion that any people has ever experienced."[17] Dewey spies an underlying conformity lurking behind the celebration of "individualism":

Nowhere is the decline of the old-fashioned individual and individualism more marked in leisure life, in amusements and sports. Our colleges only follow the movement of the day when they make athletics an organized business, aroused and conducted under paid directors in the spirit of pure collectivism. The formation of theatre chains is at once the cause and the effect of the destruction of the older independent life of leisure carried on in separate homes . . . The press is the organ of amusement for a hurried leisure time, and it reflects and carries further the formation of mental collectivism by massed methods. Crime, too, is assuming a new form; it is organized and corporate.[18]

As someone born in Vermont in 1859, Dewey came of age in a time and place that allowed him to experience American culture before the corporate mentality had fully consolidated its grip on the public imagination. The model of individuality Dewey conceptualized, however, was by no means fixated in a nostalgic look back to recover the way things were before "corporatization" had reduced American individualism to an economic relation. Dewey elaborates on the rationale of his criticism:

I have said that the instances cited of the reaction of the growing corporateness of society upon social mind and habit were not given in order to be either deplored or approved. They are set forth only to call out the picture of the decline of an individualistic philosophy of life, and the formation of a collectivist scheme of interdependence, which finds its way into every cranny of life . . . But because the purpose was to indicate the decay of the older conceptions, although they are still those that are most loudly and vocally professed, the illustrations given inevitably emphasize those features of growing standardization and mass uniformity which critics justly deplore.[19]

Dewey does not want readers to lose sight of the fact that "the things that are criticized are the outward signs of an inner move- ment toward integration on a scale never known before."[20] The "integration" was a consequence of forces unleashed by the industrial revolution; as Marx famously observed, the Industrial Age was a maelstrom that made "all that is solid melt into air." Today, this simultaneous process of integration and disintegration is known by another name—"globalization." As Dewey surveyed these new objective conditions, he concluded that his model of individuality must have built into it the capacity to change as conditions themselves changed. Individuality was envisioned above all as a revisable form of identity. It was rooted in the recognition that keeping open the possibility of constant psychological growth was an evolutionary necessity for the perpetuation of a democratic species of selfhood. Without the living presence of this vital educational dimension, democratic culture could not possibly hope to reproduce itself.

Dewey traces the tradition of American individualism to the pioneer or frontier model of American individualism based on plentiful land and natural resources. It was a model organically derived from incredibly favorable conditions and for this reason remained hegemonic for centuries. However, as historian of the frontier Frederick Jackson Turner demonstrated, by 1893 the physical frontier had vanished. As the Industrial Age and the corporate ascendancy reached their zenith in the 1920s, frontier individualism had morphed into consumer individualism. Dewey was making the case that, as a practical matter, the first and second models of American individualism were obsolete. What was needed then was a third way, a meaning narrative that would transcend the limitations of the previous two models of individualism. From a methodological standpoint, then, we might be justified in asserting that Dewey structures his inquiry into the problem of American identity on the basis of a Hegelian dialectic of thesis/antithesis/synthesis.

How does the third way of "democratic individuality" purport to transcend the limitations and contradictions of America's two previous models of individualism? Dewey first advises that "it is impossible to develop integrated individuality by any all-embracing system or program. No individual can make the determination for anyone else; nor can he make it for himself all at once and forever."[21] Dewey's insistence on the interpretive open-endedness of his model of individuality is surely one of its most distinguishing features. Dewey wants us to resist the desire to embrace a totalizing model of individuality because, in addition to other factors, he considered the "quest for certainty" itself part of the problem his model was intended to surpass.

It bears repeating that Dewey theorizes individuality as having an intrinsic social nature; he rejects the notion that the individual exists prior to the social realm or exists in permanent opposition to something called "society." Far from seeing the "individual" in an antagonistic relationship to "society," Dewey unsettles this binary opposition and theorizes the social realm as performing a vital educative function. He describes individuality as a "potentiality, a capacity for development." It represents a "distinctive way of feeling the impacts of the world and of showing a *preferential bias in response to those impacts,* it develops into shape and form only through interaction with actual conditions; it is no more complete in itself than is a painter's tube of paint without relation to a canvas"[22] (my italics). By emphasizing the perpetually unfinished, always-in-the-making dimension of individuality, Dewey affirms its affinity with democracy, which is also perpetually unfinished and always-in-the-making.

The "preferential bias" he notes refers to the proposition that not all values should be treated as morally equivalent. While democratic individualities may, at times, care about or be actuated by commercial or "pecuniary" values, they cannot care *only* about those values without jeopardizing the integrity of their democratic selfhood. Perhaps Dewey's harshest indictment of corporate individualism, as a habitual set of cultural practices and modes of perception, was that it tended to isolate itself from any other value but economic self-interest. To illustrate the limitations of corporate individualism, Dewey introduces a useful metaphor for the purpose of reconceptualizing the individual/society binary opposition:

> To gain an integrated individuality, each of us needs to cultivate his own garden. But there is no fence about this garden: it is no sharply marked-off enclosure. Our garden is the world, in the angle at which it touches our own manner of being. By accepting the corporate and industrial world in which we live, and by thus fulfilling the pre-condition for interaction with it, we, who are also parts of the moving present, create ourselves as we create an unknowable future.[23]

When Dewey talks about accepting the corporate and industrial world, he does not mean to imply that we should acquiesce to the dominance of the business mind. Rather he means that we should not pretend that the democratic project can progress without first dealing, in a critical fashion, with the practical reality of corporate power. Dewey seems to argue that we need to engage, confront, and oppose the business mind, not in an attempt to eliminate it so much as to grasp the scope of its corrosive power and decenter that power within the negotiation of national identity.

Dewey's individuality is perfectly aligned with his theory of democracy, which he alternatively describes as a "personal way of life" and "form of moral and spiritual association." The two concepts—the principle of individuality and the principle of democratic culture—may be theoretically separable, but for Dewey they were not really empirically separable. Again, "individualities" are likened to gardens *without* fences; American selfhood, in other words, is recast as a site of human *interdependency*.

Within Dewey's framework, authentic democratic individuals will reflect a cluster of associated character traits that are best cultivated when they are socially constituted. These traits— questioning, the capacity to dialogue, to listen, to improvise, to care about the common good and other principles of social justice, to mention a few—spring from individual human potentials, but there is no guarantee that individuals will interact with their social environments in such a way that these potentials will be stimulated or come to fruition. If individuals—in conceptualizing the self/other or self/society difference—do not see themselves as a "garden with no fence about them," it is unlikely they will have the opportunity or desire to encounter a diversity of stimuli that would result in the modification of their thinking, feeling, and being. Only when exercising these social and moral capacities can individuals as citizens develop the desire and willingness to revise their previous perceptions and dare to act autonomously.

The task before us—treating corporate personhood as the new *Plessy v. Ferguson*

Let us accept for the moment Dewey's assertion that the interests of the business mind, when dominant or hegemonic, are destructive to democratic forms of identity and culture. If indeed Dewey's presupposition is valid, it would behoove us to critically investigate the doctrine of corporate personhood for the simple reason that this doctrine perpetuates the very corporate dominance which has been shown to retard the formation of democratic individualities. As previously suggested, corporate personhood could be understood as the highest legal expression of the moral ideal that the business of America is business.

The premise of the doctrine is that corporations, defined as persons, have the same rights under the 14th Amendment's equal protection clause as individual citizens. In practice, this also means that corporations "as persons" enjoy the rights afforded by the 1st Amendment's freedom of speech clause. I want to suggest that the doctrine of corporate personhood is rent with educative contradictions and that these contradictions should invite far more critical pedagogical attention than they have received to date.

To illustrate one fertile contradiction, we need only recall that one of the purposes and moral visions of the American Revolution was to eliminate the possibility that corporations—such as England's notorious East India Tea Company—would have their monopoly status institutionalized by law. The celebrated Tea Party of 1773 was an act of anticorporate civil disobedience. At the time, this defining event became a powerful symbol of the struggle against corporate monopolies. In stark contrast to this history, today's so-called Tea Party movement could be described as the creature of a public relations campaign orchestrated by corporate titans for the benefit of corporate titans.[24]

Furthermore, recall that Jefferson deliberately elevated the principle of human rights over property rights within the Declaration of Independence. He did this in large part because it would give the document a universal applicability and bolster America's putative exceptional identity. But Jefferson also wanted to elevate human rights over property rights because it would diminish the possibility that corporations might one day establish themselves as legal monopolies, as sovereign powers that existed beyond the reach of popular majorities. It is well accepted among historians that the perceived "tyranny" of corporate monopolies was one of several underlying causes of the American Revolution. Thus, in reading corporate personhood from the standpoint of America's obscured democratic tradition, the doctrine presents itself as a kind of Tory-inspired form of "economic royalism." The continued existence of the doctrine thus violates a prime tenet of America's exceptional democratic identity.

It is, moreover, commonplace to say that Jefferson played an instrumental role in placing the Bill of Rights within the US Constitution as a condition of its ratification. However, a much less known fact about Jefferson is that he actively advocated for a constitutional amendment prohibiting the establishment of monopolies. For example, in a 1787 letter to James Madison, Jefferson described what he liked about the proposed Constitution, but then said: "I will now tell you what I do not like. First, the omission of a bill of rights, providing clearly, and without the aid of sophism, for freedom of religion, freedom of press, protection against standing armies, *restriction of monopolies*, the eternal and unremitting force of habeas corpus laws, and trials by jury in all matters triable by the laws of the land."[25]

In a 1788 letter, Jefferson asserts: "By declaration of rights, I mean one which shall stipulate [among others] . . . *freedom of commerce against monopolies.*"[26] And in another 1788 letter, Jefferson maintains that the State of Virginia should insist on five amendments to the new Constitution: "1. Religion shall be free; 2. Printing presses free; 3. Trials by jury preserved in all cases; 4. *No monopolies in commerce;* 5. No standing army"[27] (my emphasis). Of course, Jefferson failed to have two of his favored prohibitions included within the Bill of Rights. Given that corporate monopolies and what might be called the "military-industrial complex" arguably tyrannize over every dimension of American life today, we have to marvel at the political wisdom reflected in Jefferson's articulation of these two negative freedoms. One can only wonder what American democracy would look like today had the Bill of Rights included in its charter the prohibition of corporate monopolies *and* standing armies. From the perspective of critical pedagogy, the larger point is that the doctrine of corporate personhood stands in direct contradiction to the American democratic tradition. And for this reason, its very existence should spawn thousands of critical interventions by classroom teachers across the nation.

Yet another contradiction presents itself for our consideration when we realize the sinister manner in which the doctrine developed out of the 14th Amendment (1868). Historians and schoolbooks alike tell us that the 14th Amendment was one of several progressive consequences of the Civil War. It was supposedly an achievement that virtually all Americans could be proud of. According to the standard narrative, at the moral heart of the amendment was the purpose of granting citizenship rights to the newly freed. Further, *all persons* born on US soil were to enjoy "equal protection" and "due process" of the laws.

Chapter four discussed the fact that the newly freed were indeed granted formal citizenship under the terms of the 14th Amendment. However, one of the consequences of The Compromise of 1876 was that the substantive content of those rights were vanquished by what could reasonably be called the tyranny of the white majority. Insofar as the newly freed were concerned, the 14th Amendment had devolved into an empty farce. It is a tragic irony of US history that, at the precise moment the 14th Amendment was being stripped of its original intent to secure civil rights for citizens long denied those rights, corporate lawyers were busy at work crafting the notion that corporations were "persons" too, deserving the same rights that individual citizens were supposed to enjoy.

Thus, the story goes that in the 1886 Supreme Court case, *Santa Clara County v. Southern Pacific Railroad*, the doctrine of corporate personhood was apparently established.[28] The disingenuous appropriation of the 14th Amendment by corporate lawyers meant that the legal protections and civil status originally intended to make citizens out of former slaves were effectively withdrawn and given over to corporations as a set of protections to further institutionalize their monopoly power. By successfully corporatizing the meaning of the 14th Amendment, corporate lawyers hijacked a sublime piece of American law rooted in the extension of human rights and transformed it into an antidemocratic device that permitted corporations to elude basic norms of democratic accountability. In this way, the doctrine of corporate personhood symbolizes the ongoing triumph of property rights over human rights in contemporary America.

For teachers searching for innovative critical pedagogies through which they might contribute to the reconstruction of American democracy, I want to recommend that in formulating these projects, we need to remember the democratic vision and unsung heroism of Charles Hamilton Houston (1896–1950). We need to remember him not only as the civil rights attorney who designed the theoretical blueprint to dismantle the Plessy doctrine decades before the Brown decision reversed it, but we also need to remember Houston as a public pedagogue of the highest order. It is impressive that Houston, acting in his capacity as Dean of the Howard University Law School during the 1930s, redesigned its curriculum and turned the purposes of the law school toward the task of training students to go forward into the world to challenge racist, unjust institutions, such as the doctrine of "separate but equal" which formed the basis of the *Plessy v. Ferguson* (1896) decision.[29] In refusing to accept the bland and depoliticized law curriculum he inherited, Houston courageously succeeded in breaking down the artificially contrived boundaries that prevented Howard Law School from fulfilling its role as an instrument of democratic reconstruction.

Just as Houston envisioned his effort to dismantle the Plessy doctrine as a decades-long project, today cadres of teachers across the nation should similarly define their efforts to interrogate and expose the antidemocratic features of corporate personhood as a decades-long project. While lawyers can work to dismantle the legal edifice of the doctrine, democratic-minded teachers have a responsibility to introduce their students to the many ways in which corporate personhood usurps America's democratic possibility at the cultural level. In treating corporate personhood as the new Plessy, as the next great hurdle in the fragile unfolding of America's democratic story, teachers as cultural workers can surely do their part to intensify their students' awareness of this glaring yet obscured cultural contradiction.

Notes

1 Calvin Coolidge, "The Press Under a Free Government" in *Foundations of the Republic: Speeches and Addresses* (Freeport: Books for Libraries Press, 1926; reprint ed., 1968), pp. 183–90, pp. 187–8.

2 For a lively book that seeks to restore luster to Coolidge's legacy after decades of distorted interpretations by "liberal" historians, see Thomas B. Silver, *Coolidge and the Historians* (Durham, NC: Carolina Academic Press, 1982). Silver does not deny Coolidge's fealty to big business, he celebrates it. For an engaging critical look at Coolidge's relationship to big business, see William Leuchtenburg, *The Perils of Prosperity* (Chicago: University of Chicago Press, 1958).

3 See Collen J. Shogan, "Coolidge and Reagan: The Rhetorical Influence of Silent Cal on the Great Communicator." *Rhetoric & Public Affairs*, Vol. 9, No. 2, 2006, 215–34.

4 I am indebted to the work of Stuart Ewen for this strand of my argument. See, for example, *Captains of Consciousness: Advertising and the Social Roots of Consumer Culture* (New York: McGraw-Hill,

1976; and more recently), *PR! A Social History of Spin* (New York: Basic Books, 1996).

5 For a comprehensive account, see Thom Hartmann, *Unequal Protection: The Rise of Corporate Dominance and the Theft of Human Rights* (New York: Rodale/St. Martin's Press, 2002).

6 See "The Leadership of Business." In Thomas C. Cochran and William Miller, *The Age of Enterprise: A Social History of Industrial America* (New York: Haper Torchbooks, 1942/1966), pp. 323–53.

7 "Coolidge Prosperity." In Frederick Lewis Allen: *Only Yesterday: An Informal History of the 1920s* (New York: Harper & Row, 1931), p. 160.

8 Coolidge, *Foundations of the Republic*, p. 188.

9 Walter Lippmann, *Men of Destiny* (New York: Macmillan, 1927), p. 17.

10 Bruce Barton, *The Man Nobody Knows: A Discovery of the Real Jesus*. Chicago, IL: Ivan R. Dee. 2000. First published in 1925 by Bobbs-Merril.

11 Frank Presbrey, *The History and Development of Advertising* (New York: Doubleday, 1929), p. 625.

12 Ibid., p. 620.

13 John Dewey, "The United States, Incorporated," in *Individualism Old and New*, p.18.

14 "Ibid., p. 18.

15 Ibid., p. 21.

16 John Dewey, "The Lost Individual," in *Individual Old and New*, pp. 29–30.

17 John Dewey, "The United States, Incorporated," p. 21.

18 Ibid., 21.

19 Ibid., 24.

20 Ibid., 24.

21 John Dewey, "Individuality in Our Day," in *Individual Old and New*, p. 81.

22 Ibid., 81.

23 Ibid., 82–3.

24 Scholars and journalists alike provide ample evidence for making this assertion. See, for example, Jane Mayer, "Covert Operations: the billionaire brothers who are waging war against Obama." *New Yorker,* August 30, 2010; Frank Rich, "The Billionaires Bankrolling

the Tea Party," *New York Times*, August 28, 2010; Matt Taibbi, "The Truth about the Tea Party," *Rolling Stone*, September 28, 2010.

25 Letter from Thomas Jefferson to James Madison, December 20, 1787. Quoted in Thom Hartmann, "Jefferson Considers Freedom against Monopolies a Basic Right," in *Unequal Protection: The Rise of Corporate Dominance and the Theft of Human Rights* (New York: St. Martin's Press, 2002), 70–1.

26 Ibid., pp. 70–1.

27 Ibid., pp. 70–1.

28 I say *apparently* because Thom Hartmann's in-depth analysis of the case demonstrates that no mention of corporate personhood is directly or indirectly mentioned in the text of the decision (reference cited in fn 25).

29 For an excellent biography of Houston, see Genna Rae McNeil, *Groundwork: Charles Hamilton Houston and the Struggle for Civil Rights* (Philadelphia, PA: University of Pennsylvania Press, 1983).

CHAPTER SEVEN

The military-industrial complex

Perhaps no other piece of public rhetoric in circulation today has attained greater iconic status within the nation's political lexicon than Dwight Eisenhower's educationally pregnant phrase, *the military-industrial complex* (MIC).[1] First identified in his 1961 farewell address, President Eisenhower described the MIC as a seemingly intractable problem that carried with it a set of "grave implications." Surely then it's a good thing that today, 50 years later, increasing numbers of Americans are familiar with the phrase. What is less evident is whether this general familiarity translates into a full appreciation of the phrase's stunning political, educational, and even gendered implications. The purpose of this chapter is to investigate these implications and to suggest how the phrase might be recruited to serve as a meaningful piece of democratic rhetoric, one that can be mined pedagogically to heighten awareness of militarization as a threat to America's democratic identity.

In his final speech-act as chief executive, Eisenhower informed the nation about the ominous presence of a new "conjunction" of power between the government's military establishment and private arms industries—what he called the "military-industrial complex." His message contained not only a warning but also a rare official critique of an emerging civic conundrum: that while the military may be needed to defend the nation, it should not come to define it. This core tension, or dread possibility, is what animates

Eisenhower's Cold War jeremiad. Remarkably enough, instead of asking his fellow Americans to fear the Russians above all else, as might be expected in that anxious and fearful phase of the Cold War, Eisenhower asked Americans to fear a new source of internal danger.

> We have been compelled to create a permanent armaments industry of vast proportions . . . We annually spend on military security alone more than the net income of all United States corporations. Now this conjunction of an immense military establishment and a large arms industry is new in the American experience. The total influence—economic, political, *even spiritual*—is felt in every city, every statehouse, every office of federal government. We recognize the imperative need for this development. Yet we must not fail to comprehend its grave implications. In the councils of government, we must guard against the acquisition of unwarranted influence, whether sought or unsought, by the military-industrial complex. (My emphasis)[2]

Few American presidents have been more qualified than Ike to evaluate the "unwarranted influence" of militarization on the formative values and processes of American identity and democracy. In the early 1930s, for example, the then Major Eisenhower was tasked with writing reports on "industrial mobilization" for the Department of War and reports on war profiteering for the War Policies Commission established by Congress. Through this latter responsibility, he studied the scandal-plagued history of military/commercial relations in which corruption was the norm in the Mexican/American War, the American Civil War, the Spanish/American, War and in World War I.[3] After having grappled with these thorny issues for several decades, what became particularly sobering for Eisenhower was his growing realization that the tentacles of militaristic culture were beginning to compromise the spiritual values of the nation's democratic character. Owing to excessive militarization, Eisenhower told the nation that the spiritual integrity of American democracy had been placed in far more serious jeopardy than most realized.

Much of the basis of this "democratic spiritual integrity" was the seventeenth century Enlightenment principle which held that a societies' civil authority should always exercise supremacy over the military authority.[4] It was the inclusion of this moral principle into the Declaration of Independence and U.S. Constitution in the eighteenth century which supplied Americans with tangible evidence that their experiment in constructing a new political identity was indeed exceptional. In effect, then, Eisenhower was concerned that if the militarizing "anti-enlightenment" tendencies he identified were to go unheeded by American citizens for too long, then military values and points of view would gain supremacy over civil values and points of view. Were this to occur, the democratic moral identity of the nation would be menaced and our exceptional experiment would have to be deemed a failure. Engaging Ike's rhetoric from a genealogical perspective in this fashion encourages us to think about the evolution of national purpose and the dissonances in national identity not as stable and objectively existent entities but as moving formations capable of permanent transformation (not unlike jazz improvisations).

As a counterpoise to the bureaucratic momentum of the MIC, Eisenhower asserted that educational institutions in particular must beware of the "weight of this combination." He feared that a preponderance of MIC influence would compromise the independence of the curriculum and bend research projects exclusively toward militarist ends, a process which, among other things, would distort quests of "intellectual curiosity." Eisenhower advised the nation that educational institutions and, by extension, teachers, had to remain separate from the interests of the MIC if they hoped to cultivate an "alert and knowledgeable citizenry" whose sensitivity to such issues was the only guarantor of ensuring the "proper meshing of liberty and security."[5]

It is promising that many scholars and journalists write with clarity about the moral problems the MIC poses to the nation's fragile democratic prospect. The high quality of this literature affirms the proposition that this piece of public rhetoric already tacitly functions as a generative theme of American political culture. What makes this piece of rhetoric "pregnant" in an educational sense—what gives it pedagogical traction, what enables it to "produce questions"—are precisely those cultural contradictions roiling within its ever-expanding boundaries. When we name and dissect these contradictions in accord with a Freirean method and when we grasp the historical tensions these contradictions contain, disruptive if not unpredictable questions are likely to be formed about the meaning of the MIC in the contemporary world and the ways in which this "peculiar institution" poses a danger not only to American democracy but also to democratic processes across the globe. As a piece of public rhetoric, treated dialectically and ironically, the phrase can be tapped to radically question and transform the very thing it names.

While the treasure-trove of literature on the MIC is too vast to summarize in these pages, it could be generalized that most of these authors write from a radical democratic perspective. Despite the myriad angles of emphasis that these works necessarily reflect, they share a common assumption: that the continued existence of an expanding MIC represents a death knell to the nation's democracy and to the fantasy of American exceptionalism as a secular meaning narrative.[6] Before undertaking the task of identifying the core contradictions housed within the concept of the MIC, however, it will be useful to first discuss a few benchmark texts that provide analyses of and updates to Eisenhower's concept. In the final section, as part of a feminist-informed pedagogy of demilitarization, I reconceptualize the "complex" within our phrase as a psychological category, as a problematic psychological condition. While not denying the validity of interpreting the "complex" sociologically as an external institution, I develop the case that the ironic reversal of the term's meaning can help to expose the hidden politics of gender operative within a militarized version of America's exceptionalist hero complex.

Putting the "Academic" back into the military-industrial-academic complex

As Henry Giroux and James Ledbetter bring to light in their definitive and attractive interpretations of the MIC, Eisenhower and his speechwriters initially constructed their linguistic hyphenation to read, the "Military-Industrial-Academic Complex." While the Academic descriptor was dropped probably for stylistic reasons by the time Eisenhower actually gave his farewell address, a careful reading of the text leaves no question that the schools, especially institutions of higher education, were expected to be future arenas of conflict given the burgeoning militarization of American society.

Giroux should be recognized as the first educational theorist to write a book specifically about the pedagogical potential of Eisenhower's presidential jeremiad.[7] In painstaking forensic detail, Giroux provides a sobering update that lends credence to Eisenhower's fears about the culturally decadent influences of militarism on higher education: "As higher education comes under the powerful influence of military contractors, intelligence agencies, right-wing think tanks, and for-profit educational establishments pushing militarized knowledge and values, the interests of a militarized state and economy begin to coincide too closely with higher education."[8]

Here, it is important to evaluate the content or substance of "militarized knowledge and values" with a healthy dose of what Cynthia Enloe calls "feminist curiosity."[9] For instance, if we read gender into the phenomenon that Giroux accurately describes (the imposition of "militarized knowledge and values" into higher education), we can begin to ask questions about the degree to which this discourse is freighted with masculine values and psychic resonances (e.g. the efficacy if not beauty of violence, obedience to authority, enchantment with technology, etc). In the following paragraphs, the associations between masculinity and the militarization of culture will be further elaborated.

Eisenhower's discussion of how the formation of a technological-elite might transform the independent character of higher education is worth quoting at length:

> Today, the solitary inventor, tinkering in his shop, has been overshadowed by task forces of scientists in laboratories and testing fields. In the same fashion, the free university, historically the fountainhead of free ideas and scientific discovery, has experienced a revolution in the conduct of research. Partly because of the huge costs involved, a government contract becomes virtually a substitute for intellectual curiosity. For every old blackboard there are now hundreds of new electronic computers. The prospect of domination of the nation's scholars by Federal employment, project allocations, and the power of money is ever present and is gravely to be regarded.[10]

To demonstrate the degree to which the boundaries of the MIC have been expanded since Eisenhower's farewell, Giroux cites a list of federal project allocations whose collective aims mandate the militarization of "intellectual curiosity." For example, the Department of Homeland Security allocates a $70 million scholarship and research budget, while the University of Southern California has created the first "Homeland Security Center of Excellence" with a $12 million grant. Meanwhile, the National Academic Consortium for Homeland Security led by the Ohio State University joins more than 200 universities in their various security-related projects. It is important to grasp the fact that the MIC has penetrated higher education in epic proportions, perhaps beyond what even Ike could have imagined. Giroux summarizes the stakes involved: "The academy is increasingly stripped of its democratic commitments and values, which are clearly jeopardized as its civic mission is relegated to the interests of the military-industrial complex . . . democracy succumbs to the ideology of militarization and becomes synonymous with the dictates of the national security state."[11] Another dimension of what could be described as the "unwarranted influence" of military values on public education can be seen in the provision within the No Child Left Behind (NCLB) legislation which compels schools which accept federal monies to permit the military access to students' private information and to the schools themselves for purposes of recruitment.

It is significant for the purposes of this inquiry to note that the 1962 manifesto of the Students for a Democratic Society (SDS), the Port Huron Statement, devotes a separate section to the antidemocratic consequences of the "Military-Industrial Complex."[12] Soon after its publication, the Port Huron Statement became the founding charter of the "New Left." One of its key platforms was the demand to put an end to education as usual; that is, an end to universities across the nation operating as willing accomplices to the interests of the MIC. Its principal author, Tom Hayden, would eventually become an anti-Vietnam war activist and state senator from California. Hayden was deeply influenced in his thinking by the radical pragmatic sociologist, C. Wright Mills. Among other things, Mills' book *The Power Elite* (1956) provided an extensive analysis of the "revolving door" phenomenon in which ex-military officials would routinely assume leadership positions within the corporate arms industries. Of course, this is but one of many examples of the "disastrous rise of misplaced power" that Eisenhower highlighted in his speech.[13]

The opening sentence of the Port Huron Statement served notice that the nation's youth were disenchanted with American life. They were searching for something beyond the material comfort afforded by an affluent yet anxiety-ridden warfare state. "We are people of this generation, bred in at least modest comfort, housed now in universities, looking uncomfortably to the world we inherit."[14] Adopting language that echoes Mills and lends further substance to Eisenhower's "grave concerns," the statement succeeds in fleshing-out the organic relation between militarization and the slow-motion degradation of American democracy. The Port Huron author's declared: "Decisions about military strategy, including the monstrous decision to go to war, are more and more the property of the Military and the industrial arms race machine, with the politicians assuming a ratifying role, instead of a determining one."[15] The membership of the SDS correctly assumed that the rise of a garrison state mentality among American citizens would likely be preceded by Congress abdicating its role as the "determining" civil authority authorized to declare war. In fact, Congress would soon abdicate its role as the determining civil authority two years later with the passage of the Tonkin Gulf Resolution (1964), legislation which effectively turned authority to initiate war over to an Executive branch already in thrall to the interests of the national security state.

A glance at the record of U.S. covert interventions abroad in the post-1947 period confirms the idea that the Constitution was patently ill-equipped, by an "enlightened" design, to carry out imperial policies *legally*. This prohibitive legal condition therefore inspired the architects of the "American century" to create a "state within a state," a dubious constitutional formation whose origin can be traced to the National Security Act (1947).[16] This creative, if unconstitutional, maneuver allowed foreign interventions to proceed secretly or covertly in order to avoid established constitutional procedures (congressional authorization and public debate) which were deemed too cumbersome for effectively disciplining America's post-1945 global empire.

What is also prophetic about the Port Huron Statement is the manner in which it describes the destructive consequences that America's "permanent war economy" was having on the nation's democratic identity. In his farewell, Eisenhower alludes twice to the negative spiritual effects of militarization on American identity.

However, in doing so, he limits his speech to raising *implicit* questions about the functional relationship between militarization and the despiritualization of American democracy. Part of the beauty of the Port Huron Statement is that it takes these implicit associations and develops them conceptually with remarkable clarity. The authors acknowledge, for example, that the development and proliferation of modernized atomic weapons infinitely more destructive than those detonated over Hiroshima or Nagasaki, rather than causing a popular uproar among the American people, was met instead with mute resignation: "Most Americans accept the military-industrial structure as "the way things are." And while "one simple miscalculation could incinerate [sic] mankind these facts are but remotely felt."

> A shell of moral callous separates the citizen from sensitivity to the common peril: this is the result of a lifetime saturation with horror . . . A half-century of accelerating destruction has flattened out the individual's ability to make moral distinctions, it has made them understandably give up, it has forced private worry and public silence.[17]

Just as the youth of the 1960s came of age under the "shadow of the bomb" and were "saturated with horror," today's youth have been saturated with fear as part of a deliberate MIC-orchestrated public relations campaign to legitimize a post-9/11 permanent war society.[18]

If, for a moment, we assume that the American public has been and is now being readied to accept the normalization of a permanent war society, at the very least this should prompt educators to develop permanent educational strategies to expose and resist this authoritarian trend. Nel Noddings, for example, argues that critical war studies ought to be integrated into the curriculum far more than it has to date. Rather than using the study of war to romanticize its attractiveness and heroic appeal, she urges a program of study that would prepare students to think about how actual participation in war frequently leads to the loss of one's moral identity. "If we claim to educate," Noddings declares, "we must encourage people to reflect on what war does and might do to the human beings engaged in it."[19] When killing other human beings is as easy as a mouse-click away, as is increasingly the case, and when our youth are steeped in "playing" with ultraviolent virtual war games in their video absorption, images of war are rendered more "virtuous" than horrific, making war itself more thinkable while making the souls of others a distant, cyber abstraction. It is a well-accepted fact that the activity of play is regarded as a primary vehicle through which children develop a sense of moral imagination and empathy for others.[20] Therefore, should America continue its pattern of waging permanent war, would it not be altogether fitting that the one activity that cultivates moral imagination and empathy for others—play—would be sacrificed on the altar of militarism?

The difficulty of mapping the expanding boundaries of the military-industrial-academic-media-sports-entertainment-complex

When Eisenhower gave his farewell address in 1961, the conceptual boundaries of the MIC were relatively easy to comprehend. This is no longer the case. We are indebted to several authors in particular for jarring us into a realization of the magnitude with which the MIC has expanded since Ike's farewell. These authors demonstrate how "the complex" has managed to work its way into every nook and cranny—read: every congressional district—in the nation.[21] The question is no longer *if* Eisenhower would deplore these post-1961 developments, for he certainly would. Today, the more pertinent question is: How does the expansion of the MIC pose a danger not only to a decent notion of "domestic tranquility" but also to our self-conception as a democratic people? To address these questions, let's briefly revisit the standard model used to frame the MIC.

According to the conventional model of the MIC, there is first of all the state-sponsored defense establishment, including the Army, Navy, Air Force and Marines, and their various intelligence services, including the Central Intelligence Agency (CIA) and the National Security Agency (NSA). As previously mentioned, critics refer to this institutional structure as a "state within a state," for the simple reason that together, these institutions exercise many powers that states do, particularly its war powers and capacity to manipulate the political processes of other sovereign nations. Owing to their secret, off-the-books character, these activities are secretly funded and are conducted without the knowledge of the American people and, in many cases, without the knowledge of congressional oversight committees.

On the corporate side of the MIC institutional structure, there are the arms merchants, such as Boeing, Lockheed, McConnell-Douglass, Northrop Grumman, General Dynamics, General Electric, and Raytheon, and so on. It should be noted that none of the authors who attempt to wrap their conceptual arms around the enormity of today's MIC argue that the conventional model has lost its explanatory value; it is just that these traditional boundaries have become limited instruments given the ubiquity of today's MIC.

As Jeremy Scahill has shown regarding the private security firm Blackwater/Xe, a large part of the MICs recent expansion consists of the wholesale privatization or corporatization of the war function. In 2008, for example, he estimates that there were 100,000 private contractors in Iraq, representing an almost one-to-one ratio to active duty U.S. soldiers. Moreover, Scahill reports that the U.S. government in 2000 spent $17.4 billion on private intelligence contracts; a figure which increased dramatically in 2008 to $42 billion.[22] Not only are these mercenary personnel paid far more than government soldiers, they enjoy an extraconstitutional legal status that gives them immunity from the Pentagon's Uniform Code of Military Justice (UCMJ), meaning that the accepted rules of engagement and accountability do not apply to their activities.

Based on Scahill's research and analysis, it is now evident that Secretary of Defense Donald Rumsfeld's (2001–2006) controversial decision to send only 120,000 U.S. troops to invade and occupy Iraq in 2003, against the advice of Army General Eric Shinseki, who recommended 350,000 troops, had everything to do with his ambitious plan to privatize America's war-making function. Why would Rumsfeld want 350,000 US troops in Iraq if his prior intention was to turn many of the activities of war over to corporate security contractors? One can only wonder: Would Ike look upon this recent innovation in defense policy as a rational, cost-efficient reform—or as a symbol of constitutional betrayal?

In an attempt to capture the hegemonic character of this expanding network of State and corporate power, Nick Turse likens today's MIC to the 1999 sci-fi film, *The Matrix*. The film features a plot in which a mysterious secret cabal controls everything that happens in the world and only a few individuals have somehow managed to escape its near total domination. Because the cultural power of "the matrix" within the film is so ubiquitous, its presence is paradoxically difficult to detect. Similarly, Turse concedes the difficulty of capturing the hegemonic character of an ever-expanding MIC.

> But only Hollywood has managed to capture the essence of today's omnipresent, all-encompassing, cleverly hidden system of systems that invades all our lives; this new military-industrial-technological-entertainment-academic-scientific-media-intelligence-homeland security-surveillance-national security-corporate complex that has truly taken hold of America.[23]

While this hyphenated construction accurately enumerates present day dimensions of the MIC, Turse rightly deems this "too unwieldy for general use," and prefers instead to use the simple moniker, "the Complex." The larger point is that an ethos of militarization now seems to have attained hegemonic status within American political culture. Assuming the validity of this claim, there seems little reason to debate whether or not Eisenhower's worst fears about the MICs "unwarranted influence" have actually come to pass. They have—and with a vengeance. The question could thus be recalibrated: What specific aspects of MIC expansion would Ike find most deplorable? We could expect that Ike would first note the continuation of astronomical levels of military expenditure (estimated as $1 trillion from 2001 to 2011).

Beyond the continuation of this predictable pattern, however, there are perhaps two novel areas of MIC expansion that would raise Ike's republican ire. First would be the MIC's elaborate and costly public relations campaigns to appeal to youth culture, to educate youth desire around a manly ideal, and second, Ike would no doubt take exception to the MICs seamless penetration into every recess of the civilian economy. As one of the nation's most adept cartographers of today's MIC, it's worth examining how Turse attempts to remap its expanding boundaries:

> Most striking in this new age of corporate-military-entertainment meldings are those by-products of the Complex's effort to

project a cool, hip image, including military-crafted simulators that have become commercial video games; NASCAR events that feature race cars sponsored by branches of the armed services; slick recruiting campaigns that use the hottest social networking technology to capture the attention of teens; and involvement with civilian outfits popular with the young, like Starbucks, Oakley, Disney; and Coca-Cola. Just like the fictional Matrix, the Complex is nearly everywhere and involved in most everything, and very few people aren't plugged into it in some way, shape or form. Above all, as in the movie, most people are hardly aware that this "real Matrix" even exists.[24]

According to Turse, public relations or disinformation campaigns reside at the core of the new and improved version of the MIC: "Today's military-corporate complex is nothing if not sophisticated. It uses all the tools of a modern corporation: publicity departments, slick advertising campaigns, and public relations efforts to build up the armed forces."[25] As a disseminator of militarized knowledge, values, symbols, and images, it is clear that the Pentagon has implemented their own sophisticated pedagogies of war, in an attempt to educate the nation's increasingly unemployed youth about what it means to be cool, hip, and manly.

Rereading the "Complex" psychologically: Toward a theory of America's civic neurosis

It is customary to conceptualize the MIC as an external institutional structure. This sociopolitical economic structure did not exist on the American historical stage when the stage was originally built but rather crept onto it incrementally. By the midpoint of the twentieth century, the MIC established itself as an institutional fixture. As we have seen, Eisenhower conceptualized this development as an historical *discontinuity*, an emergent structure of power and interest that joined up the armed forces of the State with arms merchants located in the private or corporate sphere. It is true that, in past US wars, private commercial enterprises always entered into contractual relationships with the government to procure various goods and services. Previously we noted that, in the 1930s, Eisenhower studied the history of these military/commercial relations. Decades later in his farewell address, Eisenhower wished to say that what had once been episodic relations between these two separate domains had now become permanent. At a sociological level of analysis, then, it is necessary to define the MIC as an external institutional structure.

Yet, even as we appreciate the obvious necessity of this conception, I want to suggest an alternative way of thinking about this expansive structure of military power and culture. I argue that the project of decentering the cultural power of the MIC within the negotiation of American identity can be invigorated by conceptualizing the military-industrial *complex* as a psychological category, as something *internal* to individuals. What would it mean then to treat the "complex" within our phrase as it is treated within psychoanalytic theory, as a *problematic psychological condition*?

According to Freud and Jung, it was axiomatic that everyone has "complexes." That is, everyone has within themselves a constellation of affects (ideas, fears, identifications, and projections) that are unique to their own life histories. The type of complex I want to put under the microscope is not the classic Freudian Oedipal complex. It is rather what could be called America's "national hero complex," a phenomenon particular to our political culture and to the grand narrative of American exceptionalism. A core component of this complex (roughly equivalent to Freire's concept of a "thematic universe") includes a set of gendered identifications of masculine and feminine values and traits which are ordained in varying degrees within the dominant culture. According to psychoanalytic theory, the possibility of a complex breaking out into a neurosis arises when individuals remain unconscious of their own unique constellation of affects. When such an absence of awareness occurs, individuals may become captive to the intrusive and often debilitating power that these ideas, fears, identifications, and projections can exert over their lives. In this regard, what can happen to individuals may be extended, with due caution, to an understanding of what can happen to a culture's civic self-conception.

Here, Plato's analytical distinction between the "psyche and the city" is relevant. This heuristic gives coherence to the idea that the individual and the larger civic imaginary (the city) are *mutually interpenetrated entities or significations*. Plato argued that if you want to get an accurate picture of the character of any political regime, examine the psychological profiles of the individuals contained within it, for the State is none other than its collective individual psychologies writ large.[26] Taking a cue from Plato then, we could conjecture that the affects or traces of the military-industrial *complex*—understood as an internalized overvaluation of masculinity—are likely to be implicated within the souls of many American citizens.

A close reading of the farewell address reveals that what Ike feared most, and what he meant when he talked about the spiritual erosion of America's democratic heritage and identity, was that the values, perceptions, and habits of mind of militarism might someday be *internalized* by many individual Americans. In fact, a day after his farewell, Ike held a press conference in which he said that an inordinate preoccupation with military solutions would produce an *"insidious penetration of our own minds,"* so that no other possible solutions to the nation's challenges would be perceived.[27] If Ike's worst fears concerning the internalization of militaristic cultural values have materialized today, as many astute observers maintain, that is, if military authority and its values have begun to rival or surpass civil authority and its values, it follows that many of us would eventually become walking contradictions: virtual citizens inhabiting a militarized, and militarizing, democratic republic.

To the extent this scenario is recognizable today, it suggests that the values of the (MIC) have indeed been internalized by a critical mass of Americans. For this reason, as we seek to develop more robust pedagogies of demilitarization, it would be unwise to rely exclusively on an externalized sociological conception of the complex (as indispensable as this explanatory frame is). By adopting a psychoanalytic definition of "complex," as that which signifies a pattern of emotions, perceptions, wishes, fears, values, identifications, and projections, yoked together in uneasy tension, we will be positioned to investigate how many of us have come to "host" the values of the MIC as a cultural site of heroic/masculine veneration.

On this point, it is significant that within the space of two paragraphs of his speech, Eisenhower invokes the term "balance" no less than *nine* times! The repeated use of balance in this context beckons us to ask what it would mean if we were to interpret balance not in a physical sense, as in "bringing the priorities of the federal budget into balance," but rather in a psychological sense. Read psychologically, Eisenhower's strategic repetition could be interpreted to mean that he thought American identity was in jeopardy of becoming *imbalanced* should the militarization of American society continue unabated. Indeed, at the end of this section of the farewell, Eisenhower observes: "Good judgment seeks balance and progress. Lack of it eventually finds imbalance and frustration."[28] Surely, "imbalanced" is a useful psychological metaphor to begin to describe a neurosis, whether individual or collective in nature. When examining the psychological and moral ideal of balance from a gendered perspective, one can hardly escape being intrigued by the interpretive possibilities that open up.

For example, as feminist critics of the war system remind us (such as Nel Noddings, Betty Reardon, and Cynthia Enloe), masculine-oriented discourses and values are invariably invoked to justify excessive military spending or military "solutions" of any kind. In turn, these same policies contribute to the erosion of institutions of public care, institutions that are often defended on the basis of a feminist ethic of care. Although in the passage below Enloe refers to the central mechanisms through which men in *leadership positions* negotiate their relation to war through the prism of the feminine, her point is relevant to the larger American culture: "Masculinization often is fueled by key players' anxieties and fears of feminization. Any person or group of people who think that if they are perceived as 'feminine' they will lose political influence, credibility, or respect, are likely to take steps to avoid being perceived that way: they will stay quiet about their genuine reservations . . . they might even cast doubt on the manliness of those who are criticizing military solutions (diplomats, pacifists, 'the French')."[29]

Readers will recall in Chapter five that a public controversy arose between Theodore Roosevelt and William James in which Theodore Roosevelt snidely cast doubt on James's manliness for his opposition to American imperialism in the Spanish/American turned Philippine/American war. One way to frame their dispute is to appreciate the extent to which their stances reflected contradictory interpretations of cultural heroism and, by extension, contradictory interpretations of American exceptionalism. To illustrate: In Teddy Roosevelt's view, the practical meaning of American exceptionalism as a heroic ideal gave *license* to imperialism, while in William James' view, the heroic ideal of American exceptionalism *prohibited* imperialism. Both interpretations are marked by gender, but only

James' could be called feminist-friendly. Once again we see evidence that the discourse of American exceptionalism contains conflicting internal tendencies that can be clarified through the use of gender as an analytic category. This interpretive conflict points to an obvious question: Is the privileging of masculine values the core ideological ingredient for sustaining our permanent war society? There is a good reason to believe that it is.

The theoretic contours of what I am calling America's conflicted hero complex or America's civic neurosis can be approximated by reference to an over-valorization of masculine values and principles and a corresponding marginalization of feminine values and principles. Chief among these militarized masculine traits is a desire to control, dominate, and conquer. This gender-inflected desire translates into cultural practices that can be found at both the individual and collective level. However, one notable difficulty in naming this complex and exposing its internal tensions, is the comforting belief (or illusion) held by many that the US role in the world is never controlling, dominating, and conquering for self-interest or for profit. Instead, such instances of violent force are frequently rationalized on the basis of protecting the integrity of a presumed universal moral ideal that has itself become lodged in the minds of many as transcendent signifier (i.e. American exceptionalism).

However, according to some commentators, notably Noam Chomsky, Chalmers Johnson, and Andrew Bacevich, the discourse of American exceptionalism has routinely been invoked deceptively. A glance at the historical record affirms that the sense of moral superiority underpinning the imperial strand of this discourse has been used, as it was used in the invasions of Vietnam and Iraq, to serve as a convenient fig-leaf to conceal the State's baser, imperialistic geo-strategic motives. At another level of analysis, the imperial strand of exceptionalist ideology permits many Americans to deny their nation's status as an empire even as the US armed forces maintain at least 725 military bases around the world.[30]

Having conducted various conceptual ground-clearing exercises up to this point, it is now time to identify the existence of the "other half" of America's conflicted hero complex. It is the presence of this other half which enables us to give shape and meaning to the cultural contradictions sequestered within the phrase. The capacity to identify this primary contradiction derives primarily from a prior awareness of a set of historically anchored democratic principles, themselves products of American history. Without this element of historical awareness to use as a symbolic fulcrum to set against its contrary cultural significations, there would be no basis for identifying the existence of any contradictions within the phrase whatsoever. It is this value-laden fact of an American democratic and antimilitarist *tradition* still alive in the minds of many that allows us to frame the MIC as a rhetorical repository of contradiction; one whose empirical existence as an institution, in both its external and internal dimensions, stands as a contradiction to the democratic project.

In naming the contradictions within the phrase on the basis of an historical analysis, let us recall that Freire's principle of conscientization is defined not only as a process of "learning to perceive contradictions" but also as a quality of mind dependent upon an "intensification of one's historical awareness."[31] Without an historical awareness of the nation's democratic heritage, these contradictions by definition cannot come into view; with this awareness, the contradictions cannot easily be ignored without expending energy to repress one's awareness of them. This repression—which manifests itself as a "passion to ignore"—is itself a symptom of the civic neurosis we are attempting to theorize. Put differently, the ethos of militarization, is predicated not only on the supremacy of the masculine values and the repression of the feminine values, but also on the repression of the nation's democratic, anti-imperial heritage.

As we have seen in Chapter six, Jefferson argued unsuccessfully for a constitutional amendment that would have prohibited the United States from organizing and funding "standing armies." Moreover, the Declaration of Independence includes a stinging rebuke to the principle of standing armies: "[The King] . . . has kept among us, in Times of Peace, Standing Armies without the consent of our Legislatures. He has affected to render *the Military independent of and superior to the Civil Power*"[32] (my emphasis). Jefferson was far from alone in thinking that standing armies, whether of British or American origin, were intrinsically destructive to the foundational principles of democratic republics.

As Arthur A. Ekirch's classic study of the antimilitarist tradition in the United States affirms, most State constitutions, before and after 1776, contained provisions prohibiting standing armies.[33]

Many of the framers whose names we recognize today, such as Sam Adams and John Quincy Adams, John Jay, James Madison, Richard Henry Lee, George Mason, Elbridge Gerry, Edmund Randolph, and Patrick Henry, were deeply suspicious of standing armies and of military authority in general. In short, Americans developed an acute understanding that the standing armies strewn across Europe functioned as linchpins of monarchical power, and for this reason, they were perceived by the generation of 1776 to stand in direct contradiction to the purposes, values, and identity of the newly forming republican nation. Bacevich affirms this crucial historical consciousness: "The Founders, the commander of the Continental Army not least among them, disparaged standing armies as inconsistent with republic virtue while posing a visceral threat to republican institutions."[34]

James Madison expressed this common sense attitude in 1787 during the Constitutional Convention:

> In time of actual war, great discretionary powers are constantly given to the Executive Magistrate. Constant apprehension of War, has the same tendency to render the head too large for the body. A standing military force, with an overgrown Executive, will not long be safe companions to liberty. The means of defense against foreign danger, have been always the instruments of tyranny at home. Among the Romans it was a standing maxim to excite a war, whenever revolt was apprehended. Throughout all Europe, the armies kept up under the pretext of defending, have enslaved the people.[35]

Another example of how this enlightenment principle found its way into the nation's public discourse is seen in George Washington's farewell address (1796). It is noted for its admonition to the nation to remain neutral in the face of Europe's endless warfare and free from any "entangling alliances" with friends or foes alike. Virtually identical to Eisenhower's farewell, Washington warned future generations of Americans to, ". . . avoid the necessity of those overgrown military establishments which, under any form of government, are inauspicious to liberty, and which are to be regarded as particularly hostile to republican liberty."[36]

This brief historical glimpse is not recounted for the purpose of arguing that the United States should return today to a policy of "no standing armies," as if we could push a magic reset button to perfectly synchronize national defense policy with our democratic heritage. Rather, it is to suggest that the vast scope and aesthetic spectacle of today's MIC exercises a deforming though largely obscured influence on America's democratic identity. One of the many negative consequences of this influence is that it tends to encourage chronic dispositions of historical amnesia regarding the nation's founding principles.

Largely because of this historical amnesia, the democratic myth of cultural heroism is barely negligible today as a viable meaning narrative. Teachers as cultural workers therefore need to recover the memory of democracy's historic past as a precondition for identifying how the MIC and its cultural myths of heroism exist in contradiction to democratic myths of heroism. So long as these historical amnesias remain intact, and so long as the discourse of militarization and its cultural affects are regarded as benignly genderless, it is difficult to see how the cultural power of the MIC can be decentered within the negotiation of American identity. In thus appropriating the rhetoric of the MIC dialectically and ironically, the phrase can become figuratively "pregnant" to the extent teachers identify and draw-out the latent contradictions gestating within its symbolic boundaries, an inquiry which may well give birth to some good questions and some beautiful ideas—and actions.

Notes

1 See James Ledbetter, *Unwarranted Influence: Dwight D. Eisenhower and the Military-Industrial Complex* (New Haven, CT: Yale University Press, 2010). The author includes the full text of the farewell address in the appendix of his book (pp. 211–20). Other versions of the address, such as Richard Hofstadter's *Great Issues in American History: From 1865 to 1980* (New York: Vintage Press, 1982) are abbreviated.

2 Ibid., 215–16.

3 Ibid., 47–9.

4 The following sources explicate this crucial historical tension between civil and military authority: Charles DeBenedetti, *The Peace Reform in American History* (Bloomington, IN: Indiana University

Press, 1980); Lois Schwoerer, *"No Standing Armies!" The Antiarmy Ideology in Seventeenth-Century England* (Baltimore: Johns Hopkins University Press, 1974); Arthur A. Ekirch, Jr. *The Civilian and the Military* (New York: Oxford University Press, 1956).

5 Ledbetter, 216.

6 The MIC does not seem to pose a challenge to religious oriented narratives of American exceptionalism but only to those strands identified with the democratic project. For a comprehensive overview of the many tensions operative within this narrative, see Michael Kammen, "The Problem of American Exceptionalism: A Reconsideration." *In the Past Lane: Historical Perspectives on American Culture* (New York: Oxford University Press, 1997), 169–98.

7 Henry Giroux, *The University in Chains: Confronting the Military-Industrial-Academic Complex* (Boulder, CO: Paradigm Publishers, 2007).

8 Ibid., 22–3.

9 See Cynthia Enloe, *Globalization & Militarism: Feminists Make the Link* (Lanham, MD: Rowman & Littlefield, 2007), 51, 143–4.

10 Ledbetter, 216–17.

11 Giroux, 23.

12 See http://coursesa.matrix.msu.edu/~hst306/documents/huron.html (subsequent references will be cited as *PHS*).

13 The "revolving door" between the Bush Administration (2001–2008), the arms merchants and the Pentagon is given a stunning update by Scahill, fn 21, p. 53.

14 *PHS.*

15 *PHS.*

16 One of the best primers on the origins and genesis of the "national security state" is Saul Landau's *The Dangerous Doctrine: National Security and U.S. Foreign Policy* (Boulder, CO: Westview Press, 1988).

17 *PHS.*

18 See, for example, Chalmers Johnson's discussion of the Pentagon's "Office of Strategic Influence" set up in 2001 to conduct "information warfare," whose mission included operations to manage/deceive public opinion about the war. Once the existence of this office was made public, it temporarily ended, but a new position was created to serve the same purpose: Deputy Undersecretary of Defense for "Special Plans." Chalmers Johnson, *The Sorrows of*

Empire: Militarism, Secrecy, and the End of the Republic (New York: Metropolitan Books, 2004), 298–9.

19   Nel Noddings, "The Psychology of War." *Critical Lessons: What Our Schools Should Teach* (New York: Cambridge University Press, 2006), 36–63.

20   See, for example, Martha Nussbaum, "Cultivating Imagination: Literature and the Arts." *Not for Profit: Why Democracy Needs the Humanities* (Princeton: Princeton University Press, 2010), 99–102.

21   My own thinking on the MIC and its expansion is indebted to the following authors (in alphabetical order): Andrew Bacevich, *Washington Rules: America's Path to Permanent War* (New York: Metropolitan Books, 2010); Noam Chomsky, *Hegemony or Survival: America's Quest for Global Dominance* (New York: Metropolitan Books, 2003); James Der Derian, *Virtuous War: Mapping the Military-Industrial-Media-Entertainment Network* (New York: Routledge, 2009); Henry Giroux, *The University in Chains: Confronting the Military-Industrial-Academic Complex* (Boulder, CO: Paradigm Publishers, 2007); Chalmers Johnson, *The Sorrows of Empire: Militarism, Secrecy, and the End of the Republic* (New York: Metropolitan Books, 2004); James Ledbetter, *Unwarranted Influence: Dwight D. Eisenhower and the Military-Industrial Complex* (New Haven, CT: Yale University Press, 2010); Eugene Provenzo Jr, "Virtuous War: Simulation and the Militarization of Play," In *Education as Enforcement: the Militarization and Corporatization of Schools*, eds, Kenneth J. Saltman & David A. Gabbard (New York: RoutledgeFalmer, 2003), 279–86; Jeremy Scahill, *Blackwater: The Rise of the World's Most Powerful Mercenary Army* (New York: Nation Books, 2007); Nick Turse, *The Complex: How the Military Invades Our Everyday Lives* (New York: Metropolitan Books, 2008).

22   Scahill, 53–6.

23   Turse, 16.

24   Ibid.,17.

25   Ibid, 18.

26   See Joe Sachs, trans. Plato, *Republic* (Newburyport, MA: 2007), 129 or 434d–35c.

27   Ledbetter, 96.

28   Ibid., 214–17.

29   Enloe, 52.

30   Johnson, 4–5, 153–4, 189–90.

31 Paulo Freire, *Pedagogy of the Oppressed* (New York: Continuum Books, 2010), 109.

32 Pauline Maier, ed. *The Declaration of Independence and the Constitution of the United States* (New York: Bantam Classics, 1998), 55.

33 See Arthur A. Ekirch, Jr "The Founding Fathers Reaffirm Civil Supremacy." *The Civilian and the Military* (New York: Oxford University Press, 1956), 18–31.

34 Bacevich, 243–4.

35 Max Farrand, ed. *Records of the Federal Convention of 178,* Volume I (New Haven, CT: Yale University Press, 1966), 465.

36 "George Washington's Farewell Address." Richard Hofstadter, ed. *Great Issues in American History: From the Revolution to the Civil War, 1765–1865* (New York: Vintage Books, 1982.), 214–19.

CHAPTER EIGHT

The personal is political

The personal is political achieved iconic status in the late 1960s and 1970s as a defining symbol of the second wave of the American feminist movement. It is important to appreciate why these four simple yet incendiary words, strung together as a slogan, galvanized millions of feminists across the nation into a potent cultural and political force. At a practical level, the phrase lent thematic coherence to the idea that women were oppressed by dint of having to assume the heaviest burden of labor within the private domestic sphere—notably housework and childcare. Proceeding on this general theory, radical feminists declared that henceforth all of the oppressive hierarchies enacted on a daily basis in the private sphere, enactments which had eluded political scrutiny in the past, including issues pertaining to sexuality, would no longer be immune from critique and potential transformation.

The personal is political thus encouraged feminists to critically theorize and challenge the interlocking web of hidden power relations characteristic of the patriarchal order. Carole Pateman discusses how this defining feminist insight worked to trouble the conventional boundaries separating public from private: "Feminists have emphasized how personal circumstances are structured by public factors, by laws about rape and abortion, by the status of 'wife,' by policies on child-care and the allocation of welfare benefits and the sexual division of labor in the home and workplace. 'Personal' problems can thus be solved only through political means and political action."[1] It should be noted that most feminist political theorists do not argue that the public/private distinction should be abandoned altogether. Rather most of these thinkers insist on radically reconfiguring the distinction by extending analyses of power relations to include the private domestic sphere; moreover, they contend that the fulfillment of democracy demands that they do so.[2]

Few can doubt that the institutionalization of women's oppression grows out of a complex brew of economic, political, and historical factors. But one cultural factor that could be called foundational—that which prompted the ascendancy of the slogan to begin with—was the prior theoretical division of social existence into "public" and "private" domains. Once more, as we've seen in earlier chapters, one of the nation's defining civic predicaments can be traced to the ancient Greeks.

In the Greek conception, the "public" domain, the *polis*, was constructed as an exclusively male space in which all questions of power and politics were to be decided. As a male habitat, the *polis* was privileged as the public realm of "culture" and "reason" and thus "freedom." In contrast, the private domain, the household or *oikos*, was designated as the realm of necessity (in which physical labor and mere survival were the primary activities) and thus it was understood as the realm of dependency and unfreedom. Within this habitat, females were defined more as reproductive bodies than as conscious moral beings, and because they were presumed incapable of reason, as a class, females were relegated to a private, nonpolitical location.

Critical second-wave feminists pointed out that the creation of this "nonpolitical" realm in Greek antiquity was itself an artificial invention, a strategic power move par excellence. Jean Bethke Elshtain affirms these Greek-inspired political boundaries: "The relations and activities occurring within and serving as the raison d'etre of the *polis* were defined as existing outside the realms of nature and necessity. The free space of the *polis*, though apart from necessity, existed in a *necessary* relation to those activities lodged within the private realm, held by Greeks to be the realm of unfreedom."[3]

The immediate problem feminists faced was that the public/private binary had succeeded for thousands of years in establishing a social imaginary which structured how Westerners negotiated their understanding of who they were in the political order and where the realm of culture and freedom was located and where it was not. Restricted within these historically enforced boundaries, what other choice did feminists have but to create a new set of meanings around a counter-foundational narrative such as "the personal is political?" How else to push back against centuries of official exclusion?

It is also worth mentioning that the development of a women's social movement in the 1960s and 1970s could be called organic owing to the fact that the collective identity of the movement was brought into existence largely through a spontaneous and improvisational educational institution, the so-called consciousness-raising groups (CR groups). In fact, our phrase cannot be fully appreciated apart from understanding its vital connection to the development of the CR groups. The CR groups represented the institutional component of the women's movement and the rhetoric of the personal is political represented the ideological, personalized component: Each represented a side of the same coin. The emergence of the CR groups served several purposes, first among them was the creation of free spaces within which women could openly talk to other women (without the presence of men) about the everyday practices which filled their lives. According to the proponents of consciousness-raising, unless one saw, or learned to see, the truth value contained within a feminist interpretation of the personal is political, the ability to act on behalf of one's personal or social liberation would always remain severely constrained.[4]

Emerging in tandem with the CR groups, then, the personal is political developed spontaneously as a civic rhetoric in response to women's structurally imposed historical powerlessness. The grassroots formation of the rhetoric constitutes an important part of its democratic character. The feminist thinkers who are usually given credit for coining the personal is political—Carol Hanisch, Shula Firestone, Robin Morgan, to mention a few—contend they had nothing to do with authoring the phrase. Instead they cite millions of women in millions of private and public conversations as the phrase's collective authors. In much the same spirit, when Gloria Steinem was asked about the origins of the personal is political, she responded by saying that to assign any individual credit for its formulation would be as absurd as assigning credit to someone for inventing the phrase "World War II."[5]

Among other things, this significant component of the rhetoric—its democratic character—indicates that millions of American women began to investigate dimensions of their private lives in light of egalitarian criteria. As they developed ways of "looking politically" at their subordinated role in society, and as they began to act on the basis of these new perceptions, the phrase transformed itself into a powerful vehicle of civic pedagogy. What made the phrase pedagogical was its capacity to symbolically direct an impulse toward personal and social criticism, an ongoing orientation to one's personal experience and to the world that often resulted in "consciousness-raising." In unsettling the private/public divide and in politicizing what had been designated politically neutral space, the adroit use of this rhetoric by feminists seemed to momentarily dethrone the assumption that the national identity was an inherently male project. By declaring that the personal *is* political, and by validating the legitimacy of their subjective experiences through the CR groups, feminists not only hoped to develop better means for naming their previously unheeded desires and experiences of oppression but, in a broader sense their critique also offered a glimpse into what it would mean to create a gender-balanced and thus a more democratic America.

In the following section, I revisit Carol Hanisch's brief yet historically significant essay "The Personal is Political." My treatment of it provides a springboard for further contextualizing the phrase and for experimenting theoretically with its potent yet largely untapped pedagogical possibilities. Specifically, I argue that the rhetoric can be used as a catalyst to educate at the deeper levels of democracy—not democracy understood as an "external" institution embodied in the state—but rather democracy understood as something internal, something personal, a mode of "moral and spiritual association."[6]

Bridging the gap between feminist consciousness-raising groups and critical pedagogy

In 2006, Carol Hanisch wrote a fascinating essay about the attention that her 1969 article "The Personal is Political" continues to garner around the world.[7] She tells us the piece was written in response to mounting criticism from within the feminist movement itself. This criticism denounced the educational strategy underlying the CR groups that had sprung up across the country. Some radical feminists contended that these groups were diminishing rather than promoting the prospect of revolutionary feminist change. According to Hanisch's account, these critics charged that the CR groups' focus on personal psychological conditions only encouraged women to lose sight of the real battle, which, in their view, was to actively confront the institutional structures of capitalist patriarchy.

These critics expressed their suspicion that the CR groups were more often engaged in apolitical naval-gazing exercises than they were in transforming oppressed women into committed political activists. However, Hanisch and her cohorts saw things differently. They argued that a deeper understanding of the private dimension of women's lives was the necessary educational precondition for equipping them to eventually join or form organizations to transform those external structures. From Hanisch's perspective, the proponents of the CR groups were not unmindful of how even well-intentioned groups could unwittingly encourage individualistic remedies. Responding to those who criticized CR groups as mere vehicles of privatized therapy, Hanisch had this pithy rejoinder: "Women are messed over, not messed up! We need to change the objective conditions, not adjust to them. Therapy is adjusting to your bad personal alternative."[8] In her comprehensive and valuable analysis of consciousness-raising, Catherine MacKinnon echoes Hanisch: "[E]ffectively, the process redefines women's feelings of discontent as indigenous to their situation rather than to themselves as crazy, maladjusted, hormonally imbalanced, bitchy, or ungrateful. It is validating to comprehend oneself as devalidated rather that as invalid."[9]

What, then, did these sites of educational transformation look and feel like in practical terms? For MacKinnon and for virtually everyone else who has written on the topic, the pedagogical approaches adopted by various CR groups were variable and pragmatic.

> Springing up spontaneously in the context of friendship networks, colleges and universities, women's centers, neighborhoods, churches, and shared work or workplaces, they were truly grassroots. Many aimed for diversity in age, marital

status, occupation, education, physical ability, sexuality, race and ethnicity, class, or political views. Some groups proceeded biographically, each woman presenting her life as she wished to tell it. Some moved topically, using subject focuses such as virginity crises, relations among women, mothers, body image, and early sexual experiences to orient discussion . . . Although leadership patterns often emerged, and verbal and emotional skills recognizably varied, equality within the group was a goal that reflected a value of nonhierarchical organization and a commitment to confronting sources of inequality on the basis of which members felt subordinated or excluded.[10]

MacKinnon's description of the CR groups closely parallels the ways in which Hanisch outlines their principles, methods, and purposes. Her discussion of these principles leaves little doubt that they are consistent with the language and values of democratic liberalism. "We have not done much trying to solve personal problems of women in the group. We've mostly picked topics by two methods: In a small group it is possible for us to take turns bringing questions to the meeting (like, which do/did you prefer, a girl or boy baby or no children, and why? What happens to your relationship if your man makes more money than you? Less than you?). Then, we go around the room answering the questions from our personal experiences. Everybody talks that way. At the end of the meeting we try to sum up and generalize from what's been said and make connections."[11]

To place this description in the context of democratic pedagogy, we need only to remind ourselves that, similar to Freirean theory, it is grounded in a question-based, problem-posing approach, one in which the "curriculum" is not imposed from above but rather emerges autonomously from below, from the participants themselves. While these groups reflected divergent pedagogical approaches, a common feature that linked them together was that women's personal experience was not only validated but also privileged as a starting point for inquiry.[12] In making sure that "everybody talks" in a dialogical fashion about their experiences, the CR groups strived toward a nonhierarchical moral ideal. Because the CR group approach is anchored in questioning and dialogue and seeks to make one's personal experience a primary site of critical inquiry, it is broadly comparable to the distinction Freire constructs between problem-posing education as "biophilic" (life-loving) and banking education as "necrophilic (death-loving)."[13]

Hanisch's representation also indicates that the process of "summing up, generalizing and making connections" is precisely the moment in which women (or anyone one else, for that matter) begin to see that their individual experiences both fit into and rub against larger social structures and patterns. Metaphorically speaking, this process has a positively destabilizing effect on identity as one's imagined "mobile" self undergoes recalibration to fit the wider perception. The activities of "everybody talking" (nonhierarchical dialogue), summing up, generalizing, and making connections (doing philosophy) are at the heart of the consciousness-raising process. Broadly construed, then, consciousness-raising can be defined as a quality of being that is synonymous with learning to be critical—an orientation which contains a future-directed, perpetually unfinished quality that encourages ongoing psychic growth. In one sense at least, consciousness-raising and Freire's conscientization are similar orientations in which one learns to perceive contradictions and to "take action against the oppressive elements of reality." However, the notable difference that appears to separate the two concepts is that Freire omits gender as a unit of analysis within his theory, a lacuna which has elicited sympathetic criticism from both Kathleen Weiler and bell hooks.[14]

If it is the case that these "private" CR groups assisted women in liberating themselves from the psychological constraints imposed by patriarchy, and if they imbued participants with new desires for engaging in political activism, they would invariably create substantial "public" effects in the wake of these activities. In refuting arguments about the alleged privatizing consequences of the CR groups, Hanisch appears to jettison the conventional reading of the public/private division: "I believe at this point that these analytical sessions are a form of political action . . . it is at this point *a political action is to tell it like it is*, to say what I really believe about my life instead of what I've always been told to say. So the reason I participate in these meetings is not to solve any personal problem. One of the first things we discover in these groups is that personal problems are political problems. There are no personal solutions at this time. There is only collective action for a collective solution"[15] (my emphasis).

Generally speaking, *parrhesia* is the Greek concept for "telling it like it is."[16] Hanisch's use of an English language equivalent of the term tacitly captures the meaning of this uniquely democratic virtue and thus represents another conceptual bridge linking the CR groups' pedagogical approach to democratic pedagogy. As Hamish attests, the CR groups provided women with the necessary space within which they could recover their voices and thus their ability to "speak truth to power" (to employ a modern colloquialism to approximate the meaning of *parrhesia*).[17]

Another democratic quality that can be found in Hanisch's discussion of the CR groups' educational approach is her obvious regard for the dignity of the other. In this case, "the other" represents those "oppressed" women still laboring under the deceptive enchantments of patriarchy. Just as some of her feminist critics raised serious doubts about the political efficacy of the CR groups, Hanisch criticized some within the feminist ranks for taking action for action's sake, without giving sufficient forethought to the underlying political meaning those actions might have. For example, while participating in the controversial protest at the Miss America Pageant in 1968, Hanisch took exception to those "radical" feminists who carried banners intended to demean the beauty contestants. "I wrote about how the anti-woman faction of the protesters detracted from our message that ALL women are oppressed by beauty standards, even the contestants. Signs like 'Up Against the Wall, Miss America' and 'Miss America is a Big Falsie' made these contestants out to be our enemy instead of the men and bosses as who imposed false beauty standards on women."[18]

Hanisch's essay is also significant for the way she frames the CR groups' educational purposes in strikingly nondoctrinaire terms. For instance, while addressing the thorny dilemma of women within the CR groups who, for many complicated reasons, resisted overt displays of political activism, Hanisch offers this advice to would-be feminist revolutionaries: "I think we must listen to what so-called apolitical women have to say—not so we can do a better job of organizing them but because together we are a mass movement. I think we who work full-time in the movement tend to become very narrow. What is happening now is that when non-movement women disagree with us, we assume it's because they are 'apolitical,' not because there might be something wrong with our thinking."[19]

The presence of at least two democratic dispositions can be detected in this passage: A willingness to listen to those with whom we disagree, on the one hand, and on the other, Hanisch reflects an obvious sense of fallibilism in relation to her own assumptions and truths. Both of these democratic qualities, particularly when combined with the methods and aims outlined in the preceding pages, help to furnish the educational conditions in which persons are more likely to develop the capacity to revise, to create new forms, and therefore to actually be democratic.

According to Jim Garrison, for example, the human capacity to listen needs to be understood as a cardinal democratic virtue, indeed, one that ought to be seen as the *sine qua non* of growth itself. A democratic theory of listening, Garrison explains, "requires that we acknowledge a prominent role for risking and reconstructing our social habits in open dialogues across gender, racial and ethnic differences."[20] In Garrison's hands, listening turns out to be a far more nuanced and active orientation to the world and to ourselves than we tend to think. For example, rarely is listening discussed as a form of action, as in "listening = critical reflection as an action." It is as if our recognition of the interiority of listening somehow cancels its potential to be regarded as a stimulus for action. Yet, of course, the process of listening constituted the experiential guts of CR group activity; without the presence of active listening, participants could not learn from the experiences of others and would squander opportunities to broaden their own thinking and thus their ability to act. The value of Garrison's interpretation (based on the theories of John Dewey and Hans-Georg Gadamer) is that it reconnects listening to an active sense of agency, which, in turn, is connected to the ongoing process of risking and reconstructing one's social habits. "Dialogues across difference are disturbing. Listening is dangerous. It places us at risk and leaves us vulnerable, so why listen? Because others may have what we need in thought, action, and feeling and we might not even know it."[21]

Richard Bernstein, writing within the tradition of American pragmatism, develops "fallibilism" as a democratic virtue crucial in maintaining an attitude of openness to continuous growth.

> A fallibilistic orientation requires a genuine willingness to test one's ideas in public, and to listen carefully to those who criticize them. It requires the imagination to formulate new hypotheses

and conjectures, and to subject them to rigorous public testing and critique by a community of inquirers. Fallibilism requires a high tolerance for uncertainty, and the courage to revise, modify, and abandon our most cherished beliefs when they have been refuted.[22]

In Hanisch's 1969 article, as well as in her 2006 retrospective, a refreshing sense of critical fallibilism attends to everything she writes. Her impressionistic yet theoretically adept account of how the CR groups conducted themselves, including her discussion of the moral principles which animated their respective trajectories, constitutes an ideal representation or model of what these educational sites were empirically and what they might become as future possibilities.

The CR group tradition is relevant for educators today because it represents a prototype of what a critically oriented gender-conscious democratic education looks like in practice. Despite the fact that the CR groups are not comparable in certain respects to democratic-friendly State-sponsored public school classrooms—here again, the public/private divide separates the two educational spheres—their respective aims and methods could still be said to run along similar conceptual tracks. Similar to democratic education at its best, the CR groups tended to treat one's personal experience as both a source of inquiry and as a catalyst for personal transformation. In addition, the feminist pedagogy animating the CR groups was dialogical, nonhierarchical, *parrhesiatic*, egalitarian, improvisational, and tended always to question inequalities wherever they were perceived to exist. This brief overview suggests that democratic teachers may need to "listen to" the insights afforded by the core concepts of feminist theory if we wish to better define and fulfill our own ends.

Making the personal political: The education of desire and purpose in the formation of democratic selfhood

John Dewey devoted his storied career to the historical project of weaning Americans away from what he considered to be our overly "State-centric" misunderstanding of democracy. The argument here is that the feminist rhetoric of the personal is political can serve as a theoretical compass to direct our pedagogical attention beyond a mere State-centered approach to the education of democratic citizens and toward a more personalized approach. Before developing this case further, however, we need to gain insight into why and how Americans were conditioned to adopt this problematic perception. Dewey identified two main causes underlying the formation of this socially constructed habit.[23]

First, the existence of a vast geographical frontier made it easier for many Americans to not really care about the cultural and educational task of debating the meaning of national identity or in seeing the benefits that could be derived from the debate itself (such as creating broader conceptions of the common good). With a seemingly infinite amount of land at the nation's disposal, Dewey noted that from the pioneer days up to the stock market crash of 1929, for most Americans, there seemed to be no appetite much less a moral imperative to wrestle with abstract notions of national purpose. Dewey wrote that for centuries the frontier's existence enabled a form of excessive individualism that imagined itself as the already finished moral equivalent of the common good— practically speaking, this species of selfhood was entirely of, by, and for itself. Writing in the midst of the Great Depression, then, Dewey was convinced that given the nation's radically transformed circumstances, it was no longer viable for Americans to live within an image of individualism and by extension, national identity that was defined in large part by its celebration of civic detachment.

The second cause Dewey identified as a factor inhibiting the development of American democracy resided ironically in the ingenuity of both the constitution's mechanical structure and the moral purposes set forth in the Preamble. The document's much-heralded checks and balances, its election cycles, its elasticity, its separation of Church from State, and its truly exceptional democratic rhetoric, produced a political culture in which too many came to believe our politics functioned like a Giant Clock. Once the mechanism was metaphorically wound-up, it would propel the nation's civic life ad infinitum in harmony with the Preamble's democratic vision. "The depth of the present crisis," Dewey warned, "is due in considerable part to the fact that, for a long period we acted as if our democracy were something that perpetuated itself automatically; as if our ancestors had succeeded in setting up a

machine that solved the problem of perpetual motion in politics."
As a counterpoise to the timid liberal republicanism the US
Constitution is well known to have encouraged, Dewey articulates
a humanistic, personalized conception of democracy.

> We can escape from this external way of thinking only as we
> realize in thought and act that democracy is a personal way of
> individual life; that it signifies the possession and continual use
> of certain attitudes, forming personal character and determining
> desire and purpose in all the relations of life.[24]

Here, we glimpse the essence of Dewey's conception of democracy.
It is not defined as an external institution located "out there"
symbolized by the State, but as something "in here" embodied
personally as a set of lived attitudes, desires and purposes. Let's
pause and consider the key analytical distinction that lies at the
center of the momentous paradigm-shift Dewey introduces; that is,
the distinction between democracy defined as virtually synonymous
with the external institutions of government and democracy
defined as a set of embodied spiritual and moral ideals. Recently,
Sheldon Wolin has described this significant analytical distinction in
language that reinforces Dewey's arguments: "The democratization
of politics remains merely formal without the democratization
of self. Democratization is not about being 'left alone' but about
becoming a self that sees the values of common involvements and
endeavors and finds in them a source of self-fulfillment."[25]

Wolin's assertion deserves close attention. For our purposes, its
primary value is that it raises a tricky educational question: How
can democratic teachers educate students to want to care not only
about the common good of the nation but also, in a cosmopolitan
sense, to care also about the ecological health of the planet? It
seems apparent that unless we attend to the prior education of this
emotional connection to and love for the world, as Hannah Arendt
so eloquently puts the issue, students will be denied opportunities
to experience common involvements and endeavors as sources of
self-fulfillment.[26]

For many reasons, then, it is a matter of great consequence
whether Americans learn to see democracy primarily as an
(internal) moral quality or as an (external) set of electoral processes

and official buildings (put crudely but accurately). We need to fully grasp the pedagogical implications that accompany this sea change in perception of what democracy is—and what it is not. To be sure, a personalized conception of democracy requires for its development a radically different kind of education than what we are used to seeing. How then to define and theoretically unpack the spiritual and moral dimensions of democratic personhood? Once defined and situated in a contemporary educational context, how can the capacities or potentialities of this formation be jostled into shape and drawn out pedagogically?

Before investigating these questions directly, it may be useful to state that when Dewey defines democracy as a mode of being rooted in certain moral ideals, he conceives of democratic education above all as a form of moral education. Thus, we could say, owing to the inherent personal character of morality, that democratic education is a site in which the personal and the political necessarily intersect. For some, such an assertion may seem unremarkable. For others, however, especially for those swayed by today's technocratic climate of presumed educational objectivity and political neutrality, Dewey's moral education for democracy could seem like a recipe for enlisting teachers to engage in forms of ideological indoctrination. The question of how democratic political educators might position themselves in relation to the predicament of indoctrination will be addressed in the following paragraphs. But first I want to offer a few preliminary remarks in order to situate this ethical dilemma in its specific American context.

To begin, it cannot be overemphasized that Dewey claimed that the depth of our crisis with respect to democracy was traced in "considerable part" to the flawed idea that most Americans unselfconsciously held, namely, the assumption that democracy was something located outside of us as individuals. For Dewey, this dominant assumption had the practical effect of draining democracy of its personal and therefore of its moral (human) content. The meaning of democracy, in effect, was narrowly construed as a noun, and hence this limited social imaginary precluded democracy from being defined and *experienced* in its active form as a verb. Dewey cautioned that there could be no quick method for unseating the cultural power of this habitual perception, save for persuasively highlighting democracy's true status as a moral ideal. "For to get rid of the habit of thinking of democracy as something institutional and external and to *acquire the habit of treating it as a way of personal life* is to realize that democracy is a moral ideal and so far as it becomes a fact is a moral fact. It is to realize that *democracy is a reality only as it is indeed a commonplace of living"*[27] (my emphasis).

Considering Dewey's democratic conception of education, it is stunningly apparent that for teachers to journey metaphorically toward the deeper layers of their students' psyches and to seek to draw out desires to engage the democratic values and to form democratic ends, they need to divest themselves of the conventional thinking that democracy can be meaningfully taught through a focus on the mechanical procedures of the State, such as learning how a bill becomes a law, and so on.

Learning to *be* democratic, as opposed to learning *about* democratic mechanisms and procedures, requires the cultivation of several interrelated personality traits. This cultivation is grounded far more in the mobilization of new desires and new purposes than it is in inculcating or implanting pieces of knowledge into students from external sources. The formation of democratic citizens depends on how these desires and purposes are drawn-out, turned around, sparked, or rechanneled, to mention a few metaphors commonly deployed to capture liberatory educational processes.

Learning to be democratic involves learning not only to question but also to find pleasure and meaning in its subversive beauty, for example, to appreciate its capacity to destroy obsolete ideas and to create new ones. Democratic theorist Cornelius Castoriadis claims that questioning forms the very basis of democratic culture and without the presence of this vital principle within democracies, they will inevitably devolve into one form of tyranny or another.[28]

As has already been suggested, teaching for democracy involves developing in students a passion for public affairs, for caring about people outside one's private orbit, the vital precondition for continually expanding one's image of the common good. It means always pursuing "knowledge of conditions as they are,"[29] a principle that put into practice guarantees to generate civic controversies for student consideration and debate. Being democratic means learning to engage in dialogue, especially with those who think differently than we do; this disposition, of course, is impossible to actualize without an ability and willingness to listen. It also means learning to exercise our imaginations so that we can continually revise our perceptions of ourselves and of the world. It means developing a sense of the moral equality of all human beings and to think deeply about what it means to say that everyone has a right to live in dignity under conditions of justice.] Surely, democracy also involves learning how to debate competing interpretations of justice and every other contested democratic principle.[30] It means having faith in the possibilities of human nature to transcend social determination. It means learning to appreciate and honor the role of dissent and dissenters as a requirement for the progressive renewal of democratic culture.[31] Although this roster could include other valid developmental qualities crucial to democratic culture, I hope this impressionistic snapshot is sufficient to suggest the direction teachers need to move toward in order to reframe the purposes of a personalized democratic education.

In reviewing these character traits, we could conjecture that all of them are innate to human beings as potentialities, as part of the psychic equipment of the human inheritance. However, there is absolutely nothing innate about their conscious social development. None of these capabilities come fully developed in any of us. Without their active and sustained development, and without a public commitment to the cultivation of these personal yet civic-oriented virtues, democracies must inevitably degenerate into a sea of isolated empty-shelled noncitizens, a transformation not unlike how Plato describes the devolution of democracy into oligarchy and tyranny.[32] It is precisely democracy's vulnerability to the internal disease of collective ignorance—in contrast to Dewey's ideal of "public collective intelligence"[33]—that is cited as the main reason why the legitimacy of democratic republics is said to hinge upon the quality of education these regimes choose to provide their young.

With these preliminary background remarks in mind, we are now positioned to consider how democratic educators can best negotiate their relationship to the issue of indoctrination in education. This predicament thickens considerably when we apply the personal is political not only to the task of educating for democracy as a mode of being but also as a heuristic device to illuminate the kind of teacher-identity required for teachers to educate for democracy at these so-called deeper levels.

Teachers as lovers or managers?
Reflections on the impossibility
of teacher neutrality

Let's begin with an obvious statement of fact, but one that some may find controversial: that the dominant educational regime operative today—NCLB, and its ideological progeny, NCLB-ism—is nothing if not an elaborate form of indoctrination. Since its inception we have witnessed the demotion of both civic education and the humanities nationwide.[34] Are we to believe that the demotion of these noble curricular traditions somehow represents a politically "neutral" law and policy? Would it not be justified to regard this *absence of caring* in relation to the personal and civic development of the nation's youth as a kind of "indoctrination"? Furthermore, would it not be safe to assert that NCLB retards the civic literacy of students not only by slashing instructional time in these subject areas but also by the dreary reduction of the K-12 social studies curriculum to the rote memorization of isolated facts? Arguably, the real question is not *if* NCLB represents a form of indoctrination but rather *how* it indoctrinates and to what effect, personally and civically. As Elliot Eisner cogently demonstrated decades ago with his concept of the "null curriculum," that which is *absent* from the curriculum can have as powerful a shaping influence on identity formation as that which is "in" the curriculum.[35]

The most important question, therefore, is not whether NCLB represents a form of indoctrination but rather how teachers who implement a robust democratic moral education might situate themselves in relation to the problem of indoctrination. Rather than trying to reinvent the wheel with respect to this complicated negotiation, it may be wise to briefly consider the incredibly rich debates that broke out among radical democratic educators during the 1930s over precisely this issue. When George Counts presented a series of controversial papers on the subject of indoctrination at the National Education Association conference in 1932, he created a legendary ruckus in progressive educational circles. Counts' message hit the audience like a thunderclap:

> If progressive education is to be genuinely progressive, it must emancipate itself from the influence of class, face squarely and

courageously every social issue, come to grips with life in all its stark reality, establish an organic relationship with the community, develop a realistic and comprehensive theory of welfare, fashion a compelling vision of human destiny, and become less frightened than it is today at the bogies of *imposition* and indoctrination.[36]

The intensity of interest aroused by these controversial words prompted several faculty members at Teachers College Columbia University, led by Counts and William Heard Kilpatrick, to launch a new journal, *The Social Frontier*. It would be the journal's mission to provide a public forum for educators to think through this vexatious ideological predicament and more generally to consider the educational challenges posed by the project of social reconstruction.

James Giarelli provides a comprehensive examination of these debates which he maintains are as relevant today as they were in the 1930s. Giarelli frames the core problem:

> There is no such thing as an objective, value-free, or neutral education. But does this mean all education must be some form of indoctrination? Is any attempt to influence, impose, guide or direct the educated about some point of view about the nature of the good life, even if this point of view is supported by reasons and evidence, an instance of manipulation?[37]

According to Giarelli, based on their responses to these questions, the social frontiersmen cannot be considered a monolithic bunch. Despite their general agreement on the ideal outcomes of democratic education, degrees of difference emerged regarding the best methods to be employed to attain these ends. Giarelli observes that standard interpretations of *The Social Frontier* debates divide their disagreements into two camps. One group "demanded a well-defined social vision (democratic socialism), and advocated a no-nonsense program of indoctrinating students into the norms and attitudes of democratic collectivist citizenship." The other group, which included Dewey, "believed that democratic ends could not be achieved through nondemocratic means and that the democratic faith required a belief that the natural workings of creative and critical intelligence on the social issues at hand would lead to a commitment to democratic ideals."[38]

Giarelli points out that this either/or picture is too simplistic. It tends to overlook the "dialectical" interpretation that coalesced as a result of the creative tensions that came to the fore within the pages of the journal as these thinkers wrestled with the question of indoctrination. He argues that *The Social Frontier*'s legacy, at least as it has influenced critical educational theory over the last several decades, inspired pedagogies that consciously seek to engage these various tensions rather than ignoring them. As a consequence of these historic debates, Giarelli writes that theorists have sought to respect the "means-end continuum," and they have attempted to "overcome indoctrination through methods of dialogue, demystification and participation, and by analyzing how the schools and social life both limit and sanction creative thought."[39] On my reading, Giarelli is exactly right to identify the chief "dialectical" value of *The Social Frontier*'s legacy as that of a tart recommendation for democratic educators to learn to live with and thrive from a permanent lack of closure with regard to the question of indoctrination.

Given these notorious complications, perhaps a personalized democratic education could be best framed as a form of "critical indoctrination."[40] The problem which immediately arises with this designation, however, is that when such an education is done well, it doesn't comport with textbook images of indoctrination. In fact, when done well, a paradox comes to light: democratic education may be said to indoctrinate students so that they may avoid being indoctrinated. The question thus arises: What label can we invoke to capture this phenomenon? Owing to the paradoxical quality of this interpretive dilemma, three additional caveats need to be offered, the outlines of which Giarelli has already mapped. First, democratic education could be called critical indoctrination based on the assumption that a self-identified democratic culture must, in some fashion, introduce/impose and promote the democratic values and principles within its educational institutions if it hopes to reproduce itself as a democracy.

Second, a democratic education questions its own purposes; at their best, democratic educators question their own cherished doctrines. Thus if we are going to define this type of education as indoctrination, its posture of ongoing critical analysis would seem to keep its practitioners alert to the most egregious examples of this phenomenon which, after all, is intrinsic to all education. That the development of the critical faculties is so vital to democratic education also suggests the degree to which democracy requires philosophy as a condition of its own possibility. For, if philosophy symbolizes the impulse toward self and civic interrogation, as in the Socratic tradition, it is this very quality of self-criticism that renders cultural democracy revisable.[41]

The third reason why a democratic education could plausibly be framed as a critical indoctrination is that all of the democratic traits and dispositions previously enumerated—questioning, passion for public affairs, dialogue, listening, revisability, honoring dissent, etc.—rely for their coming into being on an educational process of "drawing-out" rather than on "implanting" or "depositing" knowledge and information. The developmental (and noncoercive) image of "drawing-out" is crucial here because it refers to education as the stimulation of latent human capacities such as the desire to know and to question. The legitimacy of a democratic education is anchored in its ability to spark curiosities and to inflame desires to know—where exactly these inquiries lead is a secondary concern. Thus, the value of democratic education is at once not only political (citizenship) but also personal and philosophical: We want students to embark on their own autonomously authored knowledge quests, an end-in-view which can never be attained simply by depositing finished pieces of knowledge into students from external sources.

In attempting to come to grips with the issue of indoctrination in democratic education, we arrive finally at the question of teacher-identity. It has been said previously that the rhetoric of the personal is political can and should be seen as a valuable resource in terms of giving point and direction to what it means to teach for democracy as a mode of being. But the phrase also has implications in terms of illuminating the kind of teacher-identity that's required to catalyze democratic education to its higher levels.

For good reason, the social frontiersman blasted the idea and practice of teacher neutrality. Dewey, for one, stated that the practice of teacher neutrality had the destructive effect of "keeping the oncoming generation ignorant of the conditions in which they live and the issues they have to face."[42] It is perfectly obvious that when Dewey called for teachers to make education "an instrument in the active and constant suppression of the war spirit," when he urged teachers to resist "every subtle appeal of sinister class interest," and when he admonished teachers to define themselves as the "consecrated servants of the democratic ideas," he was abandoning the very idea of teacher neutrality.[43]

How can teachers be "consecrated servants of the democratic ideas" and maintain their neutrality? No doubt, an impossible task! The term *consecrated* after all, is an iconic religious symbol aligned with the concept of the *holy*. In a sense, then, we can interpret Dewey's *holy charge* to teachers as an expression of his conception of democracy as a secular religious project.[44] Dewey believed that democracy should be capable of stirring up the same kind of emotional intensities and devotions that religions commonly inspire—however he wrote that the spiritual wellsprings of its being had yet to be fully cultivated educationally. He lamented that in failing to properly grasp the "spiritual element" of its democratic tradition, Americans also failed to grasp the transcendent dimensions of its own identity.[45] Arguably, this elevated conception of democracy and its formative influence on national identity "happens" at the permeable intersection where the personal meets the political. Today, I would like to think that Dewey would offer a toast to teachers who see in this piece of civic rhetoric a pedagogical guide both for democratizing American education and for encouraging teachers to see the love of democracy—including its consciousness-raising potential—as the animating principle in defining who they are as teachers.

Notes

1 See "The Personal is the Political." Carole Pateman, *The Disorder of Women: Democracy, Feminism and Political Theory* (Stanford, CA: Stanford University Press, 1989), 131–4.

2 It is not my intention to offer a substantive review of the feminist literature on the theoretically dense philosophical debates surrounding the public/private distinction. My reference to this conceptual divide is limited to identifying the historical and discursive origins of the phrase as a form of civic rhetoric.

3 Jean Bethke Elshtain, *Public Man, Private Woman: Women in Social and Political Thought*. Princeton, NJ: Princeton University Press, 1981/1993), 12.

4 See, for example, Catherine A. MacKinnon, "Consciousness-Raising." *Toward a Feminist Theory of State* (Cambridge, MA: Harvard University Press, 1989), 83–105.

5 Linda Napikoski, http://womenshistory.about.com/bio/Linda-Napikoski-70961.htm

6 John Dewey, "The Ethics of Democracy." *The Collected Works of John Dewey, 1882–1953*, ed. Jo Ann Boydston (Carbondale: Southern Illinois University Press, 1981), 240.

7 The article was first published in *Notes from the Second Year: Women's Liberation: Major Writings of the Radical Feminist* (New York: Feminist Revolution, 1970), 204–5. Both the original article and Carol Hanisch's 2006 "Introduction" to it can be found at http://carolhanisch.org/CHArticlesList.html (subsequent references to both titles will be cited as Hanisch 1970 or 2006).

8 Hanisch, 1970.

9 MacKinnon, 100.

10 Ibid., 83–4.

11 Hanisch, 1970.

12 For a comprehensive treatment of feminist pedagogy, see Frances A. Maher and Mary Kay Thompson Tetreault, *The Feminist Classroom* (New York: HarperCollins, 1994).

13 See Paulo Freire, *Pedagogy of the Oppressed.* (New York: Continuum Books, 1970/2010), 77–86.

14 See Kathleen Weiler, "Freire and a Feminist Pedagogy of Difference." *Harvard Educational Review* 4 (November 1991): 449–74; bell hooks, "Paulo Freire." In *Teaching to Transgress: Education as the Practice of Freedom* (New York: Routledge, 1994), 45–58.

15 Hanisch, 1970.

16 See Kerry Burch, "Parrhesia as a Principle of Democratic Pedagogy." *Philosophical Studies in Education*, 40, 2009, 71–82.

17 For an edifying feminist discussion of *parrhesia* as embodied by Emma Goldman, consult Kathy E. Ferguson's, *Emma Goldman: Political Thinking in the Streets* (Lanham, MD: Rowman & Littlefield, 2011), 24, 33, 39–40, 54–5.

18 Hanisch, 2006.

19 Hanisch, 2006.

20 Jim Garrison, "A Deweyan Theory of Democratic Listening" *Educational Theory*, Fall 1996, 46, 429.

21 Ibid., 450–1.

22 The essential features of the "fallibilistic mentality" are adroitly captured in Richard Bernstein's *The Abuse of Evil: The Corruption of Politics since 9/11* (Malden, MA: Polity Press, 2005), 29.

23 John Dewey, "Creative Democracy—the Task before Us." Eds Larry A. Hickman and Thomas M. Alexander, *The Essential Dewey: Volume 1: Pragmatism, Education, Democracy*. Bloomington, IN: Indiana University Press, 1998), 340–3.

24 Dewey, Creative Democracy, 341.

25 Sheldon Wolin, *Democracy, Inc: Managed Democracy and the Specter of Inverted Totalitarianism*. (Princeton, NJ: Princeton University Press, 2008), 289.

26 Hannah Arendt, "The Crisis in Education." *Between Past and Future* (New York: Viking Press, 1968), 196.

27 Dewey, Creative Democracy, 342–3.

28 Cornelius Castoriadis, "The Problem of Democracy Today" *Democracy & Nature*, 8, 1995, 18–35.

29 Dewey, Creative Democracy, 343.

30 Diana E. Hess, *Controversy in the Classroom: The Democratic Power of Discussion* (New York: Routledge, 2009).

31 For more on the "Socratic" connection between dissent and the revisability of democracy, see Josiah Ober, "How to Criticize Democracy in Late Fifth-And Fourth-Century Athens." In *The Athenian Revolution: Essays on Ancient Greek Democracy and Political Theory* (Princeton, NJ: Princeton University Press, 1996), 140–60.

32 This devolution is depicted in Book 8 of the *Republic*. Joe Sachs, transl. Plato, *Republic* (Newburyport, MA: Focus Publishing, 2007).

33 John Dewey, Democracy is Radical, 339.

34 Martha Nussbaum's, *Not for Profit: Why Democracy Needs the Humanities* (Princeton, NJ: Princeton University Press, 2010) is a wonderfully written philosophical analysis of why it is so profoundly important to reverse this anti-intellectual trend sweeping the United States and other parts of the world under the rationalizing discourses of globalization.

35 Elliot Eisner, *The Educational Imagination: On the Design and Evaluation of School Programs* (New York: Macmillan Publishers, 1979), 83–92.

36 George S. Counts, *Dare the School Build a New Social Order?* (Carbondale: Southern Illinois University Press, 1932/1978), 7. An outstanding resource for readers interested in learning more about the contents of *The Social Frontier*, see Eugene F. Provenzo, Jr, ed., *The Social Frontier: A Critical Reader* (New York: Peter Lang, 2011).

37 James M. Giarelli, "The Social Frontier 1934–43: Retrospect and Prospect." Michael E. James, ed., *Social Reconstruction through Education: The Philosophy, History, & Curricula of a Radical Idea.* (Norwood, NJ: Ablex Publishing, 1995), 33.

38 Ibid., 34.

39 Ibid., 39.

40 For this formulation, I am indebted to my colleague at Northern Illinois University, Dr Linda O'Neill.

41 It is meaningful that democracy and philosophy emerged as regimes of questioning at roughly the same historical moment. See, for example, Cornel West, *Democracy Matters* (New York: Penguin Books, 2004); Sara Monoson, *Plato's Democratic Entanglements: Athenian Politics and the Practice of Democracy* (Princeton, NJ: Princeton University Press, 2000).

42 John Dewey, "Education and Social Change." Eugene F. Provenzo, Jr, ed., *The Social Frontier: A Critical Reader* (New York: Peter Lang, 2011), 218–19.

43 John Dewey, "Nationalizing Education," Eds Larry A. Hickman and Thomas M. Alexander, *The Essential Dewey: Volume 1: Pragmatism, Education, Democracy* (Bloomington, IN: Indiana University Press, 1998), 269.

44 Richard Rorty articulates this Deweyan theme in *Achieving Our Country: Leftist Thought in Twentieth-Century America* (Cambridge, MA: Harvard University Press, 1998), 15–38.

45 John Dewey, "The House Divided against Itself." In *Individualism Old and New* (Amherst, NY: Prometheus Books, 1929/1999), 9.

EPILOGUE

Educating the *souls* of democratic folk

Through a critical investigation of eight pieces of public rhetoric in American political culture, previous chapters tell a story of how the negotiation of national identity consists in epic clashes between competing value systems and competing systems of cultural heroism. Today it is commonplace to conceive of American identity as a site of unremitting conflict and contestation. With the advent of the 24/7 news cycle and proliferation of media, this feature of national identity has become increasingly apparent to a critical mass of Americans. A glance at our intellectual history further reinforces this image, but from a different if not more penetrating angle: The antifoundational traditions of both American pragmatism and postmodernism seem to have made it is easier for many to acknowledge that no such thing as an "objectively existent" American identity exists.[2] The sense of impending crisis that grows out of this recognition is not going away nor should we expect it to. Instead, we should learn to recalibrate our relation to this condition of permanent crisis. If American identity is better characterized by its absences and its fluidities than by any prefixed given nature, critical pedagogues need to recognize that these open spaces, as difficult as they may seem to negotiate, also make possible a national identity formation more susceptible to democratic transformation than we tend to think.

Surely, a condition of ontological absence has always functioned as a hidden factor in the social construction of American identity, as it tends to be hidden within all national identity formations.[3] For many historical, geographical and demographical reasons, the "imagined community" of American nationhood is infinitely more fragile and dependent upon representational strategies than other national identity designations.

Democratic Transformations affirms this insight as a positive historical development. It celebrates the absences and fluidities (and fragilities) contained within the national identity, including those qualities closely associated with this condition—its festering contradictions, its vexing paradoxes, its endless ambiguities, and its tragic ironies. As indispensable as it is for educators to bring these repressed dimensions of American identity to light, while writing *Democratic Transformations*, I became convinced that in order for the book to contribute to the democratic project in education, it had to offer readers something beyond a mere chronicle of contradiction and other difficult-to-assimilate characteristics of American identity.

In every chapter, I have suggested that an ongoing critical analysis of the defining contradictions simmering beneath the surface of US political culture has the potential to serve a high educational purpose. On this point, let us recall the Socratic/Freirean learning theory underlying the structure of the book: That when individuals learn to perceive contradictions (located inside oneself and/or externally in society), they will tend to experience a heightened state of internal tension brought about by this emergent perception of opposing viewpoints and value systems. In this manner, by identifying the contradictions sequestered within each of these eight phrases, I hope to have created for readers' opportunities to frame novel questions—questions called forth and structured by the perception of these various contradictions.

The heightened states of internal tension that such questions can elicit generally do not produce comforting feelings. On the contrary, they tend to produce psychic disturbances. Yet these inner states of disequilibrium do have the advantage of being able to *propel* new desires to know into existence. To reiterate a point made in the Prologue, *Democratic Transformations* is not intended to be a tidy answer-based book nor is it intended to prescribe well-defined policy initiatives. Rather its purpose is to create the conditions for readers in which newly minted curiosities and inquiries might be sparked into being. Put differently, the *acquisition* of knowledge regarding aspects of US political and educational culture has been secondary to the prior and more crucial goal of stimulating *desires for* knowledge—wherever they may lead. While it is true that the final sections of each chapter offer various "democratic" ways of "transforming" the civic tensions identified throughout the book, such experiments in democratic renovation are meant more to prompt new ways of seeing old problems than they are to roll out a set of unimpeachable policy reforms.

As I immersed myself in the literature surrounding these phrases (which was itself an unorthodox, idiosyncratic procedure), I was invariably "taken places" I didn't expect to go. Not a single chapter ended up the way I had anticipated. I hope readers share in my experience of being taken places they didn't expect to go, by inquiries they didn't expect to launch. In the initial stages of writing *Democratic Transformations*, I clung to the view that it would be sufficient for me to identify the contradictions, paradoxes, ambiguities, and ironies that, in my view, were absolutely indispensable to understanding the conflicted dynamics of the nation's past. I assumed that the identification of these historically marginalized dimensions, coupled with the new desires to know that might be catalyzed as a result of their identification, would provide ample justification for writing the book.

Over time, however, I gradually realized that this approach by itself would not be enough. For the sake of argument (I thought to myself) even if the United States were to undergo radical democratization, these existential strands of the national identity would never be mitigated, overcome, and transcended. Suddenly, the thought occurred to me that what *could* change, what *could* help bring about greater democratization, was *how* we perceived and thought through our relationship to these liminal dimensions of national identity.[4] How might we better negotiate our relation to the contradictions, paradoxes, ambiguities, and ironies of our history far more honestly than we had to date? How could teachers turn around their students' perception of these existential qualities and experiences so that instead of denying or being revolted by them—as the dominant culture teaches—they might actually learn to learn from them?

It was during these moments of rethinking the thrust of my book that I remembered something I'd read years earlier by Cornel West regarding the intriguing conceptual affinities between democracy as a way of life and jazz as a musical idiom. Could it be possible, I wondered, that a wider appreciation of the jazz idiom could help us to think differently about these difficult-to-assimilate dimensions of the national identity? Could the development of such an appreciation enable us to see and think differently about what makes a democracy a democracy? It seemed to me that the development of such an aesthetic literacy would have profound implications for redefining American selfhood in addition to deepening our grasp of democracy as a personal way of life.

At first, I looked skeptically at this development. I was not keen about the prospect of a nonmusician theorizing about the political and educational potential of jazz music to enhance the democratic project. Despite some initial misgivings born from my own lack of knowledge about jazz, the more I studied the jazz-as-democracy metaphor, the more I was reminded how musical metaphors are employed by many of the intellectual heavyweights throughout Western history to convey their deepest insights about politics, identity formation, and the quest for justice. Soon I dispensed with my cautious reservations.

Plato, for example, theorized that music should be regarded as a vital element in the education of the young. He wrote that early exposure to musical harmony, when properly internalized, can function as a symbolic prototype to enhance peoples' ability later in life to harmonize the conflicting parts of their psyche into a state of balance—a kind of psychic equilibrium that was tantamount to the achievement of "justice."[5] Along with Plato, I think we need to take more seriously than we have the ways in which music and musical metaphors can illuminate the structure of the psyche and its dialectical relation to "the city." In a 1915 American context, John Dewey and Horace Kallen exchanged fascinating letters on the merits of conceiving of American identity as a metaphoric "symphony orchestra," even as they grappled with the centrifugal forces the notion of cultural pluralism posed to images of a unified national identity. Dewey approved of Kallen's symphony ideal with the proviso that a true national metaphoric orchestra would have to share some common aims rather than being an assemblage of instruments playing music without reference to an image of a common good.[6]

More recently, as Nancy Love argues in her innovative book, *Musical Democracy*, Jurgen Habermas and John Rawls deploy musical metaphors as a central part of their democratic justice-seeking political philosophies.[7] And as we observed in Chapter five, the primary justification I advanced for defining a reinvigorated musical education as a Jamesian "moral equivalent of war" stemmed from Horace Mann's conviction that music represented an emotionally powerful vehicle of human flourishing (a conviction shared by one of America's preeminent public philosophers, Martha Nussbaum). The legitimacy of adopting a "sonic metaphor" for advancing democratic pedagogy was further reinforced when I reread W. E. B. Du Bois, and was reminded again that musical metaphors are central to his democratic educational philosophy.

The title of the Epilogue is a riff on Du Bois' *The Souls of Black Folk*. In the first instance, the title extends Du Bois' concept of "double-consciousness" to describe not just the interior duality of black folk but the interior duality of American folk generally in reference to democracy. As each chapter has sought to demonstrate, our democratic traditions and impulses are "contradicted" by opposing cultural values (imperialism, atomistic individualism, historical amnesia, etc.). This gives all Americans a kind of double consciousness in relation to our democratic ideals. In the second instance, "Educating the Souls of Democratic Folk" echoes Du Bois' conviction that "Negro" music could impart a soulfulness (as a set of emotional attributes) to help humanize and democratize the atomistic and racist tendencies of American identity.[8]

In the final chapter of *Souls*, "The Sorrow Songs," Du Bois proposes that the greatest gift the Negro people could bequeath to America would be their musical tradition and specifically the spiritual insights this tradition could offer the nation. While it is true that Du Bois was not referring to jazz or to the blues at the time he published *Souls* (in 1903, neither idiom had been named as such), the fact remains that both of these related musical idioms grew directly out of the tradition that he was attempting to identify. Du Bois places this spiritual heritage in context:

Little of beauty has America given the world save the rude grandeur God himself stamped on her bosom; the human spirit in this new world has expressed itself in vigor and ingenuity rather than in beauty. And so by fateful chance the Negro folk-song—the rhythmic cry of the slave—stands today not simply as the sole American music, but as the most beautiful expression of human experience born this side the seas. It has been neglected, it has been, and is, half despised, and above all it has been persistently mistaken and misunderstood; but notwithstanding, it still remains the singular spiritual heritage of the nation and the greatest gift of the Negro people.[9]

When Du Bois further writes that "the gift of story and song—soft stirring melody in an ill-harmonized and unmelodious land,"[10] he's employing musical symbols to describe a culture beset with internal division and willful ignorance about the ongoing racial injustices which continued to define American culture. Significantly, he claimed that an integration of the Negro's musical spiritual heritage into the broader American culture could play an educative role in the process of fulfilling its democratic ideals. Rodino F. Anderson interprets the contemporary meaning of Du Bois' bold assertion:

> The gift is not simply the singing of songs, but the message and the expression of human experience they express. This gift of the American Negro, for Du Bois, constitutes the first genuinely aesthetic mark of American culture. To place the Sorrow Songs at the center of American culture is to place the long, hard-fought struggle of a people for the very meaning of freedom as *the* struggle of American society . . . The Sorrow Songs are, then, the freedom music of America for it is those songs that always envisioned a better place for all in potent, poignant terms.[11]

As a thought-experiment, let's take a moment to develop this line of thinking. For example, if we were to place the Sorrow Songs at the front and center of American culture and, by extension, *a greater knowledge of and sensitivity to the blues and jazz traditions*, it could very well transform our understanding of the narrative of American exceptionalism (and thus, American identity itself). First, to accomplish this feat, we would need to recognize and then overcome the culturally conditioned forms of historical amnesia that daily prevent this centering from taking place. We would need to remind ourselves that unnecessary suffering and injustice still abound and thus the struggle for social justice must remain central—never peripheral—to America's civic self-conception.

Such a recovery of historical memory would suggest that the only justification for retaining a belief in the fantasy of American exceptionalism would be premised on the condition that the repressed night-side of American culture be kept at the forefront of our historical and civic awareness. In other words, the narrative of American exceptionalism would no longer rest on our military might, our global economic power, and surely not on our presumed moral superiority. Rather it would rest on the degree to which Americans remained alert to our social inequalities and injustices and committed to the unfinished democratic project. Such a rebooting of national identity would represent a democratic version of American exceptionalism that even an unsentimental critic like Du Bois might be comfortable with.

As we have seen throughout the pages of *Democratic Transformations*, four separate but highly interrelated conceptual motifs have been highlighted as sources of civic tension and difficult negotiation within US political culture: individualism/individuality, democracy/imperialism, historical amnesia and the politics of forgetting, and the ambiguous status of American exceptionalism. Of course, the use of these four motifs as a means to "factor down" the complexity of the American cultural and political landscape is a limited framework, one intended only to approximate some of the dissonances (and prophetic visions) operative in American political culture. To bring this book to its conclusion, then, I want to map the conceptual affinities that link democracy as a personal mode of being to jazz as a musical idiom, with a specific focus on how this conceptual linkage may fruitfully elucidate the formation of individuality and the common good as complex democratic achievements.

What jazz music can teach us about the education of democratic souls

As previously mentioned, appropriating the jazz idiom as a framework for clarifying the democratic negotiation of national identity is not an original idea. Nonetheless, it is a metaphor and discourse that hasn't been nearly as appreciated, utilized, or theoretically developed as it should be. For this reason, I want to further develop the case that jazz is uniquely endowed to reveal not only democracy's distinctive character as a personality formation but also America's distinctive character as an imagined community (keeping in mind that Dewey regarded democracy and America as interchangeable terms, at least at the normative level insofar as what *should* be the case).

Regarding the hoped-for similitude or symbiosis between democracy and America, Ralph Ellison refers to jazz as a vehicle "that speaks eloquently to the United States' predicament as a still-forming nation, black, brown, beige, that is still in a state of nakedness . . . but this nakedness allows for a greater degree of personal improvisation, and with the least hindrance from traditional social forms, rituals, manners, etc."[12] Here, Ellison identifies one of the most frequently cited conceptual affinities that link jazz to democracy—that in their finest moments, both jazz and American democracy embody *forms* that have a perpetually-in-motion, improvisational quality. In the previous chapter, we observed that democracy as a mode of being relies on improvisation and revision as a means for renewing itself when old forms or ways of doing things prove untenable or obsolete. In the language of the Declaration of Independence, for example, Americans accorded themselves the right to revolution, that is, the right to create new forms. The US Constitution's amendment process similarly codifies permanent revisability as a defining feature of our democratic-inspired political culture.

Robert O'Meally captures this particular conceptual affinity between democracy and jazz with great cogency: "According to this jazz/democracy perspective, in the growing blueprint society that is the United States we are all improvisers, making it up as we go along and depending on flexibility and resiliency—both hallmarks of the music—to make our way together. In a nation requiring resiliency as a prime trait, jazz is the canonical sound track."[1] A large part of the attraction we feel toward jazz derives from our not knowing what rhythmic or melodic variations might come next; this heightened anticipation is not only pleasurable as an aesthetic delight but also analogous to the unfinished trajectory of American democracy itself.

Martin Williams, in discussing the freedom to improvise in jazz, also points out that improvising should *not* be seen as a purely individual practice. As we saw in Chapter six, while the individual is a cornerstone of democratic culture, too much of an emphasis on the self to the exclusion of others actually destroys democracy. Therefore, for improvisation in jazz to be fully realized, the group must be seen as a central part of the musical equation.

> In all its styles, jazz involves some degree of collective ensemble improvisation, and this differs from Western music even at those times in its history when improvisation was required. The high degree of individuality, together with the mutual respect and co-operation required in a jazz ensemble carry with them philosophical implications that are so exciting and far-reaching that one almost hesitates to contemplate them. It is as if jazz were saying to us that *not only is far greater individuality possible to man than he has so far allowed himself, but that such individuality, far from being a threat to a co-operative social structure, can actually enhance society.*[14]

The exciting and far-reaching "philosophical implications" of jazz to which Williams refers reminds us of Dewey's and Wolin's efforts, seen in previous chapters, to theorize a species of individuality capable of listening to others and learning from them as a means for developing affections for the common good. Williams states that jazz requires improvisational spirits and collaborative attitudes ("mutual respect and cooperation"). When these attributes are in full play, individual and group interests become not only reconcilable but *mutually educable*. Thus, the beauty of engaging in democratic deliberation is that when conflicting parties learn to learn from each other, both are transformed to higher planes of civic reciprocity, a virtual precondition for fostering conflict resolution.

The following passage from Dewey describing the communicative essence of democracy can easily be applied to the communicative or dialogical essence of jazz: "For every way of life that fails in its democracy limits the contacts, the exchanges, the communications, the interactions by which experience is steadied while it is also enlarged and enriched."[15] Good jazz, like good democracy, requires environments of free exchange, discovery and surprise, spaces in which individuals are encouraged to listen, collaborate, and revise. At their best, both forms create educative spaces in which the fulfillment of individuality and the common good can be "harmonized" at higher levels than would be possible were there no sense of mutual recognition between the individual and the group.

Reinforcing yet another dimension of the jazz/democracy connection, Albert Murray suggests that the dialogic aspects of jazz are applicable to many realms of human endeavor, including political procedures:

> As a matter of fact, the jazz musician is always engaged in a dialogue or a conversation or even argument—not only, as in a jam session, with his peers—but also with all other music and musicians in the world at large. Indeed, his is an ongoing dialogue with the form itself. He achieves his individuality by saying "yes and also" to that which he agrees, and by saying "no," or in any case, "on the other hand" to that which he disagrees. Yes, all of this is as applicable to science and engineering and political procedure as it is to music and literature and all of the other arts.[16]

The jazz musician, in short, must be just as adept at listening and dialoguing as any democratic citizen. For without this quality of dialogue or conversation or even argument, there can be no give-and-take, no enlargement of purpose and meaning, and thus no growth. The process Murray sketches dovetails with Dewey's oft-noted belief that democratic individuality is dependent upon dialogue, insofar as "each has to refer his own actions to that of others, and to consider the action of others to give point and direction to his own."[17]

Philosopher Cornel West, a self-described "jazzman in the life of the mind," insists that all jazz artists are of necessity conversant with the voices of the past, that is, they are conversant with a tradition. He attaches great import to the integral relation between "voice" and "music" as two things that could not be denied to an enslaved people: "Owing to white supremacist sanctions, enslaved Africans were not allowed to read or write. As a non-literate people, we learned to manifest our genius through what no one could take away—our voices and our music."[18] West observes that contemporary literary artist, Toni Morrison, said that she would like to write the way that Sarah Vaughn sings, to which West adds: "did not Ralph Ellison try to write like Louis Armstrong blew his horn?"[19] Expanding on the vital relation between the development of one's authentic voice and musical expression, West writes:

> The irony is that you can't find your voice unless you're bouncing off the voices of the dead. That's where tradition plays a role. There's no Wynton Marsalis without Duke Ellington. Duke is the voice of the dead. Now Wynton is in deep conversation. He's in relation so he can create by finding his own voice. He is relating to someone who has expressed his voice in such a profound way. You get this wonderful interplay between past and present, which creates a new future musically.[20]

Extrapolating from West's analysis, we could safely conjecture that democracy as a mode of being is also dependent on individuals finding if not creating anew their own voice as a prerequisite for achieving the higher reaches of democratic selfhood. Similarly, Dewey writes that the fulfillment of democracy depends on people's ability to be conversant with its memory and tradition: "democracy has been finely termed the memory of an historic past, the consciousness of a living present, the idea of a coming future."[21] Put differently, if democratic citizens have no sense of historical awareness, they cannot be viable democratic citizens. Just as jazz players need to bounce off the voices of the dead to actualize their own musical expressions, so, too, do democratic citizens need to bounce off their own traditions to actualize their own potential for civic transformation.

Jazz players and theorists alike also emphasize that part of the significance of the musical idiom resides "in the *making* of jazz," that is, in the moment-to-moment, impossible to predict construction of beautiful sounds. While jazz today is regularly put to sheet music and recited, jazz aficionados agree that the music's highest expressions occur when jazz players make or create music spontaneously in the moment. According to Kabir Sehgal, "this tradition of *making* music represents the triumph of the verb over the noun."[22] Similarly, as we saw in Chapter eight, a large part of the significance of democracy as a mode of being can also be seen in its making, in the courageous individual *enactments* of the democratic virtues without which these virtues become no more than abstract nouns written on paper, as opposed to action-oriented, soulful verbs.

Let us finally consider the relationship between the concept of swing and democracy as a mode of being. Louis "Satchmo" Armstrong (1901–71) has stated that the meaning of "swing" is directly related to the capacity of players to "cut loose" from the sheet music and to create a variation upon it. In his words: "Any average player can follow through a score, as it's written there in front of him on his instrument rack. But it takes a swing player to be able to leave that score and to know, or 'feel,' just when to leave it and when to go back to it. If he can't play away from the score, I don't want him."[23] Not surprisingly, when we compare Armstrong's interpretation of the swing concept to that of Duke Ellington's (1899–1974), we find striking similarities. Ellington provides a formal definition of the concept: "Swing is an unmechanical but hard-driving and fluid rhythm over which soloists improvise as they play."[24] In his essay explaining swing, Ellington highlights three of its crucial features.

In classical music, the composer and the conductor are all-important . . . But in swing the musician—the instrumentalist—is all-important: he must add something to the original composition and do it spontaneously—without preparation. And that's not all. Your good swing man must have a very deep feeling. If the feeling is honest, the music is honest. It is not pure showmanship that causes "Pee Wee" Russell, the great white clarinetist, to twist his eyebrows when swinging. Nor does Satchmo Armstrong sweat over his swinging trumpet for effect. A good swinger gives everything he's got each time he goes into action.[25]

Based on Ellington's conceptualization, we could speculate that to swing well, one must be one's own leader rather than being content to take cues from another, an orientation to the world which also holds true for the achievement of democratic individuality. The emphasis on "deep feeling" corresponds to the fact that democratic citizens must develop deep feelings of care for the democratic values if a viable democratic culture is to be fully realized. And if good swinging requires "giving everything one has" to each creative action one takes, it affirms the maxim that democracy cannot be anchored in a spectator view *of* the world but can only be brought about when one feels oneself to be a passionate participator *with* the world.

By way of conclusion, let's review some of the remarkable conceptual affinities that link jazz to democracy. Improvisation and revisability. Collaboration and dialogue. Individuality reconciled with the common good. The recovery of voice through the recovery of tradition. Making music versus reciting music. Being democratic versus reciting democratic procedures. The ability to swing (as a participator) versus the inability to swing (as a spectator). All of these affinities that bind jazz to democracy need to be fleshed-out conceptually and made more explicit in order to serve as a practical resource for democratic educators. Given these educationally significant linkages, the jazz as democracy metaphor seems to have the potential to transform how we think through many of the predicaments that confront the negotiation of American identity.[26]

It seems reasonable to assert that for Americans to enact a more democratic version of ourselves, we need to think differently about the contradictions, paradoxes, ambiguities, and ironies that are the stuff of our collective (and personal) experience. To date, the dominant culture and its educational institutions have been largely complicit in teaching its citizens not to recognize, much less celebrate, these existential qualities. This inquiry suggests that we need to turn this crusty old puritan page and rewrite these erotic qualities into the future fabric of America's national story.[27] In this project, the jazz-as-democracy metaphor can help us to navigate and to ultimately transform the way we *perceive* and *experience* and *negotiate* the conflicts that have historically roiled American identity. If placed in its proper educational context, this democratic sonic idiom could well alter our vicarious identifications with the symbol of America in such a way that the nation's previously untapped reservoirs of energy and daring could be drawn out and democratically reconceived.

Would it not be deliciously ironic were the souls of democratic folk to be nourished and redeemed through a recovery of that musical art form which represents America's greatest artistic contribution to the world? The development and practice of such a pedagogical art would encourage Americans to negotiate their personal and civic identities in a manner less beholden to the binary oppositions that have historically sustained the old regime of national identity. Among other benefits, a jazz-infused democratic pedagogy could offer opportunities for students to renegotiate the self/other relation and the relation between individualism and the common good, while also clarifying the meaning of democracy as a personal way of life. Considering these sublime possibilities, is it not the task before us to reawaken America's sense of democratic swing?

Notes

1 Excerpted from "The King Cake Walk" © 2000 Antonio J. García. All rights reserved. Used by permission. The presence of this musical bar by jazz composer Antonio J. Garcia is an homage to Du Bois's *The Souls of Black Folk*, a text that features musical bars before every chapter.

2 Although the literature on these subjects is vast, for an excellent overview of American pragmatism, see Cornel West, *The American Evasion of Philosophy: A Genealogy of Pragmatism* (Madison: University of Wisconsin Press, 1989). On the postmodern stance relative to the construction of American identity, see David Campbell, second edition, *Writing Security: United States Foreign Policy and the Politics of Identity* (Minneapolis: University of Minnesota Press, 1998).

3 For more on this "hidden" feature, see Campbell (fn 2) and Benedict Anderson, *Imagined Communities* (London: Verso Books, 1992/2006).

4 For a comprehensive and lucid treatment of the positive attributes of the liminal in education, see James Conroy, *Betwixt & Between: The Liminal Imagination, Education and Democracy* (New York: Peter Lang, 2004).

5 Two superb sources that elaborate on this principle are Eva Brann's, *The Music of the Republic* (Philadelphia: Paul Dry Books, 2004/2011) and Stanley Rosen's, *Plato's Republic: A Study* (New Haven: Yale University Press, 2008).

6 This exchange is discussed in Robert B. Westbrook, *John Dewey and American Democracy* (Ithaca: Cornell University Press, 1991), 213–14.

7 Nancy S. Love, *Musical Democracy* (Albany, SUNY Press, 2006), 17–66.

8 I retain the term "Negro" here in order to be consistent with Du Bois' text (which he uses despite the book's title).

9 W. E. B. Du Bois, *The Souls of Black Folk*, eds, Henry Louis Gates, Jr, and Terri Hume Oliver (Cambridge: W.W. Norton & Company, 1999), 155.

10 Ibid., 162.

11 Rodino F. Anderson, "W. E. B. Du Bois and an Education for Democracy and Creativity." David T. Hansen, ed. *Ethical Visions of Education: Philosophies in Practice* (New York: Teachers College Press, 2007), 55.

12 *Ralph Ellison's Jazz Writings: Living with Music*, ed. Robert G. O'Meally (New York: Modern Library, 2002), xii.

13 *The Jazz Cadence of American Culture*, ed. Robert O'Meally (New York: Columbia University Press, 1998), 118.

14 Martin Williams, *The Jazz Tradition*, second edition (New York: Oxford University Press, 1970/1993), 263 (my emphasis).

15 John Dewey, "Creative Democracy—The Task Before Us", eds, Larry A. Hickman and Thomas M. Alexander, *The Essential Dewey: Volume 1: Pragmatism, Education, Democracy* (Bloomington, IN: Indiana University Press, 1998), 343.

16 Albert Murray, "Improvisation and the Creative Process." In *The Jazz Cadence of American Culture*, ed. Robert O'Meally (New York: Columbia University Press, 1998), 113.

17 John Dewey, "The Democratic Conception in Education." In *Democracy and Education* (New York: The Macmillan Co., 1916/1958), 101.

18 Cornel West, "Music." *Hope on a Tightrope: Words & Wisdom* (New york: SmileyBooks, 2008), 110.

19 Ibid., 111.

20 Ibid., 113.

21 John Dewey, "The Ethics of Democracy." Jo Ann Boydston, ed., *Collected Writings, Early Works, Vol. 1* (Carbondale: Southern Illinois University Press, 1987), 240.

22 Kabir Sehgal, *Jazzocracy: Jazz, Democracy, & the Creation of a New American Mythology* (Mishawaka, IN: Better World Books, 2008), 25.

23 Louis Armstrong, "What is Swing?" in *Keeping Time: Readings in Jazz History*, ed. Robert Walser (New York: Oxford University Press, 1999), 74.

24 Duke Ellington, "Duke Ellington Explains Swing" in *Keeping Time: Readings in Jazz History*, ed. Robert Walser (New York: Oxford University Press, 1999), 109.

25 Ibid., 109.

26 For an innovative curricular resource to help students grasp the principles of democracy through a greater appreciation of jazz, consult the documentary video, *Let Freedom Swing: Conversations on*

Jazz and Democracy. The video was put together by Wynton Marsalis at the Lincoln Center Jazz Education program, in conjunction with former Supreme Court Justice Sandra Day O'Conner. It can be found at http://letfreedomswing.org.

27 Although some powerful cultural forces in the 1920s reviled jazz and denied that it had anything to do with "Culture," in 1987 the US Congress passed a resolution which stated that jazz was an "internationally acclaimed rare and valuable national treasure." Its proponents no doubt wanted to build a case for more energetic funding for public music education and for the humanities in general. Congressional Record—House, September 23, 1987, H7825–27.

ACKNOWLEDGMENTS

Although I cannot adequately thank all of my friends & colleagues who have contributed to the completion of this book, it gives me pleasure to mention a few people whose generosity over the last several years was particularly helpful.

I want to thank Bill Ayers for his energetic words of encouragement which affirmed the book's main idea at an early moment in its development. I want to thank Deron Boyles for his close reading and critique of every chapter. I want to thank Nick Young for his oft-stated belief in the potential of the book to spark critical thought, and to Bruce Novack for providing me with his unique prophetic interpretations of the American intellectual tradition. Thanks to Jim Garrison for his remarks on improving chapter five, and to Diana Hess for lending support to the book at its proposal stage. I want to thank Antonio J. Garcia, Director of Jazz Studies at Virginia Commonwealth University, for granting me permission to use the musical bar of his jazz composition, "King Cake Walk" in the Epilogue, and for generously recommending a range of additional sources to strengthen the musical strand of the book's argument.

I also want to thank several colleagues at Northern Illinois University, beginning with Al Ottens, for his insightful remarks on the Lincoln chapter. I want to thank Linda O' Neill for offering her always astute commentary for making several chapters stronger. I want to thank Jessica Heybach for our conversations over the years about the challenge of re-aestheticizing the curriculum; Jessica's pioneering work in this regard played a vital role in my adoption of the jazz as democracy metaphor as a civic aesthetic. An affectionate thank you goes out to Sarah Militz-Frielink for her inspirational support of this project and for sharing with me her insights into the poetics of the writing process. I would also like to acknowledge the support that Northern Illinois University provided in the form of a one-year sabbatical leave, 2009–2010.

Thanks to my editor David Barker and his team at Continuum for their steadfastness and patience in working with me to produce the book. Thanks also to Anindya Sen for the hard work and conceptual clarity he brought to the task of compiling the index. While I am indebted to these fine people and institutions for having helped me write the book, its mistakes and shortcomings, of course, are mine alone.

FURTHER READING

Prologue

Baldwin, James. "A Talk to Teachers." *The Price of the Ticket: Collected Non-Fiction, 1948–1985*. New York: St. Martin's Press, 1985.

Berstein, Richard J. "John Dewey's Vision of Radical Democracy." *The Pragmatic Turn*. Malden: Polity Press, 2010.

Britzman, Deborah. *After-Education: Anna Freud, Melanie Klein, and Psychoanalytic Histories of Learning*. New York: SUNY Press, 2003.

Bronner, Stephen. *Critical Theory: A Very Brief Introduction*. New York: Oxford University Press, 2011.

Brown, Wendy. *Edgework: Critical Essays in Knowledge and Politics*. Princeton: Princeton University Press, 2005.

Cobb, William, trans. *The Symposium and the Phaedrus: Plato's Erotic Dialogues*. Albany: SUNY Press, 1996.

Freire, Paulo. *Pedagogy of the Oppressed*. New York: Continuum, 1970.

—. *Education for Critical Consciousness*. New York: Continuum, 1973.

Hodgson, Godfrey. *The Myth of American Exceptionalism*. New Haven: Yale University Press, 2009.

Kammen, Michael. "The Problem of American Exceptionalism: A Reconsideration." *In the Past Lane: Historical Perspectives on American Culture*. New York: Oxford University Press, 1997.

Loewen, James W. *Lies My Teacher Told Me: Everything Your American History Textbooks Got Wrong*. New York: Touchstone, 1995/2007.

O'Meally, Robert, ed. *The Jazz Cadence in American Culture*. New York: Columbia University Press, 1998.

Pease, Donald E. *The New American Exceptionalism*. Minneapolis: University of Minnesota Press, 2009.

Unger, Roberto M. *The Self Awakened: Pragmatism Unbound*. Cambridge: Harvard University Press, 2007.

West, Cornel. *Democracy Matters: Winning the Fight Against Imperialism*. New York: Penguin, 2004.

Westbrook, Robert B. *Democratic Hope: Pragmatism and the Politics of Truth*. Ithaca: Cornell University Press, 2005.

Zinn, Howard. *A People's History of the United States*. New York: Harper Perennial Books, 1980/2010.

Chapter One

Arendt, Hannah. "The Pursuit of Happiness." *On Revolution*. New York: Penguin Books, 1963.

Aristotle. *The Nichomachean Ethics*. D. Ross, trans. Oxford: Oxford University Press, 1990.

Banks, Russell. *Dreaming Up America*. New York: Seven Stories Press, 2008.

Boyles, Deron, ed. *Schools or Markets: Commercialism, Privatization, and School-Business Partnerships*. Mahwah: Lawrence Erlbaum, 2005.

Delbanco, Andrew. *The Real American Dream: A Meditation on Hope*. Cambridge: Harvard University Press, 1999.

Detweiler, Philip. "The Changing Reputation of the Declaration of Independence: The First Fifty Years." *William & Mary Quarterly*, 19(4), (1962), 557–74.

Dewey, John. *Freedom and Culture*. New York: Prometheus Books, 1989.

—. *Individualism Old and New*. New York: Prometheus Books, 1999.

Hess, Diana E. *Controversy in the Classroom: The Democratic Power of Discussion*. New York: Routledge, 2009.

Jones, Howard M. *The Pursuit of Happiness*. Ithaca: Cornell University Press, 1953.

Lynd, Staughton. *The Intellectual Origins of American Radicalism*. New York: Pantheon Books, 1968.

Maier, Pauline. *American Scripture: Making the Declaration of Independence*. New York: Vintage Books, 1997.

Matthews, Richard K. *The Radical Politics of Thomas Jefferson: A Revisionist View*. Lawrence: University of Kansas Press, 1984.

Meyer, Donald H. *The Democratic Enlightenment*. New York: G. P. Putnam's Sons, 1976.

Norris, Trevor. *Consuming Schools: Commercialism and the End of Politics*. Toronto: University of Toronto Press, 2011.

Peterson, Merrill D., ed. *Thomas Jefferson, Writings*. New York: The Library of America, 1984.

Plato. *The Last Days of Socrates*. New York: Penguin Classics, 1993.

Wills, Garry. *Inventing America: Jefferson's Declaration of Independence*. New York: Vintage Books, 1978.

Wood, Gordon S. *The Radicalism of the American Revolution*. New York: Vintage, 1991.

Young, Alfred. *The Shoemaker and the Tea Party: Memory and the American Revolution*. Boston: Beacon Press, 1999.

Chapter Two

Boesche, Roger. *Theories of Tyranny From Plato to Arendt*. University Park: University of Pennsylvania Press, 1996.

—. *Tocqueville's Road Map: Methodology, Liberalism, Revolution, and Despotism*. Lanham: Lexington Books, 2006.

Boler, Megan. "Teaching for Hope: The Ethics of Shattering World Views." Eds., Jim Garrison and Daniel Liston. *Teaching, Loving and Learning: Reclaiming Passion in Educational Practice*. New York: Routledge, 2004.

Madison, James. "Federalist No. 10." Eds., Alexander Hamilton, John Jay, James Madison. *The Federalist Papers*. New York: Mentor Books, 1968.

Mayo, Cris. "Civility and Its Discontents: Sexuality, Race and the Lure of Beautiful Manners." Ed., Suzanne Rice. *Philosophy of Education Yearbook* 2001. Urbana: Philosophy of Education Society, 2002.

Monoson, Sara. *Plato's Democratic Entanglements: Athenian Politics and the Practice of Philosophy*. Princeton: Princeton University Press, 2000.

Paxton, Robert O. *The Anatomy of Fascism*. New York: Vintage Books, 2005.

Tocqueville, Alexis. *Democracy in America*. New York: Penguin Books, 2003.

Wolin, Sheldon. *Democracy, Incorporated: Managed Democracy and the Specter of Inverted Totalitarianism*. Princeton: Princeton University Press, 2008.

Chapter Three

Basler, Roy, ed. *The Collected Works of Abraham Lincoln*. New Brunswick: Rutgers University Press, 1953.

Bennett, Lerone, Jr. *Forced Into Glory: Abraham Lincoln's White American Dream*. Chicago: Johnson Publishing, 1999.

Blight, David. *Beyond the Battlefield: Race, Memory and the American Civil War*. Amherst: University of Massachusetts Press, 2002.

—. "The Theft of Lincoln in Scholarship, Politics and Public Memory." Ed., Eric Foner. *Our Lincoln: New Perspectives on Lincoln and His World*. New York: W. W. Norton, 2008.

Colaiaco, James A. *Frederick Douglass and the Fourth of July*. New York: Palgrave Macmillan, 2006.

Diggins, John P. *On Hallowed Ground: Abraham Lincoln and the Foundations of American History*. New Haven: Yale University Press, 2000.

Douglass, Frederick. "The Freedmen's Oration (1876)." *The Life and Times of Frederick Douglass*. Mineola: Dover Publications, 2003.

Du Bois, William E. B. "Abraham Lincoln." *W. E. B. Du Bois, Writings*. New York: Literary Classics, 1986 (1196–99).

—. "Again, Abraham Lincoln." *W. E. B. Du Bois, Writings*. New York: Literary Classics, 1986 (1199).

Guelzo, Allen C. "Apple of Gold in a Picture of Silver: The Constitution and Liberty." Ed., Gabor Boritt. *The Lincoln Enigma: The Changing Faces of an American Icon*. New York: Oxford University Press, 2001.

May, Rollo. "Eros in Conflict with Sex." *Love and Will*. New York: W. W. Norton, 1969.

Wills, Garry. *Lincoln at Gettysburg: The Words That Remade America*. New York: Touchstone Books, 1992.

Chapter Four

Ayers, William and Dohrn, Bernadine. *Race Course: Against White Supremacy*. Chicago: Third World Press, 2009.

Du Bois, William E. B. "The Propaganda of History." *Black Reconstruction in America*, 1860–1880. New York: Atheneum, 1935/1998.

Dyson, Michael E. "America Must Move Toward a Democratic Socialism: A Progressive Social Blueprint." *I May Not Get There With You: The True Martin Luther King, Jr*. New York: Touchstone, 2001.

Felman, Shoshana. "Psychoanalysis and Education: Teaching Terminable and Interminable." *Jacques Lacan and the Adventure of Insight: Psychoanalysis in Contemporary Culture*. Cambridge: Harvard University Press, 1987.

Foner, Eric. *Forever Free: The Story of Emancipation and Reconstruction*. New York: Vintage Books, 2005.

Frazier, Garrison. "Colloquy with Colored Ministers." *The Journal of Negro History*, 16(1), (1931), 88–94.

King, Martin L., Jr. *Where Do We Go From Here: Chaos or Community?* Boston: Beacon Press, 1968.

Lane, Mark and Gregory, Dick. *Code Named "Zorro:" The Murder of Martin Luther King, Jr*. Englewood Cliffs: Prentice-Hall, 1977.

Marable, Manning. "Forty Acres and a Mule: The Case for Black Reparations." *The Great Wells of Democracy: The Meaning of Race in American Life*. New York: Basic Books, 2002.

Oubre, Claude F. *Forty Acres and a Mule: The Freedmen's Bureau and Black Land Ownership.* Baton Rouge: Louisiana State University Press, 1978.

Pepper, William F. *An Act of State: The Execution of Martin Luther King.* London: Verso, 2003.

Robinson, Randall. *The Debt: What America Owes to Blacks.* New York: Dutton Books, 2000.

Sullivan, Shannon and Tuana, Nancy, eds. *Race and Epistemologies of Ignorance.* Albany: SUNY Press, 2007.

Chapter Five

Barzun, Jacques. *A Stroll with William James.* New York: Harper & Row, 1983.

Bourne, Randolph. "A Moral Equivalent for Universal Military Service (1916)." Ed., Carl Resek. *War and the Intellectuals: Collected Essays, 1915–19.* New York: Harper & Row, 1964.

Elshtain, Jean B. *Women and War.* New York: Basic Books, 1987/1995.

Ferguson, Kennan F. *William James: Politics in the Pluriverse.* Lanham: Rowman & Littlefield, 2007.

Frederickson, George M. *The Inner Civil War: Northern Intellectuals and the Crisis of the Union.* New York: Harper & Row, 1965.

Garrison, Jim, Bredo, Eric, Podeschi, Ronald. *William James and Education.* New York: Teachers College Press, 2002.

Hoganson, Kristin L. *Fighting For American Manhood: How Gender Politics Provoked the Spanish-American and Philippine-American Wars.* New Haven: Yale University Press, 1998.

James, William. "The Moral Equivalent of War." Ed., Bruce W. Wilshire. *William James: The Essential Writings.* Albany: SUNY Press, 1984.

—. "On A Certain Blindness In Human Beings." Ed., Bruce W. Wilshire. *William James: The Essential Writings.* Albany: SUNY Press, 1984.

Kautzer, Chad and Mendieta, Eduardo, eds. *Pragmatism, Nation, and Race: Community in the Age of Empire.* Bloomington: Indiana University Press, 2009.

Mann, Horace. "Eighth Report" (1844). *Life and Works of Horace Mann,* Vol. III. Boston: Lee and Shepard Publishers, 1891.

Martin, Jane R. "Martial Virtues or Capital Vices? William James's Moral Equivalent of War Revisited." *Journal of Thought,* 22, (Fall 1987), 32–44.

Miller, Joshua. *Democratic Temperament: The Legacy of William James.* Lawrence: University of Kansas Press, 1997.

Nussbaum, Martha. *Not For Profit: Why Democracy Needs the Humanities.* Princeton: Princeton University Press, 2010.

Stuhr, John J., ed. *100 Years of Pragmatism: William James's Revolutionary Philosophy*. Bloomington: Indiana University Press, 2010.

West, Cornel. "James on Individuality, Reconcilation, and Heroic Energies." *The American Evasion of Philosophy: A Genealogy of Pragmatism*. Madison: University of Wisconsin Press, 1989.

Chapter Six

Allen, Frederick L. "Coolidge Prosperity." *Only Yesterday: An Informal History of the 1920s*. New York: Harper & Row, 1931.

Clements, Jeffrey D. *Corporations Are Not People: Why They Have More Rights Than You Do and What You Can Do About It*. San Fransciso: Berrett-Koehler Publishers, 2012.

Coolidge, Calvin. "The Press Under a Free Government." *Foundations of the Republic: Speeches and Addresses*. Freeport: Books for Libraries Press, 1926/1968.

Dewey, John. "The House Divided against Itself." *New Republic*, 58, (1929), 270–1.

—. "The United States, Incorporated (1930)." *Individualism Old and New*. Amherst: Prometheus Books, 1995.

—. "Individuality in Our Day" (1930). *Individualism Old and New*. Amherst: Prometheus Books, 1995.

Ewen, Stuart. *Captains of Consciousness: Advertising and the Social Roots of Consumer Culture*. New York: McGraw-Hill, 1976.

—. *PR! A Social History of Spin*. New York: Basic Books, 1996.

Hartmann, Thom. "Jefferson Considers Freedom Against Monopolies A Basic Right." *Unequal Protection: The Rise of Corporate Dominance and the Theft of Human Rights*. New York: St. Martin's Press, 2002.

Lippmann, Walter. *American Inquisitors*. New York: Transaction Publishers, 1927/1993.

McNeil, Genna R. *Groundwork: Charles Hamilton Houston and the Struggle for Civil Rights*. Philadelphia: University of Philadelphia Press, 1983.

Rich, Frank. "The Billionaires Bankrolling the Tea Party." *New York Times*, August 28, 2010.

Rockefeller, Steven C. *John Dewey: Religious Faith and Democratic Humanism*. New York: Columbia University Press, 1991.

Saito, Naoko. "The Rekindling of the Gleam of Light: Toward Perfectionist Education." *The Gleam of Light: Moral Perfectionism and Education in Dewey and Emerson*. New York: Fordham University Press, 2000.

Chapter Seven

Bacevich, Andrew. *Washington Rules: America's Path to Permanent War*. New York: Metropolitan Books, 2010.

Butler, Smedley. *War is a Racket*. Port Townsend: Feral House Books, 1935/2003.

Chomsky, Noam. *Hegemony or Survival? America's Quest for Global Dominance*. New York: Metropolitan Books, 2003.

Cook, Blanche W. *The Declassified Eisenhower: A Startling Reappraisal of the Eisenhower Presidency*. New York: Penguin Books, 1984.

Douglass, James W. *JFK and the Unspeakable: Why He Died & Why It Matters*. Maryknoll: Orbis Books, 2008.

Ekirch, Arthur. "The Founding Fathers Reaffirm Civil Supremacy." *The Civilian and the Military*. New York: Oxford University Press, 1956.

Enloe, Cynthia. *Globalization & Militarism: Feminists Make the Link*. Lanham: Rowman & Littlefield, 2007.

Giroux, Henry. *The University in Chains: Confronting the Military-Industrial-Academic Complex*. Boulder: Paradigm Press, 2007.

Jeffords, Susan. *The Remasculinization of America: Gender and the Vietnam War*. Bloomington: Indiana University Press, 1989.

Johnson, Chalmers. *The Sorrows of the Republic: Militarism, Secrecy and the End of the Republic*. New York: Metropolitan Books, 2004.

Ledbetter, James. *Unwarranted Influence: Dwight D. Eisenhower and the Military-Industrial Complex*. New Haven: Yale University Press, 2010.

Miller, James. "The Port Huron Statement." *Democracy Is in the Streets: From Port Huron to the Siege of Chicago*. Cambridge, MA: Harvard University Press, 1994.

Mills, Charles W. *The Power Elite*. New York: Oxford University Press, 1956.

Noddings, Nel. "The Psychology of War." *Critical Lessons: What Our Schools Should Teach*. New York: Cambridge University Press, 2006.

Provenzo, Eugene, Jr. "Virtuous War: The Simulation and Militarization of Play." Eds., Kenneth Saltman and David Gabbard. *Education as Enforcement: The Militarization and Corporatization of Schools*. New York: Routledge, 2003.

Schwoerer, Lois G. *"No Standing Armies!" The Antiarmy Ideology in Seventeeth-Century England*. Baltimore: Johns Hopkins University Press, 1974.

Turse, Nick. *The Complex: How the Military Invades Our Everyday Lives*. New York: Metropolitan Books, 2010.

Chapter Eight

Bell, Hooks. *Teaching to Transgress: Education as the Practice of Freedom*. New York: Routledge, 1994.

Bernstein, Richard J. *The Abuse of Evil: The Corruption of Politics since 9/11*. Malden: Polity Press, 2005.

Boler, Megan, ed. *Democratic Dialogue in Education: Troubling Speech, Disturbing Silence*. New York: Peter Lang, 2006.

Castoriadis, Cornelius. "The Problem of Democracy Today." *Democracy & Nature*, 8, (1995), 18–37.

Counts, George S. *Dare the Schools Build A New Social Order?* Carbondale: Southern Illinois University Press, 1932/1978.

Dewey, John. "The Ethics of Democracy" (1888). Ed., Jo Ann Boydston. *The Collected Works of John Dewey, 1882–1953*. Carbondale: Southern Illinois University Press, 1981.

Eisner, Eliot. "The Null Curriculum." *The Educational Imagination: On the Design and Evaluation of School Programs*. New York: Macmillan Publishers, 1979.

Elshtain, Jean B. *Public Man, Private Woman: Women in Social and Political Thought*. Princeton: Princeton University Press, 1981/1993.

Ferguson, Kathy E. *Emma Goldman: Political Thinking in the Streets*. Lanham: Rowman & Littlefield, 2011.

Garrison, James. "A Deweyan Theory of Democratic Listening." *Educational Theory*, 46, (Fall 1996), 429–51.

Giarelli, James. "The Social Frontier 1934–1943: Retrospect and Prospect." Ed., Michael E. James. *Social Reconstruction Through Education: The Philosophy, History & Curricula of a Radical Idea*. Norwood: Ablex Publishing, 1995.

Hanisch, Carol. "The Personal is Political." *Notes from the Second Year: Women's Liberation: Major Writings of the Radical Feminists*. New York: Feminist Revolution, 1970.

—. Introduction to "The Personal is Political" (2006). http://carolhanisch.org/CHArticleslist.html.

MacKinnon, Catherine. "Consciousness-Raising." *Toward a Feminist Theory of State*. Cambridge: Harvard University Press, 1989.

Provenzo, Eugene, Jr., Ed. *The Social Frontier: A Critical Reader*. New York: Peter Lang, 2011.

Epilogue

Anderson, Rodino. "W. E. B. Du Bois and an Education for Democracy and Creativity." Ed., David T. Hansen. *Ethical Visions of Education: Philosophies in Practice*. New York: Teachers College Press, 2007.

Armstrong, Louis. "What is Swing?" Ed., Robert Walser. *Keeping Time: Readings in Jazz History.* New York: Oxford University Press, 1999.

Brann, Eva. *The Music of the Republic.* Philadelphia: Paul Dry Books, 2004/2010.

Conroy, James. *Betwixt & Between: The Liminal Imagination, Education and Democracy.* New York: Peter Lang, 2004.

Crouch, Stanley. *Considering Genius: Writings on Jazz.* New York: Basic Books, 2006.

Dewey, John. "Creative Democracy—The Task Before Us" (1939). Eds. Larry A. Hickman and Thomas M. Alexander. *The Essential Dewey: Volume 1: Pragmatism, Education, Democracy.* Bloomington: Indiana University Press, 1998.

—. "The Democratic Conception in Education." *Democracy and Education.* New York: The Macmillan Co., 1916/2000.

Du Bois, William E. B. *The Souls of Black Folk*, eds. Henry Louis Gates, Jr., and Terri Hume Oliver. New York: W. W. Norton, 1999.

Ellington, Duke. "Duke Ellington Explains Swing." Ed., Robert Walser. *Keeping Time: Readings in Jazz History.* New York: Oxford University Press, 1999.

Ellison, Ralph. *Living With Music: Ralph Ellison's Jazz Writings*, ed. Robert O'Meally. New York: Modern Library, 2001.

Love, Nancy. *Musical Democracy.* Albany: SUNY Press, 2006.

Murray, Albert. "Improvisation and the Creative Process." Ed., Robert O'Meally. *The Jazz Cadence in American Culture.* New York: Columbia University Press, 1998.

Seghal, Kabir. *Jazzocracy: Jazz, Democracy & the Creation of a New American Mythology.* Mishawaka: Better World Books, 2008.

Shapiro, Michael J. "Composing America." *Deforming American Political Thought: Ethnicity, Facticity, and Genre.* Lexington: University of Kentucky Press, 2006.

INDEX

American exceptionalism *see*
exceptionalism
Anderson, Rodino   166
Arendt, Hannah
on love for the world   148
on public happiness   9–10, 13
(*On Revolution*)   3
Aristotle   5–6
Armstrong, Louis
on the concept of swing   172

Bennett, Lerone Jr.
(*Forced into Glory*)   46–7
Bernstein, Richard
on Dewey's view of social
conflict   xvii
on fallibilism   145–6
Boler, Megan   31, 33–4
Britzman, Deborah   x
difficult knowledge   xixn.1
Brown v. Board of Education,
(1954)   15, 26, 110

Castoriadis, Cornelius   150
civic aesthetic
as difficult knowledge in
relation to American
identity   xviii–xix, 46, 177
as the emotional properties of
crisis   x, 51
civic generativity   xii
civic rebirth   39
conscientization *see also*
Freire, Paulo
as critical action-taking   xiv

and feminist consciousness-
raising   143
as heightened state of internal
tension   xvi
and historical awareness   131
as learning to perceive
contradictions   xiv, 131
constitution   xv, 3, 10, 47
and its amendment process
related to jazz   168
as an anti-imperial
document   121, 131–2
and Jefferson on the Bill
of Rights   108–9
on its mechanical structure and
the moral purposes of the
Preamble   147–8
and the primacy of civil
authority   117
and prohibition   93
in relation to Lincoln's apple
of gold/picture of silvery
imagery   41–5
in tension with the Declaration
of Independence   38–9,
61–2
Coolidge, Calvin   xv, 94–103
*The business of America
is business*   94, 96–7,
99, 108
as conservative
ideologue   95–6
Coolidge Prosperity   96–7,
100–1, 103
as moral pedagogue   100

Counts, George
  (*Dare the Schools Build a
    New Social Order?*)   152–3
Cremin, Lawrence
  (*The Republic and the
    School*)   86
critical pedagogy   xi–xii, 5, 31–3,
    109, 140
critical thinking   xi, xiv
  conscientization   xiv
  critical historical
    awareness   xiv

Declaration of Independence   xvi
  as a basis for American
    exceptionalism   108, 117
  in opposition to standing
    armies   131
  politically inventive rereadings
    of   3–4
  and the pursuit of
    happiness   10
  in relation to Lincoln's apple
    of gold/picture of silver
    imagery   41–5
  and the right to
    revolution   168
  as a site of democratic
    identification   46
  in tension with the U.S.
    Constitution   38–9, 61
democracy   xi–xii, xiv, xvii–xviii,
    xix
  business mind as threat
    to   13, 94
  and consciousness-raising
    groups   139–40
  as a Deweyan mode of
    being   146–51
  and Dewey's model of
    individuality   105–7
  and forty acres and a mule   56,
    61, 70

Gettysburg Address
  and   37–41
homo economicus as
    threat to   2
  majority rule as
    basis of   21–2
  and the moral equivalent
    of war   75–7, 80
  Plato's criticism of   25
  and the public/private
    distinction   138
  as the real business of
    America   96–8
  threatened by the Military-
    Industrial Complex   116–18,
    120–2, 133
  and the tyranny of the
    majority   25–31, 34–5
Democracy in America   21–3,
    27–30 *see also* de
    Tocqueville
Democratic education
    (pedagogy)
  and consciousness-raising
    groups   142–6
  jazz and   164–5, 167–74
  and Lincoln's apple of
    gold/picture of silver
    allegory   41–5
  and music   85–8
  and the problem of corporate
    personhood   107–11
  and the problem of
    indoctrination   152–6
  and the tyranny of the
    majority   34–5
Dewey, John   xv, xviii, 9, 102–7,
    145–51, 153
  on the communicative
    and dialogic essence of
    democracy   169–71
  on the concept of democratic
    individuality   97, 102–7

critique of the pursuit of
happiness as a moral
ideal 13–14
critique of teacher
neutrality 155
on democracy as a secular
religious project 155–6
on Jefferson's legacy 12
individuality/individualism
tension 13, 96–102
rejection of Locke's theory that
property is a natural right 12
remarks on Kallen's image
of national identity as a
"symphony orchestra" 164
theory of democracy as a mode
of being 97, 146–50
Du Bois, W. E. B xv, 64, 98
on black musical traditions as
a contribution to American
culture 165–7
citizenship 62
double consciousness as
an internal democratic
contradiction 165
interpretation of
Lincoln 47, 49–50
music 165–6
national identity 167
racist textbooks and their
destructive impact on
citizenship 62
reconstruction 61
on the tragedy of black
landlessness 61

Ellington, Duke
on the concept of swing 172
Eisenhower, Dwight xv, 115–21,
123, 125–9, 132
the Military-Industrial
Complex (MIC) 115–21,
123, 125–9, 132

on the military and its effects
on education 118–20
on the supremacy of civil
authority 116–17
Ellsberg, Daniel 30–1
Elshtain, Jean 84, 138
Enloe, Cynthia
on feminist curiosity 119
on masculine values and the
military 129
Eros
as desire for wholeness 40
as desire to know xvii
as form of love xvii
Gettysburg Address 40
relation to Lincoln's apple of
gold metaphor 40, 43, 45
eudaimonia 5–6
exceptionalism xiv
as cultural fantasy xx
democratic version of 166–7
and gender 127, 129–30
Jefferson's interpretation of 8
militarized version of 118
William James and
Theodore Roosevelt on
the conbtradictory images
of 80–1

feminist 81, 118–19, 129–30,
137–41, 144, 146–7, 156
consciousness-raising 139–41,
144, 146–7, 156
ethic of care 129
feminist curiosity 119
feminist deconstruction of
William James 81
feminist pedagogy 118, 146
*the personal is
political* 139–40, 146–7
and the public/private
division 137–8, 143, 146
second wave oof 137–8

Foner, Eric   59–60
forty acres and a mule   55–9,
   61–4, 66–7, 69–70
*four score and seven years
   ago*   37–8, 47–9
Freire, Paulo   xiii–xvi, xx–xxi,
   127, 131, 136, 142–3, 157
   see also conscientization,
   Freirean
   and conscientization   xiv,
      131, 143
   generative themes   xiii, 94,
      117
   historical awareness as basis for
      conscientization   xiv, 131
   praxis   xv
   and the tension between
      problem-posing and banking
      education   142–3
   thematic universe   xiii,
      xiv, 127
Freirean
   contradictions   xiii
   generative theme   94
   learning theory   162
   method   117
   pedagogy   xviii
   theory   142

Garrison, Jim   145
Giarelli, James   153–4
Giroux, Henry   118–20
gender   115, 145
   and domestic anxieties
      79–80
   and democratic education   146
   lack of balance in James'
      essays   82–4
   politics of   118–19, 127,
      129–30
Gettysburg Address   37–40,
   42, 44, 47–51 *see also*
   Lincoln

Hanisch, Carol   139
   description of feminist
      consciousness-raising
      groups   140–6
Hayden, Tom   120–2
historical amnesia   xiv *see also*
   politics of forgetting
   and the Declaration of
      Independence   3, 38, 44
   and its effects on the
      democratic myth of cultural
      heroism   133, 167
   and the legacy of Martin
      Luther King   70
   and the spiritual element of
      America's founding   13
historical awareness   xiv, 131, 171
homo economicus   2, 7
Houston, Charles H   110–11

imperialism   xiv, xx
   competing conceptions
      of   78–81, 129–30
   democratic antidote
      to   166–7
   feminist analysis of   80, 129
individualism   xiv, 7, 13–14, 16,
   27–8, 30, 95–7, 101–6, 147,
   165, 167, 173
individuality   xiv, xix, 13, 96–7,
   102–7, 169–70, 172–3

James, William   xv–xvi, xviii,
   75–8 *see also the moral
   equivalent of war*
   criticizes the imperial logic of
      Theodore Roosevelt   78–81,
      129–30
   on wars   75–82
jazz   xix, 93
   as metaphor of
      democracy   xix, 166,
      173, 177

and its relation to
democracy 164
and its relation to democracy as
a mode of being 168–74
and its relation to national
identity xix, 117
and the *Roaring Twenties* 93
Jefferson, Thomas xv–xvi
on the basis of American
exceptionalism 8
on education as a vehicle of
civic virtue 9, 11, 16
and Lincoln's interpretation
of the Declaration of
Independence 45
and opposition to commercial
monopolies 108–9
and opposition to standing
armies 109, 131
on public/civic happiness 8–10
pursuit of happiness xvi, 4,
6–14, 16, 45
and rejection of Locke's theory
of natural rights 6–7

King, Martin Luther xv, 66–70
*see also forty acres and
a mule*
African-American
citizenship 66, 69
and assassination of 69–70
contra the Vietnam
War 68–70
on military spending 70
as nation's soul-doctor 70
and radical analysis of
American society 66–70
Kloppenberg, James
(*Reading Obama*) 88

Ledbetter, James
(*Unwarranted Influence*) 118
Lincoln, Abraham xv, 57, 59, 61
see also Gettysburg Address

on the "*apple of gold*"
and "*picture of
silver*" 41–4
contradictions between
the Declaration of
Independence and the
Constitution 38–51
*four score and seven years
ago* 37–8, 47–9
metaphors of rebirth
in the Gettysburg
Address 39–45
relation to national
identity 38, 41–51
remarks on the meaning
of the Declaration of
Independence 44–5
Locke, John
ideology as manifested by U.S.
public schools 14
influence on
Jefferson 7–8, 12
Loewen, James
(*Lies My Teacher Told
Me*) xviii

Madison, James
letter from Jefferson
against monopolies in
commerce 109
the problem of a majority
faction resolved by
"extending the sphere"
(Federalist 10) 25–6
statement against standing
armies 132
Mann, Horace xv, 85–8, 165
the Eighth Report
(1844) 85–6, 88
and the importance of musical
education 85–8, 165
Martin, Jane Roland 81–4
criticism of William
James 81–4

the moral equivalent of war   xvi,
    75–8, 82–5, 87–8, 165
    see also James, William
music   xix, 87, 93, 170–2, 177
    and education   85–8, 164–5,
        167–9
    emotions and feelings produced
        by   85–8, 165–9
    musical education as moral
        equivalent of war   85–8

Noddings, Nel   122, 129
Nussbaum, Martha   6, 86, 165
    on eudaimonia   6
    and the relation of
        musical education to
        democracy   86, 165

Plato
    analytical distinction between
        the psyche and the
        city   127–8
    (*The Apology*)   5
    character of political
        regimes   127–8
    on the devolution of
        democracy   151
    the dialectic as basis of
        Socratic pedagogy   xvi
    dialectic defined   xxi
    eros (love)   xvii, 5, 40
    happiness   4–6
    on the harmonizing effects of
        music on the soul   164
    on the problem of
        democracy   25
    (*The Republic*)   164
    (*The Symposium*)   xvii, 40
Plessy v. Ferguson (1896)   107,
    110–11
politics of forgetting   xiv, 2–3,
    167 *see also* historical
    amnesia
praxis   xv

pursuit of happiness   xvi, 1–5,
    7–16, 44–5, 60–2

Roosevelt, Franklin D.   102
    criticism of "economic
        royalists"   102
Roosevelt, Theodore   78–82
    anti-trust legislation   98
    apologist for
        imperialism   78–82
Rorty, Richard
    (*Achieving Our Country*)   51

*Santa Clara County v. Southern
    Pacific Railroad*
    (1886)   110
Socrates (Socratic)
    corrupting the youth   5
    critical pedagogy   xvi, 5, 155,
        162
    criticism of Athenian
        self-conception   5
    happiness   5
    his execution by a democratic
        jury   25
    how Socratic pedagogy
        sparks new desires to
        know   xvi–xviii
    Socratic pedagogy as a
        vehicle for identifying
        contradictions   5, 155,
        162
souls
    conflicted nature of
        democratic   165
    of democratic folk   173
    denial of   13
    Martin Luther King as
        soul-doctor   70
    militarization and   128
    music to harmonize the
        passions of   85
    others as cyber-
        abstractions   123

perfection of 5
recognition of 80–1
recovery of democratic 93
satisfaction of 8
standing armies 109, 131–3
see also Jefferson, Thomas
Stevens, Thaddeus 56, 61
Students for a Democratic Society
(SDS) 120–2
Sumner, Charles 56, 65

de Tocqueville, Alexis xv, 21–5,
27–30, 32–5, 103
critique of American
culture 21–5, 27–30, 32–5
on the tyranny of the
majority 21–5, 27–30,
32–5, 103

tyranny of the majority 21–7,
29–35, 103

U.S. Constitution *see* constitution

Washington, George 80, 132
West,Cornel 164, 170–1
Wolin, Sheldon 30–1, 148, 169
democratization of
self 148
relation between inverted
totalitarianism and
the tyranny of the
majority 30–1

Zinn, Howard
(*A People's History of the
United States*) xviii